# THE IMAGINATIVE INSTITUTION:
# PLANNING AND GOVERNANCE IN MADRID

*To my parents and Elisabeth*

# The Imaginative Institution:
# Planning and Governance
# in Madrid

MICHAEL NEUMAN
*Texas A&M University, USA*

ASHGATE

Published by
Ashgate Publishing Limited
Wey Court East
Union Road
Farnham
Surrey, GU9 7PT
England

Ashgate Publishing Company
Suite 420
101 Cherry Street
Burlington
VT 05401-4405
USA

www.ashgate.com

**British Library Cataloguing in Publication Data**
Neuman, Michael, 1955-
  The imaginative institution : planning and governance in
  Madrid.
  1. City planning--Spain--Madrid--History.
  2. Metropolitan government--Spain--Madrid--History.
  I. Title
  307.1'216'094641-dc22

**Library of Congress Cataloging-in-Publication Data**
Neuman, Michael, 1955-
  The imaginative institution : planning and governance in Madrid / by Michael Neuman.
    p. cm.
  Includes bibliographical references and index.
  ISBN 978-1-4094-0541-2 (hardback) ISBN 978-1-4094-1944-0 (ebook)
  1. Regional planning--Spain--Madrid (Region) 2. Madrid (Spain : Region)--Politics and government. I. Title.

  HT395.S72M2765 2010
  307.1'216094641--dc22

                                                                    2010016346

ISBN 9781409405412 (hbk)
ISBN 9781409419440 (ebk)

**Mixed Sources**
Product group from well-managed
forests and other controlled sources
www.fsc.org  Cert no. SA-COC-1565
FSC  © 1996 Forest Stewardship Council

Printed and bound in Great Britain by
MPG Books Group, UK

# Contents

# List of Figures

# List of Tables

# Preface

It was a Friday. It could have been any Friday. This one was in 1994. The winter wind shook the naked branches on the *Paseo de la Castellana*, the north-south boulevard that fuses the eastern and western halves of the city. The low sun's rays streamed deep into *El Gran Café Gijon*. Inside, talk turned to cities, urbanism, and planning. The protagonists, retired housewives and a young married couple, lit up when talk turned to urbanism. Their passion burst forth for streets and plazas, their streets and plazas.

Later in the afternoon, the poet Antonio Morales was conducting his weekly tertulia at his usual window table at the same *Café Gijon*. Other writers and artists joined him in carrying on a centuries-old tradition of discussing their work, the city, politics, and the latest events. At those same tables in the early 1970s forward looking intellectuals, politicians, and bureaucrats sketched the main criteria of the new democratic institutions as Franco's dictatorship waned.

Outside, the streets and squares were filling with evening strollers. The city was theirs and they were using it. Later in the evening, down the way from the *Café Gijon* at the *Círculo de Bellas Artes*, a consortium of downtown neighborhood associations was hosting an open forum on the draft city plan. Three hundred people patiently listened for over two hours to experts. Then, as 11 o'clock at night neared, these faithful citizens who had yet to eat dinner launched into personal and emotional stories, pleas, and advice for their city, their neighborhoods, their future. This is par for the course in Madrid, a city of neighborhoods. Ask a born and bred Madrileña where she is from, and she will name a neighborhood, not Madrid.

Meanwhile in Malasaña, a nearby neighborhood, an open *tertulia* debated the artist and the city at the *Café Manuela*. Afterwards most of the *tertuliantes* ambled a few blocks to the *Café del Foro* to listen to ethnic music. The neighborhood had been recently gentrified by Madrileñean yuppies, as had Chueca, another neighborhood that adjoins Malasaña, 10 years later. This conversion swept in on the coattails of Malasaña's fame in the 1960s and 1970s as a hotbed of political protest, neighborhood activism, and alternative culture. Chueca, along with Lavapies and La Latina, took over Malasaña's role of alternative culture hotbed in the 1990s. Walking home from the *Café del Foro* at four in the morning after the last copa, the streets *Calle de la Hortaleza* and *Las Huertas* were as packed with pedestrians as Fifth Avenue in Manhattan on a Saturday before Christmas. Far from Walter Benjamin's *flaneurs*, these youths were enjoying the twilight of the *movida Madrileña*, indifferent to the cold blowing in from the *meseta* that typifies winter nights in Castile.

The *movida Madrileña* is the name of the vibrant social and cultural life that sprang to the surface in Madrid during the advent of the current democratic period. It started as an alternative for the youth in clubs such as the *Garaje Hermético* in *La Prospe*, as the neighborhood *Prosperidad* is known locally. The *movida* spread to other areas, ages, and activities, becoming city-wide. It enjoyed its apogee in the early and mid 1980s.

Earlier in the week, former regional planning director Eduardo Mangada's *tertulia* about Madrid met. Practitioners, academics and politicians convene their periodic sessions to mull over the future of the region and its institutions. Other tertulias, such as Manuel Castells', took on more worldly topics. In the 15,000 bars and cafés within the city limits chats, debates, arguments, stories, conversations— talk of all kinds—intermingle with the smoke wafting through the air. *Madrileños* love to talk, and given any chance they will, often at their favorite café. Cafés are full before work, in the midmorning for *desayuno* (extended coffee break), an *aperitivo* before lunch, the post-siesta coffee, the evening aperitivo before dinner, and the after dinner *digestivo* and nightcap. What a day it has been. What a day each of them are.

This selective day in the life touches on the social and cultural character of the Spanish capital that mark its politics and planning. Some of these, such as the café life and strolling the streets, are common to Latin societies, whether Mediterranean or American. Others such as *tertulias* originated in Madrid. In this narrative we see that the people's use and possession of the city, the role of conversation in civic life, the emphasis on the physical form of the city, the involvement of neighborhood groups, and the influence of intellectuals on politics are recurrent themes in Madrid, its politics, and its urbanism. A calm approach to life in an urbane city.

Another vision could have occupied these lines. The other Madrid, metro Madrid, the third largest city region in Europe. New universities, private research centers, and high technology industry in the periphery. Changing from a mono-centric region to a polycentric one. (Though still the most center-heavy metropolis in Europe or North America, with three of its six million residents living within the city line as of 2010.) Jammed highways, noise, and pollution. Shanty towns on the outskirts. Deteriorated and depopulating inner city neighborhoods. All the usual accoutrements of a late industrial metropolis, displaying symptoms of a dual city and designs on being a global one. But to understand why Madrid is not yet fully a global city, why it is known as *Villa y Corte* (town and court), and why it is "a city that is not a city and that is not a town, that nonetheless has much of one and much of other; but is neither a town nor a city: it is MADRID"; we must go deep inside and explore (Miguel Hernández Fernández de Bobadilla, personal communication).

This book is the result of a dozen years of research from 1992 to 2004. This period included a six month residency and was punctuated by more than a dozen other visits of a few days to one week each. The research is qualitative and interpretive, characterized by intense participant observation. In addition to surveys, in-depth interviews of one to three hours each, and archival digging; I attended numerous meetings and joined the local branch of an advocacy group, AEDENAT (*Asociación Española de la Defensa de la Naturaleza*—a Spanish version of Greenpeace), becoming an active member in their urban section. Some of the acquaintances and colleagues that I met became and remain friends. This rewarding and unexpected outcome stems from the depth of the initial immersion.

# Acknowledgements

Thanks go to the funding agencies: the J. William Fulbright Foreign Scholarship Board in New York and *the Comisión de Intercambio Cultural entre España y los Estados Unidos de America*, the Program for Cultural Cooperation Between Spain's Ministry of Culture and United States Universities, the United States Department of Education, the Gaspar de Portolà Catalonian Studies Program and the Center for German and European Studies, both at the University of California at Berkeley, the University of California Regents, and Texas A&M University, each of which provided financial support without which this research would not have been possible.

The libraries of the *Consejería de Política Territorial* of the *Comunidad Autónoma de Madrid*, the *Gerencia de Urbanismo del Ayuntamiento de Madrid*, the *Colegio Oficial de Arquitectos de Catalunya*, the College of Environmental Design and the other libraries of the University of California at Berkeley, and the Bartlett School of the University of College London were most helpful in sorting through the maze of documentation that accompanies the field of city planning. The agencies and organizations that were the subject of the research, and the individuals whom I interviewed (see the appendix) are too numerous to mention, yet each was indispensable. Inés Sánchez de Madariaga, then of ARPEGIO, S.A., Jesús Leal of the University Complutense in Madrid, and Félix Arias of SEPES deserve special mention for going far beyond any reasonable expectation by making the research far richer than it could have been otherwise.

To colleagues Manuel Castells, Peter Hall, Robert Bellah, and AnnaLee Saxenian, all the faculty, students, and staff of the Department of City and Regional Planning and the Institute of Urban and Regional Development at the University of California at Berkeley—this work owes more than might be imagined or acknowledged to you collectively. In addition to these, the scholars most responsible for intellectual contributions to this research were Martin Meyerson, John Keene, Seymour Mandelbaum, Patsy Healey, Luigi Mazza, Andreas Faludi, Judy Innes, Michael Teitz, Fran Violich, Fred Collignon, Todd LaPorte, Aaron Wildavsky, José Gavinha, and Karen Christensen. Conversations and correspondence with them over the years has enriched this work enormously. This book strives to do justice to their extraordinary contributions.

# Chapter 1

# Taming the Metropolitan Medusa

## Research Questions

How is policy made? Specifically, how is urban policy made in advanced industrial nations? We have selected a specific branch of urban policy—city planning—to explore this question. In complex polities such as contemporary cities and metropolises, social actors and factors impinge on public policy. Most actors belong to organizations and institutions, and most factors are expressed in and through them. Each metropolis has an institution of metropolitan planning that has stakeholders interacting in forums, arenas, and courts in which planning and plan making occurs. Our first cut at the metropolitan planning institution defines it as a loose assemblage of organized actors who intend to guide the future urban development of the metropolis. The institution's nerve center may be a single planning organization or governing body. More often responsibility is scattered among many organizations. The term planning institution is defined more concretely later in this chapter, in Chapter 2, and in the case studies in Chapters 4 and 5.

This poses a related set of questions. How does the institution in which public policy is made affect policy making? How does urban policy in general and spatial planning in particular emerge historically from the metropolitan planning institution? Conversely, how does the institution evolve in relation to policy? Do plans and policies shape the institution? Or does the institution shape policies and plans? Does co-evolution occur? Our hypotheses assume a reciprocal relation between the urban plans/urban policy and the planning/governance institution which plays out throughout the evolutionary life cycle of the institution.

Investigating metropolitan planning in Madrid has yielded insights that, because of the nature of its planning institution, often are obscured in the analyses of institutions that do not have professionals skilled at creating and using designs and images. The achievement of Madrid's planners (the vast majority are architects) is that they created images of the city and the metro area and employed them with perspicacity for many purposes, in addition to their customary use to shape urban development. They led the entire metropolitan planning institution and not just its principal actors (planners, policy makers, politicians) in its use of images to shape not only metro plans and not only urban form but political strategy and institutional outcomes as well.

The paragraphs that follow provide an overview of the findings of the research. They also supply a context that informs the research questions and hypotheses, as well as the research design. Madrid's modern urban planning began in 1860 with civil engineer Carlos María de Castro's expansion plan, which guided urban growth into the twentieth century. Every 20 years or so since 1920 Madrid has undergone a city planning cycle in which a plan was prepared, adopted by law, and implemented by a new institution. This preparation-adoption-institutionalization sequence, the planning institution's structures, and technical-political processes have persisted—with some exceptions—despite frequent upheavals in society. These upheavals included revolutions, civil wars, and regime changes among dictatorship, monarchy, and democracy. The city planning institution itself played a lead role in maintaining continuity, traumatic history notwithstanding. Why? How?

First, Madrid's planners invented new images for the city and metro region. Images of physical space that were social constructs, the products of planning processes. Planners also created social images that posited new identities for the growing metropolis: "Great Madrid", "Madrid Metropolitan Region", and the "Great South". Images became cornerstones of the preparation-adoption-institutionalization cycle.

Second, images were tools that coordinated planning and urban policy. In a complex, fragmented institutional milieu in which scores of organized interests competed in overlapping policy arenas, images were a cohesive force around which plans and policies were shaped. Policy negotiation based on images complemented procedural coordination methods. Indeed, images provided the basis for coordination.

Third, Madrid's politicians used urban planning as a political strategy to build institutions of planning and governance. This strategy inaugurated a shift in the mode of city planning. Formerly, planning was a process of government acting directly on the territory through master plans and regulations. Now planning is a process of government acting on other governments and organized interests through image-based plan making and strategy forming.

Fourth, planners in Madrid used images to build new governance institutions. Images began as city or metro designs or as a visual metaphor that captured a new vision. New political regimes injected their values into the institution by using the planners' images and metaphors. These images constituted the new institution that helped to realize the regime's goals.

Each plan or strategy and its images of the future marked a new period of Madrid's planning institution's history. These imagined metropolises were at the heart of the dialectic of institutional evolution: images had the dual capacity to sustain the institution across time and space and to provoke changes to it. In the dynamics of institutional change, images shaped individuals' cognition and the institution's structuration. An image endowed with this capacity to sustain and change institutions, by embodying its essential norms and by constituting the structures and processes that shape the institution, is called the *constitutional image*. Constitutional images help constitute, shape, and identify their institutions.

The empirically-based life cycle theory of institutional evolution developed in this book suggests that the constitutional image that sustains the institution undergoes a change or is replaced by a new image, leading to a new or reformed institution. A life cycle typology of institutional transformation is formulated with four variables: type of change, stimulus for change, type of constitutional image, and outcome of the transformation of the institution.

Linking this life cycle hypothesis of institutional transformation with cognitive theories of image formation and situating their synthesis within a frame of cognition as a means of structuring the institution, we arrive at a new theory of institutional evolution. The constitutional image represents the institution's thematic content and meaning within society that is replicated over space and time via the institution's structures and processes, as well as via other social networks and processes. Changing the constitutional image in the minds of the institution's members and constituents yields a change in the institution. This mental process of image manipulation suggests that institutions and their development and evolution have a cognitive basis in addition to a social basis.

Images are not used exclusively in planning institutions. All policy making institutions use them, and symbols more generally. This is so for two reasons. One is the simple fact that images and symbols play a vital role in discourse, including planning, policy, and political discourses. The other is that the way we represent policy problems and policy itself is, in the end, via images. Representational images (city plans, symbols, and metaphors, for example) are also present in our mind as mental images. As we shall argue, these mental images we see in our mind's eye are the images that need to be changed in order to change policy and institutions.

This chapter is organized as follows: statement of the research questions, summary of findings, the empirical problem to be addressed, the hypotheses, research design and method, data collection, principal findings and theoretical propositions, and finally a map for the reader indicating how the remainder of the book is organized.

**The Problem**

Between 1960 and 1981 the Madrid metro area nearly doubled in population, exploding from 2,384,000 to 4,441,000 inhabitants.[1] Like other expanding metropolitan regions at that time, Madrid faced the problems of rapid growth, urban sprawl, and their impacts. Some effects were often seen as good, such as cultural diversity, economic opportunity, and enhanced lifestyle options. On the other hand, lack of adequate and affordable housing, congestion, pollution, loss of open space, inequitable distribution of economic growth, and loss of community identity were seen as some of the ills that attended its growth.

---

1 Data compiled from national censuses of 1960 and 1981 for 20 municipalities in the core metropolitan area. See Leal Maldonado (1987).

While during the 1980s Madrid's vertiginous growth abated, it resumed in the 1990s and 2000s. According to the *Instituto Nacional de Estadísticas* (National Institute of Statistics) 2009 official estimate, the City of Madrid's population was 3,255,944. The 2009 estimate for the greater metropolitan region was 6,386,932. As a consequence, many of these problems persisted. Others problems worsened, such as the inequitable distribution of jobs, income, and environmental ills.

Urban planning fields these problems in a particular manner. Planning's take on urban policy is distinctive in several respects. First, it strives to be comprehensive by addressing inter-related issues simultaneously. Second, it takes a long term outlook. Third, it analyzes and estimates the long term impacts of current decisions and actions. Furthermore, planning explicitly considers the territorial dimensions of urban policy: land uses and their spatial distribution, as well as city and regional design. Finally, planning is inherently more political than single issue policy matters in that it intentionally tries to balance competing objectives. These features distinguish city planning and lead to specific institutional considerations in making and implementing city plans.

The institutional *milieu* of metropolitan planning is complex and fragmented. In Madrid there are 180 municipalities in the greater metropolitan region, each with numerous departments involved in spatial planning. Plus, there are regional and national government agencies, professional associations, citizens, interest groups such as labor unions, hundreds of neighborhood associations, ecological groups, the development community (developers, builders, suppliers, financiers, realtors), political parties, utilities, transportation and other infrastructure authorities, and other organized actors. In Madrid, metropolitan plans and strategies are prepared by regional government. In the past they had been made by the national government. In either case they have always been prepared by the state, and not the private or non-profit sector, or a mix thereof. Madrid's regional government has had limited direct influence on any of these actors, except municipal planning schemes and its own regional transportation, housing, and development authorities.

How to make coherent plans in an incoherent institutional setting? This kind of setting fairly overwhelms any entity's ability to deal with the urban problems confronting contemporary cities. The lack of coordinated and effective management of growth and its impacts among the many actors on the urban stage is frequently cited as the cause and outcome of growth management attempts (Innes and Booher 2010, Healey 2007, Sassen 2007, Innes, Gruber, Neuman and Thompson 1994, Alexander 1993). As early as 1911 planning pioneer Patrick Abercrombie signaled the "necessity for cooperation" in planning metropolitan areas (Abercrombie 1911). Evocative terms like gridlock and deadlock capture the morass and dis-spirit that pervade the scene. Thus, as Melnick (1991) points out, deadlock used to mean congress and president of different parties. Today "deadlock resulted from the multiplicity of commitments already made by governments at all levels ... the point is that in the 'new American political system', deadlock takes on new meaning ... government's inability to coordinate its numerous undertakings". In response, plans now contain institutional remedies—such as strategies to coordinate, in addition to its traditional remedies for urban form and urban functions.

Despite attempts to coordinate growth policy, few metropolises have means suited to the task. In many cases there is no metropolitan government. In this event a myriad of local, regional, state, and national governments, agencies, authorities, and related organizations compete in a fragmented political arena over scarce resources. Lone municipalities, the central city included, are too small to cope. Superior levels meddle with mixed results at best. Not content to accept failure, metropolises have usually experimented with different institutional arrangements and policies. At times governing growth resembles a metropolitan medusa.

In other cases metropolitan or regional government does exist. Even then, control over growth is scattered. These intermediate levels do not always exercise jurisdiction over key development factors. Autonomous agencies controlling airports, ports, rail networks, and highways act decisively to shape the metropolis. Other levels of government and the private sector shape growth as well. Tax policy, infrastructure investments, real estate development, immigration, and other domains of policy play vital roles in guiding metropolitan growth and redevelopment. The need for effective coordination remains critical.

In all cases, metropolitan planning and governance institutions are disjointed, with scant coherence regarding region-wide matters. Their lack of historical continuity in many metropolises aggravates this condition. Few have escaped major revamping(s) if not abolition over the last decades. Where they exist, these organizations measure their age in decades. Compare this to the relative stability of municipalities and nations, some enjoying centuries and even millennia of existence.

To solve the coordination problem, metro planning institutions have tried a range of partial fixes by technical-administrative tinkering with structures and rules. Through applying combinations and permutations of hierarchies, networks, markets, and civic culture (structures) administered through laws, regulations, sanctions, incentives, programs, and processes (rules); metropolitan areas have not yet discovered a stable mix that can fix the coordination problem. Nor has the assignment of a common goal or the creation of a shared vision been sufficient to effectively direct institutional actors in policy coordination. Tinkering with measures like these has been unsatisfactory because critical political, historical, cultural, economic, and symbolic issues are dealt with inadequately or overlooked completely. Mere structural or procedural patches end up as metaphorical bandaids that do not heal the underlying conditions.

Coordination is not only a technical problem. One does not merely forge links among hundreds of organizations in a region or set a common goal and *presto*— concerted action happens. Another field on which this battle is fought is symbolic. Symbols do not merely represent another thing in the semiotic sense that a sign does. Symbols are appropriated for political and governmental use because they encapsulate an amalgam of values and meaning that resonate in society and have powerful effects in daily life.

Politics is at its base symbolic (Edelman 1964, Kubik 1994, Hedetoft 1998). In Spain the Franco regime allied itself with the Catholic church and its symbols the cross and the virgin to extend its power and weave its way into the fabric of society. Symbols such as a flag or images of a single family home on a tree lined street representing the "American dream" are at the root of many policies and politics in the United States. Symbols can be objects, images, and words. Their simplicity, mobility, and malleability enable them to be affixed to and seep into the interstices of any policy matter.

Symbols are often used to spark debate and to rally people around a cause. Whether a photo (think of Frank Capra's photo of a soldier shot in the Spanish civil war and Dorothea Lange's migrant mother during the great depression), an object (think of the Statue of Liberty, the Vietnam Veterans Memorial), or an urban design (think of Le Corbusier's radiant city, Howard's garden city, Burnham's 1909 Chicago plan), symbols find their way into public discourse and eventually into policy documents.

Because symbols are charged with meaning they embody important values shared by persons and institutions. In combination with structures, rules, strategy, and power; symbols play important roles in policy and plan making, intergovernmental coordination, and institutional development. This multifold capacity of symbols to perform several tasks enables us to look at symbols, the policy documents that contain them, and institutions in new ways. It also lets us reformulate the research questions posed earlier.

How has spatial planning been used to design and build new institutions? For our case of Madrid we specify this question as: how have city and metropolitan planning been used to build their own institutions? How have they been used to build or reform city and regional government? Designing and building institutions identifies another role for planning. This role stems from the shift in planning from government acting *on* cities to government acting on government *through* cities.

Neither new institutions nor their designs appear out of thin air. They are rooted in history and emerge from specific contexts. Thus this study also looks at institutions which make public policy more broadly. How does a policy making institution evolve? Which factors lead to continuity over time and which foster change? In looking at formation and growth we see the very process of institutionalization. What enables or inhibits repeated behavior patterns to take institutional shape? Does the way this occurs change over time? Do institutions have an identifiable life cycle?

**Hypotheses**

While these questions are broad, the analytical lens is sharp. It focuses on the relation between policy making and institutional development and change. The intermediary is the symbol. In our specific case of metropolitan planning in Madrid, it was the image of the future of the metropolis contained in government plans and strategies. The image was invented by planners and diffused through symbolic networks (Ansell 1996). This city plan image was the visible, capsule version of comprehensive planning policy. It also was the cohering logic which kept the budding institution of metropolitan planning together.

Before we specify our hypotheses for the Madrilenean case, we theorize the premises and identify the research variables below. As an institution evolves or goes through a transformation, or as an organization evolves into an institution, what actually changes? See Chapter 2 for the distinction between organization and institution. We posit that among other things, its constitutional image undergoes a fundamental change. The constitutional image is specific to the institution and embraces its mission, its *raison d'être,* its ideology, and the values that the institution's members invest it with.

The constitutional image can take any number of forms. It can be a slogan: "Neither snow nor rain nor gloom of night shall stay these couriers from the swift completion of their appointed rounds"—United States Postal Service, a motto: "Veritas"—Harvard University, a symbol: mouse—Disney Corporation, an object: wedding band—marriage, or an image: municipal crest or corporate logo.

We hypothesize that as the constitutional image changes so does the institution. If the institution changes gradually, its constitutional image undergoes no change or is adjusted in minor ways. If the institution undergoes a major reform in the context of a stable societal environment, a new image first co-exists and competes with the existing image. The new image then replaces the existing one by out-competing it if the reform is a success. If the institution declines there is a loss of faith in its constitutional image. In this case the image is out of tune with the changing conditions that are causing the institution to decline. It loses meaning and deteriorates. If the institution undergoes a radical transformation in a revolutionary context, a new image displaces the old one. If the institution becomes extinct, the image is lost as well, except perhaps for historic or nostalgic reasons. In all cases the constitutional image is correlated to the changing institution. If the image does not match the institution in its phase of change, a contradiction between them occurs and leads to a crisis in the constitutional image and the institution itself.

In this formulation the change to the constitutional image is the independent variable and the mode of institutional change is the dependent variable. Now we can grasp the primordial form of a dynamic theory of institutional evolution taking shape. The constitutional image varies across the life cycle of the institution along two dimensions. One dimension was described in the preceding paragraph. It ranges from creation through stability, replacement, decline, displacement, and loss of the image. Creation occurs when a new image is invented or appropriated. Stability refers to a situation in which the image does not change or undergoes minor change. Replacement is the substitution of a new image for an old one in an intentional manner. Decline occurs when the image is becoming less relevant *vis-à-vis* its context. Displacement means the complete and rapid substitution of one image by another swept in by a radical change or revolution. The loss of a constitutional image occurs when the institution ceases to exist.

The second dimension of the constitutional image combines image strength and clarity into a composite value we call degree of imageability. The word "imageable" is taken from Lynch (1960) and used in that sense. It refers to the degree to which an external or visible image can be seen as an internal mental image in the mind's eye. An image can be clear and strong, and thus have a high degree of imageability. At the other end of the scale it can be weak and ambiguous, and have a low degree of imageability.

The dependent variable is the mode of institutional change. It varies across time in accordance with the life cycle sketched above. The term life cycle does not imply a literal organic or biological process to describe or explain the institution and its evolution over time. Nor does it imply that all institutions go through this entire sequence. Moreover it does not expect that an institution would go through the sequence in this or any other chronological order.

The mode of change ranges from the initial formation of the institution, gradual and incremental change, major reform, decline, and radical change or revolution, to extinction. See Table 1.1 for the relationship between the independent and dependent variables.

In Madrid the intervening variables that have been selected for analysis are the following: 1) the stability of the political regime, 2) the administrative structure of the policy making (metropolitan planning) institution, 3) the policy making method, 4) the impact of individual leaders at the helm of the planning institution, and 5) the influence of party politics. Another intervening variable was tested and found to be non-determinant. It was the type of political regime. Since 1860 there have been four major regime types in Spain, with at least two separate instances of each. They are monarchy, republican democracy, dictatorship, and constitutional monarchy. The last type refers to the current democratic period, of which it is the only instance.

**Table 1.1     Relation between independent and dependent variables**

| Independent Variable | | Dependent variable |
|---|---|---|
| **Change to constitutional image** | **Imageability** | **Mode of change** |
| Creation | High | Formation |
| Stability | Medium to high | Gradual and incremental change |
| Replacement | High (replacing image) | Major reform within stable context |
| Deterioration | Low | Decline |
| Displacement | Very high (displacing image) Very low (displaced image) | Radical change within a revolutionary societal context |
| Loss | Low to very low | Demise/extinction |

Since the eruption of the modern city planning and urbanism in Madrid in 1860, the intervening variables have varied substantially, allowing a full test of the hypothesis under a range of conditions. Furthermore, the intervening variables were selected because they are typically described in the literature as being responsible for effecting both policy making and the institution itself. My hypotheses and findings do not deny the effect that the intervening variables exert. Rather they suggest that the independent variable explains the nature of policy making and institutional evolution robustly and persuasively, at least in the case of Madrid's metropolitan planning. The constitutional image and its reciprocal effect on institutional evolution needs to be taken into account along with the other factors in policy making, identified here as intervening variables. The intervening variables are displayed in Table 1.2.

**Table 1.2 Intervening variable dimensions**

| Variable | Negative impact on policy | Positive impact on policy |
| --- | --- | --- |
| Stability of political regime | Short term, unstable | Long term, stable |
| Structure of planning institution | Decentralized, loosely coupled | Centralized, hierarchical |
| Policy making method | Permissive, voluntary | Directive, mandatory |
| Individual leadership | Weak | Strong |
| Party politics | Weak party, planning is a low priority | Strong party, planning is a high priority |

Related hypotheses stem from the primary one. The secondary hypotheses are:

- The more rooted a symbol/image is in its society, economy, polity, and culture; then the more it will be used by the institution and the more effective it will be.
- The more imageable an image/symbol is, then the more it will be used in planning, policy making, and institution building, and the more effective it will be.
- The more deeply rooted content is in the institution, and the more deeply content is rooted in and connected to the currency of ideas and debates in which society is engaged, then the institution has greater relevance and greater effectiveness.

The contrapositives of these secondary hypotheses are also hypothesized:

- The less rooted a symbol/image is in its society, economy, polity, and culture; then the less it will be used by the institution and the less effective it will be.

- The less imageable, that is the more vague and ambiguous, an image/ symbol is, then the less it will be used in planning, policy making and institution building and the less effective it will be.
- The more deeply rooted in structure or process and less rooted in content, then the more transitory and less relevant is the institution.

The essence of the argument can be summed up in a deductive chain of reasoning. Political actors use images and symbols to appeal to the values of society. They manipulate symbols in the course of political struggles in political forums and arenas. City planning is an institutionalized political and social activity in which planners make and implement public policy regarding the future of a specific territory such as a city or metropolis. The citizens of a city or metropolis carry in their minds images of their place, as it is and as they would like it to be, not just a single image, as Lynch (1960) suggested. Citizens use their images of the city or metropolis in the conduct of their affairs. City planners, policy makers, and politicians use images to make plans, decide policy, and build institutions.

## Research Design

This work is neither a history nor a critique of Madrilenian planning. It is an analysis of several planning episodes in order to answer the specified research questions of how city and metropolitan plans and strategies were made and how the institution of metropolitan planning evolved. The term planning episode is borrowed from Bolan (1980). Our use of the term differs in that our episodes are measured in years and are longer than the time frame used by Bolan. The research is designed to test the hypotheses laid out in the prior section.

The five planning episodes are analyzed as individual case histories from the modern era of Spanish urban planning. This era began in the 1850s with the Catalonian engineer Ildefons Cerdà's plan for Barcelona, adopted by royal decree in 1859. Engineer Carlos María de Castro's plan for Madrid, whose plan owed much to Cerdà, was adopted by royal decree in 1860. It initiated the modern era in Madrid. In each episode the independent variable is the image of the future of the city (before 1940) or metropolis (after 1940) as depicted in official city and metropolitan plans and strategies. The image is analyzed to determine the change that it undergoes, its clarity and strength (imageability), and content. The dependent variable, the mode of change to the city/metropolitan planning institution, is analyzed to identify the stage in the institution's life cycle, overall stability, and importance of the planning institution within the political regime, and its administrative structures, planning processes, and thematic content (see Chapter 2 for an explanation of these terms.) This research design allows us to assess the actual relation of the image and the institution against a backdrop of a wide array of intervening variables, each which changed markedly across the five planning episodes. We will see how the images and the institution co-evolved in the face of the historical flux of dictators who rose and fell, democracies that waxed and waned, planners and other leaders who came and went, political parties that appeared and disappeared, and planning bureaucracies that made heads roll or pushed paper.

Each planning episode is understood as a planning cycle of about five to 10 years, the time it took to conceive and prepare a plan and take the first implementation actions after adoption. Implementation means institutional development and intervention in the territory planned for. We also recount the critical political, social, economical, and cultural contexts that preceded and set the stage for each episode. Each episode closes with key follow-on events in which the plan or strategy played an important role.

The first episode takes place in the 1980s. In the mid- and late-1980s Spain was well into consolidating its democratic government which came into being after long term dictator Francisco Franco died in 1975. The new democratic regional government the *Comunidad de Madrid* and its regional planning department prepared two key strategy documents. One was a regional re-election campaign platform called *Madrid Región Metropolitana* and the second was a sub-regional development strategy called the *Gran Sur* (Great South). The strong and clear images expressed in each are the independent variables in this episode. The dependent variable is the planning institution centered around but not limited to the regional planning department. The intervening variables are the consolidating (and thus relatively stable) democratic political regimes (regional and national), hierarchical and centralized regional government and planning structure (though less so than the preceding dictatorship but more so than during the citizens' movement), the technical-political planning process, the strong individual leadership of the planning department director, key deputies, and the regional government president (in the 1980s), and the strong socialist political party that controlled the regional government and the municipalities in the zone of the *Gran Sur* strategy. This episode concludes with the initial formulations of the new regional planning law and the intended successor to the two strategies, the Regional Plan of Territorial Strategy.

The first episode cannot be understood without knowing the transition to democracy in the 1970s and 1980s and the role the urban social movement played in that transition in Madrid. Moreover, the entire history of the modern city planning institution in Madrid bears on each episode, weighing more heavily as the institution ages and matures. We present the remaining four episodes in chronological order, beginning with the expansion plan of 1860, in order to show the effect of this history.

The second episode is the first instance of Madrid city planning in the modern era, chronologically speaking. The "Plan Castro" of 1860 and its historic image of the future expansion of Madrid guided growth till the turn of that century and beyond. The formal structure of the research design is not suited for the incipient nature of city planning in Madrid at that time. While city planning became institutionalized in the apparatus of city hall because of the force of Castro's plan, there was no identifiable city planning institution per se. The length between this episode and the next official plan (Bidagor's in 1946) renders a formal analysis in line with the research design less meaningful in comparison with the other episodes. Nonetheless the pattern of a plan containing a clear image of the city, its adoption by law, and its institutionalization in government was set in place by the 1860 plan and continued until the appearance of the *Comunidad de Madrid* in 1983.

The third episode extends from 1910 to 1931. Several plans were sketched on the drawing boards but none were adopted. In this period there were rapid changes between regimes at both the national and city levels, resulting in a low priority for planning. The independent variable is the lack of strong images in these draft plans, which did not enjoy political backing. The dependent variable is the succession of city organizations in which the fledgling activities of city planning were situated. The intervening variables are the shifts among political regimes (monarchy, democracy, dictatorship), the fragmented and weak structure in which planning found itself at the city level, the lack of influence of city plans on urban affairs, the lack of a stand-out leader in city planning, and party politics that was product and prisoner of the shifts among national and local regimes. In this period it can be adduced that for this episode, the intervening variables had a greater impact on city planning than the image, at least partly because the plan images were weak.

Fourth is the episode of the Bidagor Plan (named after its author the architect-planner Pedro Bidagor) from the inception of its undertaking 1939 to its official adoption in 1946. The historical context begins with a landmark 1929 planning scheme for Madrid and the all-important civil war of 1936 to 1939. The analysis extends to the 1956 national planning law, sired by Bidagor. This law codified the principles and institutions begat by his 1946 plan.

The independent variable is the image of Madrid in the Bidagor plan. The dependent variable is the planning institution spawned by the adoption of that plan, the *Comisaría General de Ordenación Urbana de Madrid*. The intervening variables are the dictatorship at the apogee of its power, the highly centralized and all-powerful *Comisaría* and its commanding centralized bureaucracy and hierarchical structure, a highly influential planner in the person of Pedro Bidagor, and the omnipotent falange of Franco.

The fifth episode starts in 1960 at the outset of the process to prepare a new metropolitan plan initiated by the same central government-controlled metropolitan planning agency the *Comisaría General de Ordenación Urbana de Madrid*. This plan was adopted by law in 1963. The *Comisaría*'s plan lacked two key ingredients, a strong and clear image and a strong individual planner with political backing. It is in this sense a counter-example to the 1940s and 1980s episodes. While the plan making and its attempted adoption took place in the 1960s, the analysis extends to 1980 to cover the rise of the important citizen movement and the transition to democracy, and the simultaneous downfall of the metropolitan planning agency.

The independent variable in this episode is the image of the Madrid metro area in the 1963 plan. The dependent variable is metro planning institution *Comisión de Planificación del Area Metropolitana de Madrid* (COPLACO), the *Comisaría*'s successor created by the law that adopted the plan. The intervening variables are the post-apogee Franco regime at the onset of its decline, the centralized and hierarchical planning institution, the technical, directive, and mandatory planning process, weak individual planning leadership, and declining influence of one faction in Franco's regime, the falange, in the early 1960s with the concomitant rise of another, the Opus Dei. The latter part of this period (mid and late 1970s) is erratic and unstable vis-à-vis political regimes and political parties. Many revisions and replacements to the 1963 plan were attempted throughout this period. None came to fruition.

**Method and Data Collection**

The multiple levels of analysis: images, individuals, organizations, institutions, processes, and political regimes; a period of time that spans more than one century; and the complex and reciprocal relations among the variables demands a combination of research methods. Any single method would do injustice to research of this complexity. The research methods are mainly historic and ethnographic. They employ qualitative and interpretive means and supplement them with quantitative and symbolic data as necessary. Using all these methods permits the collection of a wider range of data and a more robust analysis than if one method alone were applied.

The research took place *in situ.* The author spent six months in Madrid between November 1993 and April 1994. This period was supplemented by four additional visits of one week each between the summers of 1992 and 1995, and numerous short visits between 2000 and 2009. The first and last episodes (1980s regional planning and 1960s metropolitan planning) were based on primary data and structured yet open-ended interviews of one to three hours each with principal protagonists in the planning institution (broadly defined). See Appendices 1 and 2 for the interview questionnaire and list of interviewees. The data gathering and analysis of the COPLACO and *Consejería* episodes were supplemented by direct, informal participation in one of the interest groups in the metro planning institution, attending conferences, informal meetings and meals with institution members, walking and using the city, reading the press on a daily basis, and participating in the civic culture of Madrid: its *tertulias* and café society; all in an effort to immerse myself into the daily life of Madrid and its planning.

The middle three episodes relied on primary and secondary documents and the published research of others. No interviews with protagonists nor participation in their planning, of course, was possible.

Our analysis is an ethnographic and historic thick description (Geertz 1973) of the institutional, sociological, technical, and political aspects of urban planning in Madrid. The analysis is the result of access to hundreds of official documents (many unpublished), news and historical archives, interviews with 40 principal players (some not identified in Appendix 2), attending meetings, conferences, and being an interest group member. In short this research lets the voices of the documents and the players speak for themselves, through the interpretive lenses of the research design and the researcher.

## Findings

As an episodic story—not a history—of break points in the evolution of Madrid's city and metropolitan planning institution since 1860, the findings listed as numbers one through seven below refer strictly to the overall pattern of institutional change. Specific findings for each episode are presented with their corresponding chapters.

1.  In Madrid, politicians used city and metropolitan planning as a political strategy to build the institutions of metropolitan and regional planning and governance. This held true for the first entity of metropolitan governance, the *Comisaría General de Ordenación Urbana de Madrid y sus Alrededores* (General Commissariat for City Planning of Madrid and its Surroundings), created in 1946. Its follow-on the *Comisión de Planificación y Coordinación del Area Metropolitana de Madrid* (COPLACO), created in 1963, also adopted this strategy, as did its 1983 replacement the *Consejería de Ordenación Territorial, Medio Ambiente y Vivienda* (Department of Regional Planning, Environment and Housing (later the *Consejería de Política Territorial*, now again the *Consejería de Medio Ambiente, Vivienda, y Ordenación Territorial*).

2.  Planners in Madrid in turn have used the image to build these new institutions. These images have been physical designs of the city, of the whole metropolitan region, of a part of it, or a metaphor capturing a new vision of it. These images have most often been presented in spatial plans. Recently they have appeared in strategies—regional development strategies and re-election strategies. The prominence of the image can be attributed to its inherent power as well as its nature as the tool of habitual recourse of the designers of these institutions, architects by profession.

3.  Despite the major changes brought about by the citizens' movement and the transition to democracy in the 1970s, and the other historical facts particular to each planning episode chronicled in this research, the enduring nature of some of the features of Madrid's planning institution and its parts had a major impact on the way it makes plans and strategies, on the plans and strategies themselves, and on the way they are implemented. The passing on of planning traditions and customs is part and parcel of the

planning institution's very nature and therefore has an unavoidable effect on institutional outcomes.

4. Despite the aforementioned institutional legacy, Madrid metropolitan planning has changed over time. It is more democratic. It is more equitable in its spatial, social, and economic policies. It is less autarchic and more collaborative. The very process of institutionalization also has changed. In the nineteenth and through the mid-twentieth century the institution was created by the national governments. An architect, engineer, or small team of professionals created the plan that the institution was based on, and the ruling political regime approved it and brought it to life. During the transition from dictatorship to democracy in the 1970s an inverted institutionalization occurred, in which organized citizens provided the impetus and the basis for the new institution of metropolitan government. In the current phase of democratic consolidation, policy making processes are more collaborative and involve a more diverse set of actors than before the transition. They tend to span the public, private, and non-governmental sectors.

5. These changes have brought along with them a shift in the mode of planning. Formerly, planning in Madrid was a process of government acting directly on the territory. It is now a process of government acting on other units of government, as well as other organized interests, through the territory. In sum, spatial planning in Madrid is now a governance activity, and not merely under the purview of government.

6. In Madrid, planners invented new images for their physical territory and its social counterpart. Images of physical space were a social construct, a product of one of the social functions of planning. They also were vehicles for new social images, namely new identities for the "Great South" and "Madrid Metropolitan Region". The planners also instituted a method of planning new to Spain, a collaborative and coordinated decision process called *concertación*. The new physical and social images and the new processes transformed planning institutions. In short Madrid's planners invented new ways to solve collective action and collective consumption problems. They were able to do this because they were able to construct persuasive and clear images of the new social collectivities and the new territory they were planning for. Their preoccupation with the "model of the territory" so prevalent in their documents and discourse has led to social and political consequences and have been far from idle professional musings.

7. Madrid has been accustomed to a high degree of public intervention in the planning for and actual development of the city and the metropolis. Urban planning was the top item on Madrid's local and metropolitan public

agendas. This grew out of a general and persistent belief in and reliance on the public sector. This belief varied, of course, with political swings between the left (more interventionist) and right (more market oriented). For example in the early and mid 1990s the right rose to power and precipitated a concomitant reassessment of the fortunes and prominence of interventionist planning.

## Applicability of Findings

On one hand, these findings are specific to Madrid. On the other hand, after accounting for the unique cultural, historical, and political circumstances of Spain and Madrid, which the intervening variables have done in part, these findings may have broader relevance for other cities and regions, and public policy domains other than city planning, if certain contextual conditions are accounted for. They are listed below.

First is the remarkable and non-repeatable impact of the urban social movement called the *movimiento ciudadano* (citizens' movement) that marked the last transition from dictatorship to democracy in the 1970s. The specific contributions of the grassroots citizens' movement to planning in Madrid together with the broader political changes taking place at the national level penetrated the institutional body politic of planning deeply. Some of the more important impacts specific to that episode of Madrid's history had no precedents. While the movement occurred in Barcelona and to a lesser extent other Spanish cities, it is so unique that we should not expect them to be reproducible elsewhere. It and broader societal changes were largely responsible for institutional reform. First and foremost was the transition to democracy itself. The political freedom engendered by the transition occurred hand in hand with the rise of the grassroots movement. Metro planning was no longer controlled by the central state but devolved to the municipalities and the neighborhood associations which were the building blocks of the movement. The planning of that period was led by citizens, organizers, and politically radical planners and other professionals. The claims of the movement became the goals and objectives of planning and the data upon which decisions were based. It led to the downfall of a centralized and hierarchical style of planning and its replacement by its opposite, decentralized, democratic, and citizen-led planning. Metropolitan planning was neighborhood and municipal planning aggregated at the metro scale. Yet this burst of activity, so profoundly effecting the city of Madrid's 1985 General Plan and the mid 1980s planning and strategizing by the new regional government, found its spirit and means broken in the early 1980s. It has not yet recovered and so stands in history (Castells 1981, 1983, Borja 1977).

Another factor is the degree to which architects and other physical design-oriented professionals influence planning and political institutions. Professional planners in Madrid and Spain are architects by training. Their emphasis on territory, physical form, design, and images derives from their training. Architects dominate planning practice within the planning institution. This is not to say that architects are the only ones that are able to fabricate these images that have become central to planning and its institutions. It is to highlight their training, mode of thinking, and mode of acting.

Spanish planners spend their days analyzing the physical form of the city and metropolis, and designing futures for them. The architect-planner tradition goes back to the early part of the twentieth century. From about 1840, when the national civil engineering school opened in Madrid, to the 1920s engineers led the city planning profession and local city planning programs. Before and since it has been led by architects.

The emphasis on urban form goes back to the mid nineteenth century and earlier. This tradition also exists in Italy. It is not found, or is beginning to be more than just a blip on the radar screens of North American and Western European planning. This is not the place to enter into a cross-cultural debate on the roots and merits of this type of planning. Nonetheless, it colors the planning panorama. Spanish plans and strategies are loaded with images. This accounts in no small measure for the significant place images occupy in their documents, processes, the institution itself. It stands in sharp relief against the discursive mode of policy making prevalent in North America and Western Europe.

A further condition is the degree to which the government of a territory and its populace are willing to invest in and sustain a high level of public intervention in its planning. By its very nature city planning is a long term endeavor. While planning is subject to the same political winds and fashions that affect other public policy domains, long term commitment is vital.

Furthermore, these episodes have been just that. They have been landmark events that occurred precisely during the conjunction of historical currents that enabled new ways of looking at the city and metropolis, new ways of defining and solving its problems. New or transformed institutions, regardless of the degree to which certain institutionalized traits were passed on to the new institution, can only emerge at historic junctures. Truly new images are not a matter of daily routine.

On the other hand, these findings and the concomitant theory have broad applicability. As an advanced (post)industrial metropolis, Madrid, in all its uniqueness, shares its problematic with other such agglomerations. The production of urban space is a globalized social practice that leaves few (if any) metropolises untouched. Planning, as an international endeavor, trades its stories and practices with increasing frequency in the information age. The exchange and reproduction of practices of urban development and its planning makes the Madrid scenario available to others. Madrid itself has a long record of importing planning and bureaucratic practices from beyond its borders, and exporting some as well.

Moreover, these findings, while arising from urban planning, have commonalities with any substantive public policy matter which has many players, many interests, multiple and often conflicting issues, and competing objectives are spread over a specific territory, and takes a long term, broad look at the factors affecting the problematic it is facing. Which environmental, economic, and social issues today do not fit these criteria?

The findings provide politicians and policy makers with a more solid basis for designing metropolitan planning and growth management systems. Their value increases because they apply to other multi-jurisdictional, multi-disciplinary, multi-interest policy issues imbedded in complex and turbulent environments. They also give students of planning, politics, sociology, public administration, and institutions new ways of thinking about their common turf.

Thus the audience for this research is a broad one. One audience is professionals, politicians, analysts, interest groups, citizens, scholars, and students engaged in city planning—in other words the members of the planning community broadly defined. (We refer to city planning and growth management under all its guises: regional, spatial, territorial, and town and country planning, among others. See Chapter 2 for an elaborated definition of the institution of city planning.) These actors can be active on a variety of stages, be they community, urban, metropolitan, national, or rural. On the other hand the audience is institutionalists, also broadly defined. The research is not informed by a single discipline, but rather is multi- and inter-disciplinary. It cuts across disciplines and should be of interest not only to spatial planners and public administrators, along with social and political scientists, but anyone interested in institutions.

## Organization of the Book

This first chapter has given a statement of the research questions, an overview of the problem, the hypothesis guiding the specific research, the research design, the method of data collection and nature of the data collected, and finally general findings culled from the five planning episodes.

Chapter 2 defines an institution generally and the institution of city and metropolitan planning in Madrid specifically. It goes on to review the institutional literature so as to critically appraise what other analysts of public policy and institutions have said about our topic.

Chapter 3 reviews the urban planning literature. What is remarkable is the increase in the links between the urban planning and institutional literatures since this research has been conducted. Given that planning is a highly institutionalized and politicized activity, we might expect that these links will continue to increase.

Chapters 4 and 5 detail the five planning episodes. The most recent episode is presented first in Chapter 4. Chapter 5 presents the remaining four episodes in chronological order, beginning in 1860 and ending with COPLACO in the 1970s. Chapter 6 contains intermediate reflections on the nature of and change to the planning and political processes, the legal-administrative structures of the metropolitan planning institution, and the thematic content of that institution. It presents commonalities across the episodes and distinguishing features of each.

Chapter 7 presents a more systematic analysis of Madrid's metropolitan planning institution by taking a critical look at the dialectic of institutional evolution. This dialectic traverses the enantidroma of stability and change. It presents a version of institutional evolution that borrows conceptually from punctuated equilibrium.

Chapter 8 outlines a new theory of institutional evolution based on the empirical analysis. The theory places the image at the center of institutional development and change. It represents a new point of departure for institutional analysis. Further research is needed to empirically validate the hypotheses which the theory suggests, and to suggest new hypotheses.

# Chapter 2
# Institutional Evolution
# and Cognition: An Overview

The sources for learning about the nature of the metropolitan planning institution and its relation to policy making are found in the writings on city planning and those on institutions, the latter including policy making. Our academic legacy has kept these two fields apart, with some exceptions. Accordingly this review addresses the literatures of institutions and city planning in turn. Before doing so, we set out a conception of the institution generally, then focus on government and governance institutions, and finally spotlight spatial planning institutions, specifically those of metropolitan scale. With these definitions under our belt we will be able to assess the planning and institutional literatures in their light.

Strictly speaking, institution is an object of the verb to institute. It stems from the Latin *institutum:* plan, design, purpose, ordinance, instruction, precept. These early meanings were directly related to the giving of form and order, orderly arrangement, the established order by which any thing is regulated, a system, a constitution. It has come to mean an established law, custom, usage, practice, or other element in the political or social life of a people. It is a regulative principle or convention subservient to the needs of an organized community or the general ends of civilization. Most specifically, it is an establishment, organization, or association instituted for the promotion of some object, specially one of public or general utility (a highly selective excerpt from the Oxford English Dictionary). The etymology of the word parallels its evolution in the social science literature, with its emphasis shifting from structure to process. The shift in common language preceded the shift in academic usage.

Conceptions of these establishments range from a social practice (handshake, marriage, environmental impact statement) and an individual organization (say a single university) through an interactive network or system of organizations united by a common theme (academia) or a common territory (regional planning) to a broad social arrangement (government, market, family). The individual organization and broad social arrangement conceptions of an institution are better represented in political science, sociology, economics, and organization literatures than the systems (fields, networks) of organizations view. The networks perspective represents a middle ground between individual organizations and social arrangement. This middle ground has gotten more notice now from the new institutionalism and network theory. It also got attention two generations ago during the systems movement, behind a different guise. Because our research on metropolitan planning falls in the middle ground, this review is directed in that vein.

What distinguishes an institution from a "mere" organization or system of organizations is its persistence over time and extension through space (Giddens 1984), its history of affiliation among its members (Castles 1989, Steinmo, et al. 1992), and its embedded norms that are manifest in common practices and traditions (Bellah, et al. 1991). An institution is not an organization that is transformed by leadership which shapes its values and then projects and protects these values inside and outside of the organization, as Selznick believed. "It is leadership that transforms a mechanistic organization into a purposive and committed institutional system" (Selznick 1957). Not all institutions are organizations, strictly speaking, nor are all organizations institutions. Prior to the emergence of the new institutionalism in the 1980s the two terms were often used interchangeably. They still are, particularly in common language. Even some of those responsible for the renewed interest in institutions conflate the two terms (Hall 1986, 280).

Giddens (1984, 24) states "institutions are the more enduring feature of social life".

A half century earlier, we find that "The only idea common to all usages of the term "institution" is that of some sort of establishment of relative permanence of a distinctly social sort" (Hughes 1936). The patterns of relationships among the members are well understood and followed. Classic books on organizations tend not to account explicitly or completely for the formal and informal rules and practices arising from common (institutionalized) norms and recurring patterns of iteration (Barnard 1938, March and Simon 1958). March and Simon, in the introduction to the second edition of *Organizations* (1993, 5), averred that if they were to rewrite the book today, it would be along the lines taken up by the new institutionalism. That is, attention to four broad features: "empirical observations as opposed to theoretical speculations", more emphasis on rule-based action and less on analytically rational action, "we would less often take the premises of decisions as given exogenously", and "we would accord a greater role to the historical, social and interpretive contexts of organizations".

Norms that express values are at the heart of all institutions. Bellah and his colleagues drew on a long line of public philosophy in affirming "institutions are normative patterns imbedded in and enforced by laws and mores (informal customs and practices)" (1991, 10). Norms are deeply and often implicitly sewn into the institution's fabric. Norms are well known and followed, even if not always clear or explicit. Bellah, et al. also state "institutions always have moral elements" (1991, 10–11). The public philosophers they draw on are primarily Walter Lippmann and John Dewey. Huntington agrees: "Political institutions have moral as well as structural dimensions" (1968, 24).

The scale and scope of the institution of urban planning in the public domain lies between broad social arrangements and a single organization. It has a geographic and political locus in a polity, be it a city, region, state, province, or nation. (Regions, provinces, and states are defined differently depending on the country.

Nevertheless, this definition holds for all of them.) The institution of public sector planning is not just the designated government planning agency. Nor is it just the executive branch or the entire level of government containing that agency. Instead it is a multi-organizational construct. It is all the organizations, public, private, and mixed that are implicated in planning. It spans all branches at each level of government. It is best embodied in the concept and practice of governance.

For example, the membership of the institution of comprehensive planning (growth management, spatial planning) in a metropolitan region includes executive agencies, courts, and legislatures of local, regional, provincial, state, and national governments; private sector actors involved in the growth management arena or affected by it; and citizens and civic organizations likewise engaged or affected. It includes interest groups—those with a stake in planning and development outcomes—such as those who build (utilities, government, developers, builders, unions), those who finance (investors, banks, insurers, government, utilities), and others (neighborhood associations, environmental groups, citizens, property owners) (Heinett and Kübler 2009, Healey 2007, Innes and Booher 2010, Xu and Yeh 2010).

The planning institution also includes processes used to manage growth that have become institutionalized, including making plans, zoning, reviewing development proposals, financing capital facilities, assessing environmental impacts, and so on. Processes may be codified laws and regulations or informal customs and traditions (Healey 2007, Eymeri-Douzans and Pierre 2010, Cheema and Rondinelli 2007). Metropolitan planning also institutionalizes its substantive content. Content appears in official documents such as plans and reports, laws and regulations. Content is also expressed in symbols and images, both visual (logos, plans, maps, designs, photos, etcetera) and verbal (metaphors, mottos, slogans, names, narratives, stories, and so on).

This view expands the traditional notion of the institution of metropolitan planning (Abercrombie 1945, Hall 1982). In Madrid, our case study, this definition goes beyond the status quo of its time (de Terán 1982, Ezquiaga Domínguez 1989). Over the course of this century the institution of Madrilenean metropolitan planning has grown in size. It is still growing, mainly by expanding outward geographically as Madrid itself has grown, and by encompassing a wider variety of stakeholders. In the past it has been almost exclusively a government operation. Before the advent of democracy in 1977, control bounced back and forth between city hall and national government. Since democratic consolidation in 1982, planning for metro Madrid has been delegated to the regional government *La Comunidad Autónoma de Madrid*. The city, however, has not let go of its illusions of influencing metro growth. Our research looks at an organization which also leads an institution—the regional government of Madrid's regional planning department. This organization is an institution by virtue of the fact that it carries forward the historic practices, traditions, and norms that were common to its city and metro planning predecessors; and because it has been formally designated as such by the regional government's constitution. Searle calls this type of constituting the result of a "performative utterance" (a type of speech act) (Searle 1995).

What we stress is the radical departure of this expansive definition of both institutions in general and of planning institutions in particular from pre-2000 standards in both fields. Since 2000 there has been an explosion in institutional and governance scholarship. The reader should pay close attention to the notions of identity and boundary as the research analyzes Madrid's metropolitan planning institution. Spatial boundaries and attendant place-based identities were factors that Madrid's architect-planners considered during each episode of institutional evolution. Spatial (territorial) factors were but one factor used to demarcate the institution. Others were the legitimacy of nongovernmental actors and the structure of the relations among the members.

## Institutions and Scholarship

Historically institutional scholarship has alluded to major theoretical debates in pairs, as if they met a dance. At the institution ball we have found society and the state (Hobbes 1651), politics and bureaucracy (Wilson 1888), structure and action (Parsons 1937, 1960), stability and change (Mannheim 1936), and the seemingly ever present micro and macro distinction. Different partners take the lead at different times and places in tune with academic fashion. Anthony Giddens (1984), Hannah Arendt (1958), Mary Douglas (1986), and the work of Foucault and Habermas are among the prominent examples of thinkers about institutions that overarch dualisms and conventional categories. We may think of them, as Geertz did, as "all purpose subversives".

Inserting a third partner always complicates a relationship. (I thank Arturo Soria y Puig for this metaphor.) Yet if there is one thing we know about institutions, especially political ones, it is their complexity and chaos. Which theories based on dualisms inadequately explain. Even Anthony Giddens's concept of structuration, which attempts to bridge the structure-action and micro-macro gaps in one breath, still resolves his unity in a duality, structure and agency. This is so notwithstanding his attempt to redefine structure and agency (1984). Anthropologists, including structural ones, have long inter-related the micro and macro. The infusion of cognition and discourse into social, political and institutional theory has blurred this boundary, as evidenced in the contributions of Habermas, Chomsky, Foucault, Searle, and others; as diverse as they may be on other scores.

Furthermore, Giddens's theory and others, as we will have occasion to see, discount or ignore the role of an institutions substantive content that its agents act on via individual action and institutionalized processes. By content we refer to the substance rather than the form, whether form be processual or structural. Content refers to the essential nature of the institution. It is the foundation that underlies, supports, and provides the basis for the very existence of the institution. Content is ontological, institutionally speaking.

This research steps into the dance with a new partner, content. In at least one respect content is not precisely a new partner. Analyses of institutions routinely refer to their moral content, or underlying values. They posit moral content as fundamental to the essence of institutions—separating them from mere organizations. Moral content has been unpacked carefully by a number of thinkers, as can be seen in most of the writings by Seyla Benhabib, Amy Gutmann, Alistair MacIntyre, John Rawls, Jürgen Habermas, Robert Bellah, and many others.

Content is a focal point for those who try to disentangle the notion of the public good, such as Meyerson and Banfield (1955), Bellah, et al. (1985, 1991), and Tierney (2006). Others address content through learning, in the extensive literatures on organizational learning, not covered here, and institutional learning (Zito 2010, Healey 2007, Gualini 2001, Cooke 2007). Finally, other institutionalists struggle with values and norms. Their analyses take on a range of issues from the place of values in the institutions of urban planning (Campbell 2003, Osborne 2009) to legitimacy in governance (Heinett, Sweeting and Getimis 2009, Waller and Wolff 2008). While content, broadly construed, can be observed in many publications on institutions, there is a relative silence on its role in institutional development, evolution, and design.

Nor are other aspects of content like ideas and images, laws and plans, myths and symbols, and so forth. This assertion holds more for current thinking than foundational work at the turn of the last century. George Herbert Mead's focus on morals had a long (but not lasting) influence on American sociology and the study of institutions, as did Max Weber in Europe and America. Early writing (Mead, Dewey, James, Durkheim, and Weber, for example) was slanted more toward morals while more recent work (Parsons, early and mid-career Habermas, Levi-Strauss, Goffman, and Giddens) leans more to structure and action in a technical sense—how they work. A main finding of this research is the prime role content plays in institutional formation, fixity, and ferment.

Should this surprise? By examining content we affirm the role cognition plays in institutional development as indicated by Giddens and others. Giddens (1984) employs the term consciousness rather than cognition and structuration rather than development. He draws on Erickson (1963, 1967, 1968), Garfinkel (1967), and Erving Goffman's life work to argue that an individual's unconscious and consciousness are coordinated in a self-conscious and reflexive way when interacting with others. Commonplace personal interaction leads to the establishment of routines and social integration and explains how individual and group action (agency) extend in time and space to evolve the institution.

Cognition adds force to the argument that content drives institutional life. Cognition needs to cognize something. That something is content, the intellectual substance the mind works on. Content is the mental grist for the institutional mill.

Before embarking on a more detailed excursus of content we must retrace our steps back to the origins of the disenchantment with the duality of structure and action. The discontent was seen along several fronts. Structure was seen as beholden to received and rigid views of organizations, institutions, and society. This perception masked their inner workings. Action, in turn, became increasingly restricted to the abstraction "rational action" which was divorced from culture, history, time, and space. Rational action pertained to the individual, was collectivized in functional organizations, or aggregated in markets. Rational action became associated with a variety of micro viewpoints and became increasingly quantified.

The attacks along these fronts were well mounted. At their base was the linguistic turn in analytical philosophy, which eroded the foundations of logical positivism. The linguistic turn stems from the later Wittgenstein back through Heiddeger to Nietzsche. It has breached the walls of philosophy and spread to psychoanalysis (Lacan), literary theory (Barthes, Derrida), sociology, where it is referred to as the communicative turn (Habermas), politics, where it is referred to as discursive (Gamson, Dryzek), and semeiotics (Eco). It has marked fields in which the use and misuse of language and signs are central. The linguistic fire has been fueled by the Chomskian revolution in linguistics itself.

In some disciplines such as philosophy, linguistics, and literary theory, the linguistic turn has focused on content. In sociology and political science, on the other hand, institutional researchers have taken it in the direction of delimiting action towards discourse. The latter tendency has been influenced in no small measure by Habermas's theory of communicative action (1984, 1987) and Searle's theory of speech acts (1969). Discursive and communicative approaches have risen to prominence as belief in rational action has declined, even in the face of Habermas clinging to a critical version of rationality and the upsurge of rational action theory, however much revised (Elster 1989a, 1989b, Coleman 1990, Grafstein 1992, Knight 1992). The general dissatisfaction with rational action arose, ironically, from the pillar of rational approaches to organization, Herbert Simon, in his influential article on satisficing, "A Behavioral Model of Rational Choice" (Simon 1952).

With so many attempts since to discredit or reorient rational choice theory, and its disciplinary variants decision theory, game theory, social contract theory, organization theory, social systems theory, operations research, policy analysis, and the general tumult in sociology and political science; one suspects that underlying all these efforts is a fundamental problem. Mainly, in complex public policy arenas, individuals choose as members of organizations and institutions. They choose within a swirling dynamic of history and society, politics and power that use language and symbols in concrete institutional settings, not in abstract theoretical constructs. For example, a complex policy space like city planning entails hundreds and up to thousands of actors making tens of thousands of individual choices in the process of elaborating a city plan, which itself may be composed of hundreds of documents, elaborated over a period of years at the cost of millions of dollars. There is no *single* choice involved.

Further complicating rational choice theory is the problem of representation. Most of the actors in a city plan making process work in organizations and putatively represent their organization. Those who proclaimed a new institutionalism open their analyses with a critique of rational choice (see Ostrom (1990) and Jones (1994) for persuasive ones). We will not elaborate such a critique here, as this research is not based on rational choice nor its assumptions.

Related to rational action, models of collective action also fell short in explaining the inner workings and overall logic of institutions. The assumptions of game theory, for example, did not correspond to the complexity of the real world (Dolšak and Ostrom 2003, Scharpf 1993, Ostrom 1990, Axelrod 1984). Other theories of collective action were circumscribed within economics (Hardin 1968, Olsen 1965, Buchanan and Tullock 1965, and Downs 1957). This led to an equally prodigious realm of critiques, paralleling the dis-satisfaction with their cousins in the rational action paradigm.

In the 1980s and 1990s new approaches to rational and collective action and organizations arrived with the moniker neo-institutionalism. It pointed to a renewed interest in institutions as an object of research and to new categories of analysis (Steinmo, et al. 1992, Bellah, et al. 1991, Powell and DiMaggio 1991, March and Olsen 1989, Skocpol 1985). While the new institutionalism continued to deal with structure and function, increasing attention was given to content in its various guises: symbols, signs, values, norms, myths, and their presentation in documents, images, and discourse. Attention to the design, formation, evolution, and change of institutions is also increasing (Rehfeld 2005, Weller and Wolff 2005, Gualini 2001, Goodin 1996, Ostrom 1990, North 1990). For a precursor see Samuel Huntington (1968).

## Content and its Discontents

Content refers to the substance of institutions. Content embodies meaning (being) and purpose (becoming, doing). In a sense it is a bundle of items, each item a carrier of intelligence useful to and manipulable by members of the institution. In this analogical sense, content is the institutional category containing memes. Memes are cultural analogues to biological genes. Richard Dawkins, the inventor of the meme concept, defines meme as "a unit of cultural transmission, or unit of *imitation.* ... Examples of memes are tunes, ideas, catchphrases, clothes fashions, ways of making pots or of building arches. Just as genes propagate themselves in the gene pool by leaping from body to body via sperm or eggs, so memes propagate themselves in the meme pool by leaping from brain to brain via a process which, in the broad sense, can be called imitation" (quoted in Searle 1995, 57). A meme is a cultural replicator (Dawkins 1976).

While memes come in various forms, we will limit ourselves to those that assume symbolic form and can be transmitted via symbolic communication (not limited to verbal discourse) in institutional settings. A preliminary typology of such symbols includes natural (Douglas 1970) and human (Jung 1964, 1969a), signs (Eco 1976, 1984), analogy (Chomsky 1995, Holyoak and Thagard 1995), metaphor

(Jaynes 1976), myths (Levi-Strauss 1975), and images (Boulding 1956). We will not present a critical review of the debates surrounding these objects of symbolic communication. We will comment on the dearth of institutional research on their use in the transmission of meaning in and among institutions.

In political settings institutional content can be incarnated in documents such as constitutions, laws, party platforms, plans, policies, and programs; or any medium such as a flag, anthem, or creed. Each institution has its own bundle of items that collectively make up its content that guides the conduct of the members of the institution. We can call meaning represented by this bundle an institution's *doctrine* (Faludi and van der Valk 1994). Each doctrine is associated with a specific *institutional code.*

One vehicle of content is language. The language of an institution may be a common one such as English. It can also be specialized to an institution. For example the institution of mathematics uses numbers, signs, and symbols to construct formulae and equations—its unique *institutional code.* The institutions of architecture and urban planning use images—designs, drawings, models, and the like—as their primary institutional code.

In this classification, images occupy a special position due to their link between the external represented world and the internal mental world (of the thinking subject). This is so because we have the capacity to think in images and use imagery in thought processes. We recognize from the outset that not all individuals have the same ability to manipulate images cognitively and that some persons, it is claimed, do not possess this faculty at all. In cognitive and related sciences this is a matter of debate.[1] At the least, all non-blind people use external visual images and refer to them in their mental processes, even if they are not transformed into mental images. Anecdotally we all seem to see with the mind's eye, and our languages are replete with visual metaphors for thought. We "see clearly", "see what you mean", have "hindsight", "foresight", and "insight". We "focus" the mind on something and "imagine". Seeing is believing.

Images like photos, designs, drawings, maps, and plans; and all symbols and signs stand for something else. They represent by re-presenting. Images let us describe what is and imagine what could or should be. Imaginative images are "corrective fictions" (Alpers 1983), referring to a specific use that also has deceptive or propagandistic implications. They are abstract—excerpts of a portion of their surroundings. They are synthetic—they put together visual percepts in our brain to serve a purpose. For the image as abstraction view see Jaynes (1976). His images are part of the represented whole. We "excerpt" because we can never see anything in its entirety. See also Marr (1982), Arnheim (1969). For the image as synthetic view, see Boorstin (1962) and Finkel (1992).

Images have properties that account for their proliferation and impact in contemporary society. They are malleable and can be formed, reformed, transformed

---

1    The debate rages in philosophy as well. For the contours of this debate, see Bateson (1972 and 1979) and Searle (1995b). For a psychological view see Rachlin (1994).

at will by a range of technologies. They are reproducible, transmittable, and infinitely retransmittable, and thus ideal memes, as advertising and marketing have noticed. They help people catch on to an idea. An image is also relational. It links the thing we see in the mind's eye to the external object it represents, along with its setting and associated activities. Images are far from isolated forms. We attach preconceived notions to an image, giving it meaning. Jung's work on archetypes is germane. He states "[t]he term 'image' is intended to express not only the form of the activity taking place but also the typical situation in which the activity is released" (Jung 1982, 106). Context, inseparable from the image, endows it with added meaning (Ledrut 1973). In this manner images convey socially constructed meaning (Pitkin 1967).

The meaning of an image changes depending on its context and who uses it. Nietzsche, "the first to connect the philosophical task with a radical reflection upon language" (Foucault 1971, 305) asked "who is speaking?". That is, who has power over words? Today he may have asked "who is creating and projecting the image?" Thus we can refute Searle (1995a, 76–78) who categorically states "language is epistemically indispensable" to institutions because the "[institutional] facts in question, being inherently social, must be communicable". Images exist side by side with language in the institutional repertoire of symbolic communication. Telling is the example of the later Wittgenstein, a philosopher of language, who resorted to images to explain a philosophical dilemma regarding language because language itself was an insufficient analytical tool to resolve it. He used "pictures" to describe (rather than theorize, because Wittgenstein admits he cannot theorize his way out of the muddle) the relation between language, mind, and reality. He alludes to the way images control language. "A *picture* held us captive. And we could not get outside it, for it lay in our language and language seemed to repeat it to us inexorably" (Wittgenstein 1958, para. 115). "I wanted to put this picture before him and his *acceptance* of this picture consists in his begin able to regard a given case differently: that is, to compare it with *this* rather than *that* set of pictures. I have changed his *way of looking at things*" (ibid, para. 144). Quotations are from Stein (1993, 215–216). However we should take care not to overinterpret his claims. He was constructing a metaphilosophical discourse and his picture refers to the picture of language (Stein 1993). Compare to Boulding (1956).

In fact we are moving away from language toward the image. Away from word-based DOS and internet and to icon-based Macintosh, Windows, and the World Wide Web. Where power is at stake (money, politics), images are supplanting words. Searle, who ingravidates language, goes on to say that "in real life the phenomenon are extremely complex, and the representation of such complex information requires language". We submit that images of all sorts better convey complex phenomena. It goes far beyond "a picture is worth a thousand words", as we will instantiate with our case studies.

Like words and concepts, images are dynamic. "Society continually reinvents the image" (Boulding 1956, 64). Actually it is individuals in society that make and remake images, and society (re)constructs their meanings. Whoever controls the image maintains power. Therefore a change in the image signals a change in power relations. "An image which is about to collapse of its own weight is frequently supported far beyond its time ... that attacks of the reformers produce defensive mechanisms on the part of the holders of the image [and of power]" (Boulding 1956, 122). Of course Boulding is wrong in that images do not collapse of their own weight. They collapse when they do not respond to society's view (image) of reality. The image is out of touch, out of context.

While power uses images and symbols, they can also be used against power. The Polish labor movement Solidarity created some images (the clenched fist) and appropriated others (religious and nationalist) in its struggle (Laba 1990, Kubik 1994). They acted in accord with Swidler's thesis that society uses symbols strategically to form and reshape culture to its desired ends (Swidler 1986). A spectacular example of using images against established power was the Apple computer company's one time only television commercial in the mid 1980s during the Super Bowl football championship halftime program in which a renegade from upstart Apple (at the time) smashed the giant video screen that was projecting an image of its chief rival, IBM. Society draws on "symbolic capital", including images, to perform these acts (Bourdieu 1986) and to build up stores of "intellectual, social, and political capital" (Gruber, Innes, Neuman, Thompson 1993). An example of a government agency using images in this way was the Resettlement Agency (later the Farm Security Administration) in the United States during the great depression. Photographers such as Dorothea Lange, Margaret Bourke-White, and Walker Evans, film directors such as John Ford, and writers such as John Steinbeck and Archibald MacLeish were employed by the agency to document the depression and to inform and shape policy back in Washington (Gawthrop 1993).

The image is shared among members of society or an institution and is thus a "public image" (Boulding 1956). It is an important factor in creating the "collective memory" from which societies, institutions, and other collectivities such as cities draw their public images (Halbwachs 1950). Collective memory is built in large part upon spatial images—images a people have of a place, their place, for example a city (Halbwachs 1950, 128–157). Planning and governing institutions have capitalized on collective memory to design and build cities (Rossi 1967, Boyer 1994). As we shall argue, not only have planning and governing institutions used images to design and build cities. They have also used images to shape institutions.

From an institutional point of view perhaps the most important feature/function of an image is its ability to link the micro and the macro—the individual and the institution. It is a missing piece in Giddens's theory of structuration, which proposes that minute social practices recur and extend over time and space to form and structure the institution. The practices thus become institutionalized (Giddens 1984). While Giddens assigns a key place to cognition in structuration, building on Garfinkel, Goffinan, and Erickson, he avoids the role of the image in this cognitive transformation. He offers no explanation of the broader concept of content and its part in structuration, even as he acknowledges its existence. What is missing in Giddens regarding the cognitive function of the image is taken up by Boulding's theory of the image. He posits two images: internal (mental, emic) and external (visible, edic). We change our thinking about something when our mental image of it changes. This proposition, while still contested, is now often argued in the affirmative (Bateson 1972, Heil 1983, Tursman 1995, Brooks 1994, Thagard 2005).

What we see with our eye is an image percept that is constructed in the brain (Finkel 1992). It is a "conceptually structured representation" subject to "perceptual relativity" (Heil 1983, 65, 84). Holyoak and Thagard (1995) ascribe similar cognitive functions to analogy and metaphor. They argue that a "web of culture" is use to spread meaning in society via analogy. Ansell (1997) finds the same to occur for symbols in "symbolic networks" as does Boulding (1956) for images in society—images are made public and thus subjective. Social movements have made use of symbols and images in their attempts to change the social order and build new institutions (Castells 1983, Eyerman and Jamison 1991, Castells 2004).

But these works are largely drawn from outside the fields of politics, sociology, institutions, and organizations. In politics, Lasswell (1949, 1952) and Baudrillard (1972) have produced major studies on the political use of images, symbols, and signs. Edelman (1964) makes the inverse case, that politics itself can be used symbolically. Their research has documented the instrumental use of images, symbols, etc. as strategies to attain political victory (political power), to gain passage of a policy, or to orchestrate values. They have not touched upon the use of images in the design and creation of, nor the development and evolution of, political institutions. In sociology Ledrut (1968, 1973) has constructed suggestive theories, yet these same limitations apply. Morgan (1993) discusses images and imagination in the creation, management, and change of functional organizations (with a focus on private sector firms) but not of institutions. The institutionalists, old and new, have remained silent. To paraphrase Aaron Wildavsky, if images matter, why don't we hear about them from institutionalists? (Wildavsky 1989).

Occupying another special place in symbolic communication are stories, narratives, myths, and legends. They are not so much discrete symbols as packages of meaning that relate symbols and convey a bundle of ideas in a form easy to assimilate. A story, narrative, myth, or legend connects disparate items of information together to give coherence, relevance, and meaning. Stories give context to words, symbols and actions. Without context, that is, without a story, words and symbols would have no meaning (Bateson 1979). "Narratization" gives context to events, stimuli, information within consciousness (Jaynes 1976). "Policy narratives" make sense of policy issues that reside in other institutional settings and conform to other institutional logics. These narratives enable individuals and institutions to confront complex phenomena in other institutional frames and make them useful in their own (Hajer and Wagenaar 2003, Roe 1994, Schön and Rein

1994). Myths are used in policy making and analysis as well, in the definition of policy problems (Glynn 2009, de Neufville and Barton 1987) and the adoption of policy.

Whether the symbols stand alone (signs, analogies, metaphors, symbols, images), are contextualized (stories, narratives, myths, legends, and again images), or are instrumentally packaged for institutional use (laws, regulations, plans, programs, policies, strategies); they all add up to content. Content appears in the political science literature as "public ideas" (Reich 1990, Yishai 1993), "public philosophy" (Lippmann 1955), and "ideology" (Seliger 1976). Within the schema proposed in this section these are shades of grey rather than concepts of a whole new order. Given the resourcefulness (adaptability) of institutions and the mobility and malleability of symbols, particularly images, the combination of the two as institutional images is potent and their permutation infinite. It is curious that institutional scholars have remained nearly silent about this connection.

Some have made the connection. "Institutions always have a moral content" (Bellah, et al. 1991, 10). Morals, to which we can add ideals, principles, values, and norms, provide the ontological foundation upon which content is assembled. In Parsons, central values and institutional norms were given (Bellah, et al. 1991, 290). In post-Parsonian scholarship morals are dealt with in a more strategic sense. In some instances morals are reduced to interests. In this sense he built on the work of Durkheim, Weber, and Mead to whom moral concerns were central in their analyses of institutions. Yet by assuming them as given, Parsons relegated them to a minor role in his conception of a dynamic society and his emphasis on action. In so doing he precipitated a divorce of content from the study of society and institutions. Rid of content, the social sciences zoomed in on action and structure from a technical perspective, once the troublesome issue of morals and ends were cut free. Content became the province of specialists: semioticians, literary theorists, and communication theorists. Moral issues were left to the philosophers.

According to an interesting analysis of city regions and their governance institutions by Segberg, "capital and content flows [among city regions in global networks] are difficult to organize and cannot be regulated effectively, at least not by traditional instruments and strategies". As a consequence, "regulation and control is in crisis". By his analysis, even "the term *governance* is in crisis" (2007, 6–7). Segberg's reading of content in contemporary city regions and the global economy is that it is a primary matter, along with currency and power, that flows through global networks that link institutions.

In another reading, political interests are a form of content that has long been central to political thought, particularly in pluralist and corporatist paradigms. Interests often have been treated, however, as deinstitutionalized and pertinent to individuals and their choices. Rational and mathematical treatments of interests further disembody interests and their kin preferences from meaning and distance them from institutional analysis. There has been a renewed legitimacy for the study of interests and institutions, as seen in the work on preferences (Jones 1994) and interests (Swensen 2004, Kantor 2000, Salisbury 1992, Bellah, et al. 1991, Powell and DiMaggio 1991).

The many sided nature of content and the way it is embedded in institutions makes it hard to talk about categorically in non-ambiguous or non-tautological ways. Take the example of an environmental impact statement. It is at once an institution in itself and a part of its authorizing institution. It has its own preparation process, and is a product conveying content. It is designed to shape future action of its authorizing institution and others as well. It carries in its premise and its findings the values of its parent institution.

The new institutionalism is beginning to address the intricacies of content. New institutionalists tend to consider the interplay between content and existing institutions rather than on the use of content in forming new ones. They have concentrated on myth, symbolic order, image, and ritual. That is, it refers to the institutional reproduction of symbolic orders, not the use of symbolic orders to created and reproduce the institution (Friedland and Alford 1991). According to Friedland and Alford, institutional logic is based on "symbolic orders" and rituals are used to reproduce institutional logic. Kenneth Boulding theorized the link between images and the formation of institutions 40 years ago (1956). This theme is taken up in the latter chapters of this book. It also documents the effect of myths in the institutional environment that act on the institution, not the role of myths in creating or maintaining the institution (Powell and DiMaggio 1991, Geertz 1983, 1973). So content is creeping back in, but still occupies last place in the structure/action/content triad.

Content is contextual. It is more than just imbedded in processes and structures. Content makes sense in particular settings and loses its logic outside of them. Content has a relational character that enables members of an institution to make sense to each other, and members of different institutions to understand one another despite distinct institutional interests and codes. It can be thought of as the glue that binds loosely linked networks and the oil that lubes communication channels. Anthony Giddens criticizes the "retreat into code" of the post-structuralists and post-modernists and suggests that they miss the "relational character" of language. "Such a retreat is not at all necessary if we understand the relational character of codes that generate meaning to be located in the ordering of social practices" (1984, 32).

If we accept the Arendt/Foucault premise of the source of domination—the separation of knowledge from action—then we must take knowledge/content seriously. Their split changed the historical locus of power from action to knowledge. Images are a concentrated form of knowledge and content. An image fuses content, context, and meaning into a high impact, wide-spread, and widely spreadable source of power in institutions. It also is a ready resource for those who want to fight, change, or topple one.

## Institutional Formation and Evolution

When we look at how an institution forms, the categories of structure, action, and content help us understand the mechanism. Typically we think of a political institution being created by a constitution—branches of government (structure) and laws (processes). Or any institution being created by the chronic repetition of habitual behaviors (routines) becoming fixed over time (structures). This research suggests that content and not processes or structures is the seed from which an institution grows. As the institution takes shape, its content emerges from an idea. This idea represents a change in the way of seeing the world, or perhaps just a set of issues. In essence, a change in perception. The new idea circulates and becomes part of the daily ebb and flow of an extant institution, thus changing it. Perhaps the idea sparks the inception of a new institution. Maybe it reforms an existing one. In either case content is at the core.

Research on scientific and conceptual revolutions informs this approach. Yet as most of these deal with the broad international enterprise that is the institution of science, care must be exercised in borrowing concepts directly or analogically. Thagard (1992) offers a cognitive perspective on conceptual revolutions in science. He argues that rationality and coherence of new theories explain scientific change. He opposes Kuhn (1962) whose paradigm shift is based on the primacy of sociological explanation and relativistic epistemology. Thagard's model of theory replacement has four stages: incorporation of a new concept, sublation and then supplantation and finally disregard of the old one. Kuhn's model has four stages for "revolutionary" change, which he distinguishes from "normal science": crisis of a paradigm, paradigm breakdown, coexistence of old and new paradigms, and finally rejection of the old and replacement with the new one. Foucault's (1970) study of conceptual revolutions in the social sphere, like Thagard's in science, has a cognitive basis. For Foucault conceptual revolutions are based on changes in representation, changes in the relations among signs, the thing signified, and signification. He suggests that there has been a historical shift of meaning from the object to the sign. He accords a key role to the mental image and the imagination.

Several paths exist by which institutions can form. One is by fiat. A law, constitution, or decree imposes a new institution "from above". Or it may occur "from below" by revolution or social movement, with the masses imposing a new social order. Another path is self-organization. It can be spontaneous or intentional. A spontaneous event can prompt a reform or a even a new institution. A conjunction of factors result in the binding of forces around a leader who carries an idea, image, or metaphor that captures a new spirit. Self-organization stems from the rules that evolve into an institution as a "by-product of strategic conflict over substantial social issues" (Knight 1992, 126). These issues are often about the distribution and redistribution of resources (Knight 1992, Ostrom 1990). Ostrom highlights the incremental, self-transforming nature of institutional change in her own studies of common pool resource institutions which "current theories do not take into account" (1990, 191). Recently social scientists have begun to research self-organization, taking many of their cues from natural sciences, particularly biology, and chaos and complexity theories. Ostrom (1990) and Knight (1992) are among the social scientists who do not borrow from the biologists. Knight wants to counter institutionalism's use of evolutionary accounts in biology with rational choice in economics.

Some institutions are built around innovative policy-making processes (Ostrom 1990, Healey, et al. 1996, Gualini 2004, Innes and Booher 2010). These new institutions are the trenches in the battleground of democracy to which citizens turn in the face of apathy toward "politics as usual": representative politics, special interests, negative campaigning, and the like. As voters increasingly turn away from the voting booths and the idea of representative democracy, there has been a corresponding increase in direct participation at the local level (Heinett, Sweeting and Getimis 2009, Salet, Thornley and Kreukels 2003, de Souza Brigss 2008). This effect is compounded in the flurry of committees, commissions, panels, and other groups comprising the arenas and forums of metropolitan planning. This occurs as metro areas struggle to gain control of their destinies in the absence of coherent and unitary entities endowed with sufficient political and financial resources to manage their growth and development. Although "institutionalized normative expectations" do not exist at the outset of the design of these processes (Grafstein 1992, 101), they can be created as policy is made if other institutional structuring factors accompany them.

Still another path is gradual emergence. Day to day activities become habits and convert into routines. They become imbued with commitment and value. A gradual replacement of old mores with new ones structures the new institution in subtle ways. In this manner a new institution may be created almost with our being aware of it, so gradual can the acceptance of new behavior patterns sometimes be. This is the position Knight suggested (1992). Berger and Luckmann (1966) call this gradual process "social construction". Anthony Giddens (1984) calls this "structuration". Habermas (1989) gives these ideas their furthest institutional reach, the "public sphere". While Kuhn's 1961 landmark *The Structure of Scientific Revolutions* can be read as a tract on punctuated equilibrium, in which episodes of change (scientific revolutions) punctuate long periods of institutional evolution and stability (normal science). These three paths of institutional formation are cast as representational types. They are not necessarily mutually exclusive.[2]

Most analyses of institutional change allude to two types, incremental or revolutionary. They pose two sources of change stimuli, internal to the institution and external (environmental, contextual). Change types, whether Foucault's "continuity and catastrophe" (1970, 145), Hall's "incremental or cataclysmic" (1986, 37) and other variations on the theme (Vickers 1973, Huntington 1968,

---

2   The extensive literature from the late 1960s and early 1970s on "institution building" provided rich analyses of the factors involved and patterns of institutional birth and early stages of development. For examples see Janowitz (1969), Eisenstadt (1968), and Thomas, et al. (1972).

Ostrom 1990) mirror the punctuated equilibrium model of biological evolution (Eldredge and Gould 1972) without borrowing from it directly.

Most revolutionary changes are said to come from without, resultants of external stimuli. The institution is out of step with its society or more immediate polity or field (Skocpol 1979, Powell and DiMaggio 1991). Steinmo, Thelen and Longstreth (1992) find the stimulus for change to be external as well, in the interaction of society, economy, and politics. Ideas external to the institution are introduced, either by new agents or actors already present inside it.

Incremental change is seen as emerging from within. Internal contradiction of the existing order yields unsustainable conditions (Zito 2010, Powell and DiMaggio 1991). Most analysts attribute this type of change to a change in the rules. Knight (1992) holds that conflicts over rules end up as conflicts over power. The holder of greater power sets the new rules. Immergut (1992) and March and Olsen (1989) are several among many who also stress rules and their informal counterparts, routines. Searing (1991) offers a contrasting view which stresses the roles of individuals. (The rule-role distinction is trivial if roles are taken as predictable behavior structured by ritual settings (Goffman 1974) and rules are taken, as they are in sociology and the new institutionalism, to be structured norms that constrain behavior.) The rational choice school used utility or preference optimizing or satisficing behavior among competing individuals to explain institutional change by way of decision making directed at conflict solving. Pointing primarily to rules leaves behind explanations involving structures, content, or cognition. Rule-based theories paint clear and simple yet ultimately unsatisfying portraits of the dynamic of institutional change.

The internal-external dichotomy for the source of change stimuli and the incremental-revolutionary dichotomy regarding the type of change are barely more than typologies which hide the subtle dynamics of institutional creation and evolution. They offer much description and less explanatory power. They tend not to bridge their own dichotomies and so remain at the surface of institutional contradiction and complexity. They do not heed Ostrom's recognition that "institutional details are important" (1990, 22).

Changes in perception of existing circumstances are *a priori* to changing or creating an institution. At times, extraordinary events, historical figures, changes in historical patterns, and other factors conspire to turn an on-going institution into one ripe for reformation. These confluences are often precipitated by shifts in perception, of a new problem or new perception of an existing problem. These perceptions are incorporated first into insurgent and later into prevailing ideas, discourse, stories, traditions, and so on. Changes in perception occur in the minds of individuals. The interplay of individual perception with external forces leads to a series of questions that this research explores. How do ideas accrue legitimacy in order for society to bring them to bear on institutional change? What are the circumstances that allow perception to grow into action? In other words, when does societal transformation manifest itself as a political problem of such weight as to unleash major institutional innovation?

It is in part a cognitive issue. Powell and DiMaggio (1991, 13) posit a contrast between old and new ways of conceiving cognition. The old ways were normative: values, norms, attitudes. The new, more technical: scripts, schema, classifications, routines. This distinction parallels the change in the way institutions have been written about over the course of the twentieth century. The generation of Durkheim and Mead and their successor generation exemplified by Weber and Dewey emphasized norms. Recent and current generations have been more technically analytical, withdrawing into the workings of structure, action, and code. Exceptions have been the work of Bellah, et al. (1991), Selznick (1992), Huntington (1968), and others. Mary Douglas is among these others. For her, cognition is central to institution building (1986, 167).

Institutions change and grow because of the acts of individuals. Leaders or change agents (not necessarily the same) in a position to act have a "mental set" that was changed. The change in mental set comes from a change in perception or from a change in the external environment (Brindt and Karabel 1991). Brindt and Karabel call the response to the external environment "goal displacement". Cognition is also the key in the evolution of an institution. Zucker focuses upon "institutionalization as a *process* rather than as a state, upon the cognitive processes involved in the creation and transmission of institutions ... and upon the role of language and symbols in those processes" (1991, 104).

While cognition is generally considered an internal source of transformation, it actually spans the internal and external by integrating them. Giddens's structuration is a valuable early effort along this line. Searle's exposition (1995a), of paramount importance to all institutionalists, also attempts to bridge the usual dichotomies. Yet Searle still stresses the "priority of process over product, act over object" (1995a, 56–57). A cognitivist, he focuses on the establishment of "institutional facts ... within systems of constitutive rules" (1995a, 28), accepts language and no other aspect of content (symbols, images, and so on) as "constitutive of institutional reality" (1995a, 59). He theorizes that to become an institution, X must count as Y in context C. "Count as" proffers status, institutional status. For example, a dollar bill must count as legal tender in the United States. The federal reserve imposes a monetary value status on small green pieces of paper. A city plan counts as a set of policies to be executed in San Francisco when adopted by the city council. Searle claims that an institution declines when X no longer counts as Y in C. This leaves the source of change open. Despite his insistence on the primacy of language in forming institutions and institutional facts, there is nothing to prevent a non-language element of content—say an image that is the basis of a city plan—to be the X variable.

The excellent analysis of Leblebici, et al. (1991) of changes in the American radio broadcasting industry found several bases for change. It was based on analogy (a cognitive process), on agreements between parties, and on conventions to coordinate members of the institution (radio station affiliates). Their analysis, which defines the institution as a network of a large number of individual organizations, assumes a resource dependence view of the institution.

## Life Cycles and Evolution

Of the literature reviewed above that was based on empirical research, analysts typically chose a time span sufficient for only one episode of institutional change or creation. Only a few researchers attempt to portray an entire institutional life cycle, or a general scheme of evolution (March and Olsen 1989, North 1990, Leblebici, et al. 1991, Hollis and Sweetman 2001). Analyses are most commonly short term and episodic. The decline or demise of institutions have rarely been objects of analysis. Saxenian's account of high tech industry in Silicon Valley and Boston's Route 128 is an exception to this tendency (Saxenian 1994). She finds cultural and structural causes for the decline in the fortunes of Route 128 and Silicon Valley in the 1980s and Silicon Valley's later resurgence.

Most research on life cycles and evolution has identified organizations and not institutions as the object. Kaufman (1976, 1985) used the organic metaphor of the body to derive two sources of organizational death: when an organization's boundary is no longer discernable and when they develop resource dependence problems. Overcoming these two is a matter of environmental selection and adaptability. The contributors to Singh's volume (1990) use the population ecology paradigm in conjunction with empirically based mathematical models to refine the approach of Kaufman. They borrow biological concepts such as speciation, population ecology, ecological communities, and others. Their contributions regarding organizational imprinting followed Stinchecombe (1965): "how an organization is structured and how it behaves over the period of its life span are believed to be influenced, in part, by the conditions and circumstances surrounding its formation" (Singh 1990, 183). They also suggest routines and their replication are the way organizations grow and develop, following Cyert and March (1963).

Kimberly and Miles (1980) point out the limits to biological metaphors. An organization's "life" does not follow a linear, chronological trajectory of birth, growth, decline, and death. In contrast, they and their volume's contributors do not take any single point of view on evolution. Rather they weave power, culture, trust, rules, roles, learning, structure, and other factors to illuminate their object of study. While ostensibly about organizations, their findings pertain to institutions.

## A Note on Research Variables

Most of the literature reviewed above assumes cause and effect relations (historical, not logical) among factors responsible for institutional conditions and characteristics. Rather than cause and effect explanations, this present work reveals the rich and reciprocal relations among factors that influence and are affected by an institution. Anything so complex needs to be investigated from multiple points of view (LaPorte 1993, Putnam 1993). While this research looks at internal factors as well as external ones, the main object is the institution itself. It is primarily a middle-range look from the outside—from below, above, and alongside—along with significant glances from within.

The dependent variable in this research is the institution itself. This differs from the rational choice approach, for which the institution is an intervening variable posing constraints on choice. For new institutionalism of any stripe the institution has gained status as an independent variable. It is seen as affecting actors, choice, policy outcomes, and other variables more directly than the rational choice model.

# Chapter 3
# Planning Institutions and Images: A Brief Review

## Government or Governance?

In the past urban planning was seen as the exercise of state control over the development of cities and other territorial collectivities by administrative and political institutions (Castells 1977). Planning attempted to serve the public or general interest as it wrestled with private interests that competed in the political process (Tugwell 1940, Meyerson and Banfield 1955, Altshuler 1965). As one crisis after another rocked cities worldwide in the 1960s, and again in the 1970s as part of the global restructuring of the economy, government groped for a way to satisfy the increasingly atomized and well-organized interests. In the 1980s and 1990s, some cities worsened their plight and others improved. In either case a host of problems, some carried over from the prior decades while some others were new, continued to plague most cities. Problems stemming from crime, pollution, unemployment, traffic, and social inequities had spatial consequences that spilled across the metropolis and beyond. In desperation cities found that by engaging a broader set of actors in their policy making and problem solving, that is, by sharing power, they were able to more flexibly adapt to fluid and emerging conditions. They began to shift from government to governance.

Since the mid-1990s, globalization and the emergence of global cities and mega-city regions has prompted a number of responses by the state and by the urban planning professions (UNCHS 2006, Hall and Pfeiffer 2001). These include an amplified shift towards governance, the resurgence of urban and regional design, the re-assertion of infrastructure, and the rescaling of territorial functions and government policy (Barnett 2003, Neuman 2000, 2009, Brenner 1999). Perhaps of signal importance is the recognition that most spatial phenomena are multi-scalar, and that these phenomena have "mirrors" in institutional space that reflects a spatial-institutional isomorphism (Neuman 2007, Neuman and Hull 2009). Spatial-institutional mirroring reflects the co-development and co-evolution of urban and institutional space. It points toward the integration that will need to occur for governance to be effective.

In this spirit of integration, urban planning directed its efforts on linking local and global (glocal) issues, such as livability, walkability, and their link to public health. Other glocal issues in the purview of planning include climate change, social equity, resource and capital flows, and more (Hack, Birch, and Silver 2009). These phenomena are mainly the outcomes of incremental accretion over time by the actions of billions of humans. Coupled with the irruption of new technologies, especially telecommunications, and their attendant new behaviors, they are causing massive shifts in many spheres and on many levels (Castells 2000, 2004, 2009). In the face of these challenges, in some instances planning has both retreated to the simple comforts of a century ago (new urbanism) and jumped forward by tackling sustainability fully.

Theories of urban planning have noted these shifts. Prior theories pinned planning as a public enterprise that institutionalized political conflict among the competing interests vying to shape the city's future (Meyerson and Banfield 1955, Altshuler 1965, Cohen 1969). Progressive experiments during the 1960s in Bologna (Campos Venuti 1991, 1978) and the 1970s in Madrid (Castells 1981) and Barcelona (Borja 1977) were influential in European academic circles and widely admired in practice.[1] These grassroots experiments broadened the range of interests and actors involved in planning and shifted the locus of planning activity from government to individual citizens and organized neighborhood groups. In the United States planners issued a call to advocate for under-represented interests that were shut out from the process—the poor and other marginalized groups (Davidoff 1965). These participative experiments, along with critical pedagogy (Freire 1970), manifestos (Alinsky 1969), and environmental pleas (Carson 1962, McHarg 1969, Meadows, et al. 1972) dislodged planning from its institutional center and opened it up to new possibilities. As planning moved out from the inner city to the broader metropolitan environment and the state, it was transformed into growth management, at least in the United States (DeGrove 1984). This variant extended the institutional reach of planning beyond city hall to include as many affected interests groups as possible (Innes 1992, Stein 1994, de Souza Briggs 2008). Growth management became known for its intergovernmental coordination and institutional innovations rather than for direct participation, with New Jersey's State Plan of 1992 and San Diego's Regional Growth Management Strategy of 1994 being notable early governmental exceptions (Innes, Gruber, Neuman, Thompson 1994, DeGrove 2005, Gualini 2001). In the twenty-first century, a number of American city regions have been conducting highly participative processes of metro and regional growth guidance, such as Dallas (Envision North Texas), Austin (Envision Central Texas), and urban Utah (Envision Utah).

As a result of these transformations of planning from government to governance, planning no longer is only a social practice carried out by a state apparatus that embodied and applied the ideology of the socio-political order (Ledrut 1968a

---

1    These super-participative experiments were not imitated due to their historic specificity. Non-reproducible political and social conditions joined to produce the transformations of these cities, along with several others. In Bologna a communist government encouraged strong and direct participation in the planning and realization of its remarkable urban transformation and recovery of the historic center. In Spain, Barcelona and Madrid were not the only cities to experience social movements. Yet the two were considered leading cases (Borja 1977).

and 1968b, Castells 1969, Marris 1987). Ledrut refers to planning as "a means of social control of urban form" (Ledrut 1968b, 43, in Castells 1971, 199). Castells qualifies this mode of control as "*interventions dependent of administrative and political institutions, that is, of institutions invested with authority*" (Castells 1971, 199, emphasis in original). The decline of direct participation in large cities after the fervor of the 1960s and 1970s dissipated and the rise of a more complexly articulated interaction of interests in a back and forth rather than a strictly top-down or bottom-up manner pointed to a planning-led change in urban and growth politics.

In this new context, students of cities and their planning emphasized the new arrangement of sociopolitical relations among interested parties to the planning process (Feagin 1979, Castells 1983, Mollenkopf 1983, Fainstein, et al. 1983, Popper 1988). New interests and actors worked their way into the process and changed power relations. The presence of these new actors and the bureaucratic locus of the new interactive processes, especially agenda setting and coordination, also changed certain aspects of power relations by shifting policy making from the political to the administrative sphere. Political parties and electoral politics held less sway over land use and urban policy issues. Powerful interests and planner-bureaucrats skilled at designing and managing these processes gained their own gravity. The process mavens became the new power brokers.

Efforts at finding a political consensus among interests via critical communicative discourse (Forester 1980, 1989) and conflict resolution and negotiation processes (Susskind 1981, Susskind and Cruikshank 1987) became central. North American theorists of earlier generations reflected the pluralist and pragmatic paradigms of politics that prevail in their politics and political science (Dahl 1961, Banfield 1961). Planning theory of the time concerned itself less with the city and government acting directly on the city. It privileged interaction among the players of the game (Innes 1995).

Discourse, as a method of professional practice and a tool of research, provided an alternate framework. Engaging in reflective discourse about basic assumptions let interests from disparate backgrounds reflect across several frames of reference and better understand each other's underlying premises (Schön and Rein 1994). Conflict resolution theory held this to be interest-based consent rather that position-based compromise. Another way to traverse across frames embedded in differing and conflicting institutional logics is narrative policy practice (Roe 1994). Policy "narratives" acted as bridges across complex policy space by weaving positions, interests, and contexts into a coherent story in terms understood by the players. In urban planning discourse, plans performed "communicative work" by packaging this disparate discourse into a coherent narrative in an institutional context (Healey 1993, Mandelbaum 1990). Faludi also noted this change in the plan's function from conformance to performance (Faludi and Korthals Altes 1994). Conformance put the government plan at the heart of regulatory and implementation processes. Land use and development decisions had to conform to the plan. Conformance placed a premium on the plan's ex post use. A conformance plan's post-adoption value was higher than its pre-adoption value. A performance plan, in contrast, was a type of "single text negotiating document" which focused participants' attention and amalgamated their interests. Governance plans placed the plan at the core of the policy making process. Performance placed a premium on the plan's ex ante value. Performative governance plans are based on communicative theories of practice that place a premium on words, talk, text, and images.

Since the middle of the 1990s, however, as the scale and complexity of governance expanded to the mega-city region and beyond, planning practice scattered across disciplines, sectors, interests, and scales (Salet, Thornley, Kreukels 2003, Ross 2009). On one hand this placed a premium on consensus building across realms, however useful the outcome of consensus building was. On the other hand, chaos, complexity, and fuzzy reasoning entered into the theoretical debates, putting in to question the utility and effectiveness of the planning enterprise (Haughton, et al. 2010, Innes and Booher 2010, de Roo and Porter 2007, Healey 2007, Christensen 1999). Reflective theorists who observed practice closely have noted that under a highly qualified set of conditions and a limited set of expectations for effective outcomes as measured by the actual improvement of place, then collaboration and consensus building can enhance civic and institutional capacity as well as deliberative democracy (Throgmorton 1996, Forester 1999, Hajer and Wagenaar 2003, Healey 2006, Innes and Booher 2010). As urban space and its planning get messier, their outcomes become sketchier.

## From Plan Making to Planning without Plans

Planning in any case was not neutral, objective, or value-free. It was not merely a technical venture or instrument of politics. Planning imparted its own ideology and values, such as participation, equity, and sustainability. Norms were reinserted into planning practice and theory. Planning ideology blended its professional heritage with the leading visions of the good society at the time when the public sector was presumed to arbitrate the public good (Meyerson 1961, Reiner 1963, Choay 1965). Planning's ideology has always strived to make the city function more effectively, to deliver infrastructure and services more efficiently, and to make it a safer and more healthy place to live in (Cerdà 1867). The physical form of the city has also been a leading concern of planning ideology throughout the history of modern city planning, whether for aesthetic reasons (Sitte 1889), functional (Adams 1935), environmental (McHarg 1969, Spirn 1984), symbolic (Rossi 1966, Venturi, Scott-Brown, and Izenour 1972), or an amalgam of reasons (Howard 1898, Bacon 1967, Lynch 1981).

Urban form, spatial design, and the disposition of land were synthesized in the plan document. Through the plan and its implementation, which was mainly done by zoning and development regulation, planning conferred its own values or doctrine (Faludi and van der Valk 1994). Planning's ideology was not independent from the society in which it was developed. At the same time planning was subservient to powerful interests in society. Planning's mentality and practice were imbued with disciplinary control over urban spatial order that served economic and development factions (Boyer 1983). The dialectical interplay between planning's and society's ideologies was a staple of practice and scholarship. It mirrored the equanimity between professional and scholarly concerns about form and its representation in city plans. Professional and scholarly syntony lasted until the 1960s. The plan and planning process were two sides of the same coin. Plan making was planning (Kent 1964).

During the last generation, however, theory emphasized process over substance, procedures over the plan (Hall 2002). Critical about this shift and the lack of substance were marxist-influenced scholars emerging from Paris in the 1960s. They admonished a link between procedural planning theory and urban theory so that the former would acknowledge and incorporate the decisive historical, political, and economic conditions that shape the city, all the while maintaining the most fundamental aspect of planning—process—central (Castells 1977). Planning theory emphasized a micro-analytical view of process disembodied from the complex milieu that surrounds planning. It analyzed "planners' stories", "a planner's day", "telling stories", "reading plans", "social constructions", and the like (Mandelbaum 1990, 1991, Innes 1992, Healey 1992a, Forester 1993). For a time, the object of planning—the city—and its practice medium—the plan— dissipated into talk.

Planners had to talk about something. Parties to the planning process needed to debate some topic of substance. Prior to the 1970s planning put most of its substantive eggs in one basket, the plan. The laws that enabled the plan, its background documents of data and analysis, and implementing regulations and programs were secondary to and supported the plan. The plan, because it bundled comprehensive urban policy into a package, became the centerpiece of debate in the political arena of planning. In the language of conflict resolution theory it was a "single text negotiating document" (Moore 2008).

The plan typically offered as its centerpiece (and often as its literal centerfold) an image of the future physique of the city in the form of a land use map and/or a pictorial rendering of the city's spatial layout—a city design. This graphic image served the dual purpose of representing the city and being the focal point of the planning institution. The image depicted the city's problematic as the planners saw it and proposed remedies. Classic texts, whether theory or history, placed the plan, or the people and ideas that shaped it, front and center (Adams 1935, Kent 1964, Hall 1982, 1988). Another set of classic works questioned whether planners' dreams of rational practice could cope with the vicissitudes of actual administrative and legislative politics (Meyerson and Banfield 1955, Altshuler 1965, Mollenkopf 1983, Boyer 1983). Were high-powered interests in and out of government contrary to those advanced in the technical and therefore ideal plan? Were these interests simply too strong for the planners to handle? Were they able to sidestep the plan? Put another way, were planners too weak and naive to put forth viable proposals? Was the plan relevant? Theory continued to mount its critique on the ability of planning to handle the new problematic, until the new urbanism re-emerged in the 1990s and gathered strength in the new millennium. Accompanying this rise of physical planning was the use of images in plans (Neuman 1998). Planning theory drifted further from the city, further from urban theory, and further from planning practice and the plan (Fainstein 2005, Mandelbaum, Mazza and Burchell 1996). Theory dug deeper into process and found it was built on words. Its gap with practice widened (Innes de Neufville 1983).

Meanwhile practice tried to tackle the new problems stemming from the successive urban crises of the 1960s, 1970s and beyond. During this interval urban "renewal", highway programs, untamed politics, and a new set of ills came out from the shadows and invaded the streets and media. Riots, poverty, homelessness, crime, and drugs swept the cities. They overwhelmed the words and numbers of technical, systems-based, bureaucratic plans which were replete with data, goals, and policies but out of touch with the new reality. Moreover they were devoid of physical form proposals or images that could have offered a vision, a way out. In response planners and urban policy makers invented new ways of planning and lured in new stakeholders. In so doing it began to recover some of its prior stature. Part of the new found stature was owed to the invention of new flexible tools other than the plan: impact fees, enterprise zones, land banking, transferable development rights and the like. Another source came from working with and using new means to mediate the interests that stymied planners and plans in the past: advocacy, consensus, conflict resolution. In so doing planners adopted the language and means of those interests—entrepreneurship, strategy, collaboration, and consensus. Throughout this period fascination with the new tools mounted while the plan receded from view.

**Recovery of Plan Making**

Only in the 1980s, when a new breed of planner began to recover physical planning and design traditions from the turn of the century, did the plan begin to make a comeback. These planners combined physical planning with the new approaches listed above to prepare a new type of physical plan. The renewed interest in physical plans and urban designs underscored the importance of the image of place (Calthorpe 1993, Duany and Plater-Zyberk 1991, Katz 1994, Krier 1992). The image turned out to be the missing ingredient from the 1960s through the 1980s. The new urbanism put the image of the new image/suburb/town back into the plan and put design back into planning. The "master designer" method has prevailed in the new urbanism. The planner-client relation has been a dyad. New urbanists have yet to fully incorporate the new discursive techniques that surged concurrently with it.

## Whither the Institution?

One way to examine how urban planning has treated the city and the image is sketched schematically in Figure 3.1. Apex A represents the city. Apex B represents the planning institution. Apex C represents the image. The relation between the planning institution and the image (of the city, in the plan) is represented by side BC. Contemporary scholars have tended to focus on the processes within the planning institution and how they mediate urban actors. The objects of their analyses falls mainly along the side AB, with a preponderant emphasis on the process (a subset of apex B) and less attention to urban theory (apex A). For counterpoints on how planning mediated urban *change* (with less of an emphasis on urban *actors*) see Feagin (1979) and Healey, et al. (1988b).

In the early part of the twentieth century planning leaders on both sides of the Atlantic consciously strived in their practice and their writings to build the fledgling

Figure 3.1 **Conceptual relationship among objects of analysis in city planning**

institution of city planning. Their benchmark was the plan and its image of urban form. So intertwined was the plan with planning that no one thought to explicate the exact role of the image in the development of the institution of planning. The plan was their bread and butter. Daniel Burnham alluded to the power of a plan: "a logical diagram once recorded will never die" (Hall 2002, 174). Hall's book itself is a testimony to the ideas (content) that drove and still drive planning, and to those who shaped and used them. In the United States, the birth of modern city planning is usually linked with the amelioration of bad housing and health conditions, the progressive movement in local government, and the use of the police power in controlling unwanted land uses. Yet the Great White City of the Columbian Exposition in Chicago in 1893, Daniel Burnham's famous 1909 plan for Chicago (and earlier plans he prepared for cities such as Cleveland and San Francisco), and New York City's zoning ordinance of 1916 also led to the consolidation of the city planning institution in the U.S. This latter set projected planning on two fronts, design plans and zoning. Their effectiveness was based on the powerful images of the future, for example Burnham's renderings for the Chicago plan and Hugh Ferris's for the New York zoning ordinance have become icons of planning. They continue to resonate today, and are often exhibited in museums and galleries and reproduced in popular magazines.

Such was the link between plan and diagram that there was no differentiating between the two terms. Theorist-practitioners as late as Kent (1964) affirmed the importance of the plan.

From the academic view the abyss into which plans seemed to disappear owed to the twin onslaught of procedural planning theory and systems theory. The first focused on decision analysis and was supported intellectually by micro-analytic rational action models within a pluralist political paradigm. The pluralist model focused on atomized interests and actors. Pluralism and rational action mutually reinforced each other. Both traced their heritage to the utilitarian-pragmatic philosophies dominant at the time. The second was fueled by general systems theory and its cousin cybernetics. These approaches led academics and practitioners to retreat from the plan and the idea of comprehensive planning (Rittel and Webber 1973, Wildavsky 1973). This followed a general retreat in the social sciences and humanities from paradigms purely rational, systematic, universal, modern. In this post-modern, post-structuralist, post-fordist context, which to an extent still pervades the social sciences and allied professions such as planning, planning theory and practice has maintained its procedural bent, now spiced with urban design.

The first strain of rational action theory to take hold under that name in planning theory was in Meyerson's and Banfield's classic study of public housing in Chicago (1955). It was followed by Meyerson's students at the University of Pennsylvania, Paul Davidoff and Thomas Reiner, in the form of a politically sensitive rational choice theory (1962). Altshuler's study of planning in Minneapolis questioned the viability of planners to actually implement such a model (1965). These studies and many that followed placed their gaze on "who said what?" and "who did what?".

Interests and preferences were the common denominators. A brief interlude of systems planning tried to place the whole enterprise in a wider context but tended to detach political and other nuances from planning (Ackoff 1974, Chadwick 1971, McLaughlin 1969).

*How* planners and interest group stakeholders in planning processes talked amongst themselves in an effort to mediate interests was the crest of the next wave of planning theory. It took the who and what of Meyerson and Altshuler to the next step. Theorists applied new tools of analysis to the new forms of practice. Both planted their discursive roots firmly in the soil of philosophy's linguistic turn. Participation and consensus-seeking was one path it took (Hayward and Watson 1975, Clavel 1986, Susskind 1981, Susskind and Cruikshank 1987). Hayward and Watson's volume of analyses comparing planning in three European nations conceived of planning as a decision making technology that was "an instrument of rationalization for the system rather than a process of socio-political change from within" (1975, 455–459). For them planning was a consensus building instrument of the state—the "regulatory reproduction of the status quo" (1975, 455–459). Critical discourse and attention to power was another route taken by theorists, based on the communicative action theory of Habermas (Forester 1980, 1989, 1999).

A road less travelled was taken by scholars who based their work on Michel Foucault. In an extension of Foucault's method and ideas, Boyer attempted to show how the "apparatus of planning" and its quest for "disciplinary control" was driven by prevailing ideologies and powerful interests (1983). Her work claimed that the constraints placed on the profession were too strong for it to have an impact of its own. Planning could at best "dream" it was creating a better urban order according to its own standards. The standards and norms of the economic and political interests prevailed. Those in power merely used planning as one of their instruments. The book traced the "discourse of city planning" and not the image (1983, 282). In Boyer's interpretation, city planning intervened at the behest of more powerful social forces. Rabinow applied foucauldian technique in his excellent history of the development of the French colonial city planning institution (1989). His analysis, in which the institution was a dependent variable, showed that the planning in colonial Morocco was structured by the importation and application of modern (French) technologies of social control such as statistics and welfare programs. The account refers peripherally to the plan and its image as part of the ensemble of control technologies.

**Research Design**

In their research designs, scholars influenced by Habermas typically assigned, whether consciously or not, the institution of planning as an intervening variable. They accorded the communicative processes of planning status as the dependent variable. In this they followed Habermas himself, particularly his writings from the 1970s and first half of the 1980s (Habermas 1979, 1984, 1987). It should be noted that early in his career Habermas did view societal institutions such as the public sphere and government (he did not analyze urban planning directly in his major publications) as the outcomes of social forces. In this sense institutions were dependent variables (Habermas 1989 (1962) and 1974 (1971)). He changed his research subject dramatically, heavily influenced by the linguistic turn in philosophy, and linguistics itself.

Those influenced more by Foucault tended to assign the institution dependent variable status. In Boyer (1983) the institution as such was not the dependent variable. She refers instead to the "planning mentality" or the planning profession, and not the institution as we have defined it. They designated the processes of interaction, especially those with a cognitive basis, from which the institutions were formed and perpetuated as the independent variables. Macro-social factors, while not denied their importance, were intervening variables.

For most other researchers the planning institution was an intervening variable in their hypotheses. Policy (and strategy, plans, programs) was typically the dependent variable. Politics, or some other disposition of power driving the system, was one form the independent variable took. Another form of the independent variable was the discursive and communicative acts of planners as they assembled stakeholders in the planning process. Those who came closest to treating the planning institution as a dependent variable, as an outcome of planning or politics, were a disparate bunch. Kent (1964) analyzed in detail the inter-relation between the urban general plan, the planners, the planning process, and urban politics. Faithful to the practitioners' canon of the era, he duly recorded the role of the plan diagram and image. His normative program described how to make the plan, how to staff the planning function, and how staff was to advise politicians and citizens. It did not describe how the plan and its "major physical design proposals" were to be used to build the institution of city planning. According to Kent, the plan was a tool to apply policy determined by the city council. An astute planner and politician himself, he nonetheless kept politics (ends) and planning (means) separate.

Benveniste (1989) could be read as a reply to the surety of plans and planning advocated by Kent. With Kent he assumed and advocated a dyadic relation between the planning staff and the client. As with Kent, Benveniste's client was the political authority, which he named the Prince, after Machiavelli. Benveniste's planners differed, however, in that they helped to devise ends in a political negotiation process. He sent a mixed message by also counseling a limit on planners' authority. They should stay within the technical sphere, believing that "planning cannot substitute for ... political institutions" (Benveniste 1989, 45). Recognizing the importance of a plan and its image, he saw the institution (an independent variable) as constraining plan formulation and provided advice on how to best prepare, adopt, and implement limited-scope plans and planning (dependent variable).

Marris's analysis of planning in England showed a modified cognitive approach was used in all three of his models of planning: design, strategy, and entrepreneurship (1987). He found in his case studies that when planners changed from one model of planning to another, it involved changes of perception on the part of the participants. The participants used metaphors of the planning process as a cognitive device to make sense of the model or to justify their switch from one model to another. For example, the 1960s and 1970s model of planning was based on the metaphor of structure. This was introduced by the political left to connote the arrangement of power relations in the urban process. The metaphor changed to entrepreneurship as the conservative Thatcher and Major governments of the 1980s and early 1990s took control. Their administrations de-emphasized public sector intervention and substituted empowerment of the private sector. The change within the planning institution was a result of these changes to the planning process, coupled with the effects of broader changes in the paradigms of political and social action.

As planning scholarship on both sides of the Atlantic continued to develop, three overall trends could be observed. The first was an amalgam of the positions of Kent, Beneviste, and Marris. That is, they posited or even advocated either a public sector approach, or a private sector approach, or mixed public-private partnerships (Wiewel and Knaap 2005, Dodge and Montgomery 1996). The best examples were rooted in studies of practice, including comparative analyses (Healey et al. 1997, Albrechts et al. 2001).

The second trend was to continue the line of analysis that highlighted communication, deliberation, and discourse (Throgmorton 1996, Flyvbjerg 1998, Balducci 2000, Salet, et al. 2003, Sanyal 2005, de Souza Briggs 2008, Innes and Booher 2010). In a class of its own sits a theoretical-philosophical treatise analyzing how planning theory can be situated in a linguistic-philosophical context directed toward pragmatic planning practice (Harper and Stein 2006). Taken together, these and related works tend to accord the communicative aspects of planning processes as the independent variable in research, and procedural outcomes or transformations as the dependent variable.

The third tendency was evidenced in research that attempted more holistic portrayals of the practice of planning. These usually employed multidisciplinary methods and theories. Moreover they shied away from causal analysis and recognized the panoply of contexts and circumstances that frame planning (Hillier 2007, Healey 2007). Their thick descriptions and interpretations echoed the complex and multifarious character of planning practice. Increasingly, scholarship addressed institutions and their governance (Hoch 1994, Albrechts, et al. 2001, Madanipour, Hull, Healey 2001, Faludi and Waterhout 2002, Davoudi and Strange 2009, and many of the others cited above).

**The Image and the City**

Most research on planning has located itself along the side AB of the triangle in Figure 3.1. Most of these analyses have regarded the planning process as the dependent variable. Only a few have regarded the planning institution as the dependent variable. In fact, few deal with the formation or development of the institution of planning at all (as we have defined the word institution). Even fewer have addressed the interaction of planning institutions with the image of the city, side AC of the triangle in Figure 3.1.

The benchmark work on the image of the city is still Kevin Lynch's *The Image of the City* (1960). He found that people hold in their minds an image of the city that was essential to their functioning and emotional well-being in the city. Others have contributed to our storehouse of images of the city without necessarily studying the image itself. For example there are "world cities" (Geddes 1915, Hall 1966), "global cities" (King 1990, Sassen 1991), "edge cities" (Garreau 1991), and "megalopolis" (Gottmann 1961). Creating images for an information society which is less place-bound are Webber's "non-place urban realm" (1964) and Castells's "space of flows" (1989). More recently, the panoply of terms describing metropolitan and larger urban regions has been reviewed (Neuman and Hull 2009). There is no shortage of excellent texts documenting the relation of the image of the city, the form of the city, and city planning, side AC in Figure 3.1. The better historical overviews include Benevolo (1967), Morris (1972), and Kostof (1991).

The method used in the Lynch study was one of interviews in which respondents were asked to draw maps or diagrams representing their image of the city. Using diagrams limited the representations of the image to physical ones. Lynch synthesized his respondents' diagrams and found that their images of the city were composed of several elements: landmarks, edges, nodes, paths, and districts. Lynch found that the images his survey respondents had of their urban environments shared common features. "It is these group images, exhibiting consensus among significant numbers, that interest city planners" (1960, 7). He referred to this as a "public image", paralleling Boulding (1956). Lynch admitted the limits of the public image. "It would be impossible to generalize from these, [small sample sizes—30 people in each of three cities] and to say that a 'true' public image of the particular city has been uncovered" (1960, 152). He indicated that he and his colleague Gyorgy Kepes were not aware of Boulding's work at the time (Banerjee and Southworth 1990, 248).

Lynch did not explain how the mental image of the city is formed, nor found that interviewees held a "single comprehensive image of the entire environment" [city] (1960, 85). Nor did he analyze the relation of the image to planning processes, planning institutions, or politics. He reasoned that any use of the image by planners would be by a planner-designer, presumably at the drawing board (1960, 115). Lynch's work liberated planners from abstract models of the city based on plans and land use classifications. It injected the very real sense of the way people experienced cities. Ledrut mused on this distinction. He referred to the "concrete model" held by citizens and contrasted it to the "abstract model" held by planners (Ledrut 1973, 356–359, quoted in Gottdiener and Lagopoulos 1986, 234). Lynch translated the residents' perceptions in a way that he, trained as an architect, could excel: as images.

Twenty-five years after the book's release, Lynch reconsidered the findings and addressed their shortcomings (Lynch 1985). Some of them were taken up by his students. How the mental image was developed was studied by Banerjee (1971). While Lynch assumed a static mental image, Smith found that it changed over time (1971). In another study Lynch modified his analytical method and applied it to the metropolitan region (1976). Later studies by others affirmed Lynch's self-critique and extended it. For Rossi (1966), Venturi (1967), and Venturi, Scott-Brown and Izenour (1972) the symbolic aspects of the image were at least as important as its physical dimensions. Ledrut (1973) placed the image in its social context and indicated that *out of context the image loses its meaning*. For Ledrut the image and its context are inseparable. The image conveys its context.In this Ledrut paralleled Jung, whose findings came from his psychological and cultural studies. Jung stated that "behavior results from patterns of functioning, which I have described as images. The term 'image' is intended to express not only the form of the activity taking place, but the typical situation in which the activity is released" (Jung 1986, 106). Additionally, Ledrut found that people have not one but many images of the city. The multiple images match the multiple meanings that cities have for their inhabitants and users. They are polysemic.

Lefebvre (1991) gave the image and the city an even wider setting. It carried symbolic, social, historical, political, cultural, and economic meaning. He railed against the use of the image as a tool of abstraction. Abstract representations of space (plans, etc., prepared by experts) had to conform to the abstract criteria of global social practice in order to be effective. He did not believe they represented the real meaning and aspirations of the city or its citizens. Faludi claimed that images can outlive their usefulness (Faludi and van der Valk 1994). In the growth of new towns, for example, the image of the new town no longer belonged to the planners who created it. It was ceded to and taken up by the residents, who modified it along the way. The transfer of an image was accompanied by a change in power relations. The citizens gained and the planners lost power. The keeper of the image is the holder of power.

Lynch's last major work, *Good City Form* (1981) presented his most sophisticated synthesis of urbanism. It coincided with thinkers such as Lefebvre, Ledrut, Castells, Rossi, and others regarding the unity of the conception and production of space. Lynch explicitly left planning theory and thus its political considerations to others. His concern was a normative theory of the city as expressed in its physical form. Yet he maintained, along with Mumford, that the mental image precedes form. "Only if we can project that [new] image shall we be able to find a new form of the city" (Mumford 1961, 4).

## The Image and the Planning Institution

Of the few scholars of the image of the city, fewer still have adumbrated a relation between it and planning, represented by side BC of the triangle in Figure 3.1. Much scholarship remains to more fully relate the image to the planning institution, in particular its creation and evolution. To our knowledge, no one has formed a hypothesis posing the image as an independent variable and a planning institution as a dependent variable. Given the role of the plan and the plan's image of the future of the city in the overall development of the planning profession and the daily exercise of planning practice, this is perplexing. Into the image-planning chasm created by the dearth of scholarship fall pertinent questions as to the real nature of the making of plans and planning policy, and to the creation and change of planning institutions.

Some of the causes of this chasm can be explained by the emergence of highly analytical modes of planning based on quantitative models, of increasingly detailed and prescriptive laws and regulations, and of the residual influence of the rational decision model. Analytical modes changed the nature of the master plan, at once leading to the shunting of the image from the plan and to the plan's downfall as an important planning tool. Analytical models contrasted with the synthetic models used in design, and with the use of images in the early twentieth century era of practice led by designer-planners. The disregard of the image in contemporary planning and urban theories becomes increasingly questionable in light of the return of physical planning on the American and British scenes in the last 20 years, at least (Kelbaugh 1990, Duany and Plater-Zyberk 1991, Solomon 1992) and the ubiquity of geographic information systems (GIS) in the analysis of urban space and in the structuring of planning processes.

There have been some notable exceptions, however. Some have continued the seminal work of Lynch (Nasar 1997, Banerjee and Southworth 1990). Vale and Warner (2001) collected essays and studies on the role of city images in the popular media, with particular attention to city marketing and urban life. They also addressed the role of the image in urban design. Monclús's and Guàrdia's volume (2006) examined the role of the image of the city in city marketing and urban culture, with a stress on major international expositions and events. In that volume, Silver's essay spotlights the use of negative images about suburban sprawl and positive images about traditional city design in the genesis of the new urbanism in the United States. Most edited volumes of research on images and the city portray images as a marketing tool (Donald and Gammack 2007, Theirstein and Förster 2008, Metaxas 2009).

In Europe, several studies have noted the relationships between images of place and urban planning. In Flanders, Albrechts identified how a new law and a new institution was created as a result of the specific image of the Flemish Diamond (1999). Faludi showed general and theoretical aspects of this relation (1996), stressing a strategic approach framed by powerful images. Neuman found that in Madrid, planners used images to propel planning strategies and political campaigns (1996b). This approach was summed up as "the development of spatial logic and metaphors that can command attention and carry persuasive power in complex political contexts" (Albrechts, Healey, Kunzmann 2003, 127). Additionally, an obscure article articulates the direct relation between the use of the city image in public administration and city planning (Neascu 2009).

Images of place routinely appeared in urban plans. Yet plans conveyed much more information and knowledge than just images. Furthermore, the intellectual and substantial content of a planning institution was made of more than plans alone. (See Chapter 2 for a discussion of institutional content.) Its content also was contained in reports, surveys, models, laws, regulations, programs, standards, and other textual documents. It was also present in maps, plan drawings, designs, illustrations, photos, videos, and other images. Content was not static, collected in documents and images. Institutional actors use content and form their knowledge of the object of planning from it. Content is changed as it flows through institutional channels. Yet the importance of content has been given scant yet increasing attention in contemporary theory. John Friedmann acknowledges its role in "sustaining social movements" and "spurring action" yet shied from pinpointing its role in planning itself. His principal transmitters of content are "utopias" (Friedmann 1987, 225, 343). Yet a few writers still see content as central. Hall's history of planning states "Ideas are central and front of stage" (Hall 1988, 6). In Hall's view leading planners transformed ideas/content into practice, building the legacy of the planning institution along the way. In this fashion knowledge became the basis for decisions and action (Friedmann 1987, Innes 1990).

### The Separation of Knowledge from Action, and of Theory from Practice

Planning theory has tended to separate knowledge from action as evidenced by the subtitle of *Planning in the Public Domain: From Knowledge to Action* (Friedmann 1987, see also Innes de Neufville 1987). Doing so has perpetuated a long line of enlightenment thinking that nourishes the epistemological roots of endeavors such as planning and design. Hannah Arendt identified knowledge with command and action with obedience to command. She claimed that the separation of knowing and doing is the root of domination (Arendt 1958). This reasoning is picked up in the historical studies of Michel Foucault and his theorizing on power and knowledge (Foucault 1978, 1979, 1980). Friedmann's knowledge before action parallels Patrick Geddes's survey before plan (Geddes 1915). Friedmann cloaked a radical "transactive" program for planning in a model similar to the choice theory advocated by Davidoff and Reiner a generation earlier (1962). He emphasized linking a scientific and technical knowledge to societal guidance via politics. He set up a consulting role for planners in which they advise decision makers: "These specialists, experts at mediating knowledge and action, I shall call planners" (Friedmann 1987, 4). In this normative prescription for "radical" planning, references to vision, images, and institutions do not appear, after excepting macro-institutions such as the market, government, and society.

The split of knowledge from action, of content from process in planning theory, while pronounced in the 1990s, has experienced a reconciliation. Case studies that generated theories and hypotheses can be seen in the work of many of the contemporary theorists cited in this chapter, as well as others. While the primacy of process was held firm under the grip of Habermas's theory of communicative action, the communicative paradigm has unearthed fertile soil for a cadre of theorists using rubrics such as discourse, consensus building, debate, story telling, equity planning, and interactive planning. This paradigm has served as the conceptual framework to structure the disparate facets of "content". But to disregard images in any of their forms or isolate them from discourse results in a partial analysis. Rodowick's claim provides a valuable insight: that "electronic and digital arts are rapidly engendering new strategies of creation and simulation, and of spatial and temporal ordering, that linguistic philosophies are ill-equipped to understand" (Rodowick 1991, 12, quoted in Boyer 1994, 490).

Boyer, writing on North American city planning, claimed "the past failures of the architect-planner to build images of the city reflect the refusal to allow the past to be experienced with the present in a new constellation. In consequence our modern [North American] cityscapes show little awareness of their historical past" (1983, 286). We can add that the present failures of planning theorists to build theories incorporating images reflect their refusal to allow planning's past to be experienced with its present. We can rest somewhat easier knowing that practice has gone ahead of theory by re-incorporating the image. A consequence of this disparity is the estrangement of practice from theory and the consignment of the latter to the tower.

Practitioner-theorist Aldo Rossi closes his influential book with the observation that the politics of the city cannot be separated from the planning and architecture that constructs it. His politics is about choices. "Who ultimately chooses the image of a city if not the city itself—and always and only through its political institutions" (Rossi 1982, 162). It is to this choosing of the image we now turn, in the episodic story of city and metropolitan planning in Madrid.

# Chapter 4
# Planning, Images, and Madrid's New Regional Government

Our exploration documents five discrete episodes in the evolution of Madrid's metropolitan planning institution. The episodes stretch back to the middle of the nineteenth century. The episodes are presented in chronological order, with the exception of the most recent episode, which is presented first, in this chapter. It begins in the 1980s, at the end of the transition to democratic government in the post franquist era. The new autonomous regional government, the *Comunidad de Madrid*, was formed in 1982. In 1983 it adopted its constitution and held its first elections for the regional assembly and president. This initiated a period of institutional consolidation of the democratic gains made during the transition between 1975 and 1983. Since institutional consolidation began in 1983 government has been seeking a two-fold balance. The first is among its levels (local, provincial, regional, and national). The new intergovernmental equation must factor in the appearance of the new intermediate level, the regions. The second balance government has been seeking is between the public and private sectors.

This is not a conventional history, nor even an institutional one. We chart the evolution of the institution at five specific periods of change. New directions, new organizational structures, new politics, fresh personalities, and invented images are just some of the defining characteristics of each episode. The episodes selected test the hypothesis of whether the incidence of the invention of a new image has an effect on the evolution of the metropolitan planning institution. We will show that the relation is a reciprocal one. The image embodies salient features of the institution while at once changing it along new dimensions.

This first episode, from 1983 to 1995, occurred during a moment of ferment, as all of society was changing rapidly after the death of Francisco Franco in 1975. Franco was dictator for over 35 years. It is a case in which the regional planning department created two new images. One was of the region, which it called *Madrid Región Metropolitana*. The other aggregated seven municipalities in the southern part of the metropolis outside of Madrid city, which it called *Gran Sur* (Great South). These new images were used to shape and implement an electoral campaign strategy in the first instance and an economic and territorial development strategy in the second. Both were used to reform the institution of metro planning in the context of a stabilizing political, economic, and institutional environment.

**Madrid Comes into its Own**

In the mid-1980s Spain was awash with big events that would project it on the international stage. The country had just hosted soccer's World Cup in 1982. Spain made the agonizing decision to join NATO and the welcome decision to join the European Community as a full member. Seville began preparing for its World Fair, Barcelona for the summer Olympics, and Madrid for being Cultural Capital of Europe. All three were to be celebrated in 1992. The country was bursting outward, opening all of its doors wide. Change was in the air.

In Madrid the pace was as furious. The *movida Madrileña*, a full swing seven day a week, all night till dawn social life, captured much more than the youth's collective imagination. It set the pace for the entire city: art, culture, society, politics, sports, and business. The Reina Sofia Museum (MNCARS) and the Thyssen-Bornemisza Museum were in the works. Local art and music scenes exploded. Neighborhood and city-wide fairs, fiestas, and traditional celebrations returned to pack the streets. A citywide flea market *El Rastro* became a social and mercantile bazaar *de rigueur* —a weekly festival for scores if not hundreds of thousands. The *Real Madrid* football club won five national championships in a row. Multinationals located or expanded in Madrid to take profit from and fuel the economic recovery. Their activities shot real estate prices and skyscrapers sky high. Madrid, in a word, boomed. *Madrileños* even borrowed the term, referring to "el boom".

In this midst, Madrid breathed a collective sigh of relief in 1985 after a dozen years of severe economic crisis, political turmoil, and widespread social unrest culminating in the famous citizens' movement. Unemployment began a long-awaited downturn after reaching a peak of 23 percent in 1984, after having risen steadily from five percent in 1975. (23 percent was still several points below Barcelona and Bilbao, Spain's second and third largest cities.) Its population, 12 percent of the national total, contributed 13 percent of the nation's jobs, (16 percent of service and 19 percent of advanced service jobs) and nearly 15 percent of its gross profits (Consejería de Política Territorial, 1991b).

Although Franco's death in 1975 brought freedom and democracy, the political transition was rocky. Short-lived governments, the making and breaking of political parties, an attempted coup, Basque separatist terrorism, and the birth of autonomous regions were some of the waves crashing on the rocks. Not until the socialists gained power in 1982 did the seas begin to calm. In Madrid the socialist victory was by 1983 complete. They occupied national, regional, and Madrid city governments along with a majority of surrounding towns, being nearly absolute in the working class towns to the south and east. The convergence of the socialists at all levels of government in Madrid brought a degree of stability unseen in years. A hugely popular mayor, Enrique Tierno Galvan, was elected in 1979 and re-elected in 1983. His popularity and his policies opened up the city to the people, capitalizing on the energy of the citizens' movement. The regional and national presidents, Joaquín Leguina and Felipe González, were both re-elected for multiple terms.

Smooth political waters in the early 1980s made for smooth economic sailing. A vivid illustration of the boom that followed is the rise in the average price of a buildable vacant lot in the metropolitan area. In 1985 the price did not exceed 12,000 *pesetas* per square meter. By 1989 it reached 70,000 *pesetas*, nearly a six-fold rise in four years. Average metropolitan home prices more than doubled from 1985 to 1987 from 53,000 to 117,000 *pesetas* per square meter. Average metro office prices rose in the same period 350 percent from 78,000 to 271,000 *pesetas* per square meter (Consejería de Política Territorial 1989c).

Madrid, in the context of adapting to a global economy reliant on knowledge and information technologies, became the financial and service capital of Spain. From 1970 to 1985 the share of banks headquartered in Madrid rose from 29 to 50 percent (68 percent including banks held by other entities whose headquarters were in Madrid). 31 of 32 foreign banks that opened nationwide from 1978 to 1987 chose Madrid for their headquarters. 67 percent of investment funds, 63 percent of investment corporations, 73 percent of the capital of financial institutions, 82 percent of money market brokerage houses, and 92 percent of individual brokers were based in Madrid. In 1975 the Madrid Stock Exchange accounted for 53 percent of the national volume, by 1985, 79 percent (Estevan 1988).

Value added by such a concentration of capital brings with it support services and industries and their employees. Value subtracted by this concentration was the economic and social marginality of workers without training and the displacement of small businesses, landlords, and homeowners from strategic growth sites. During the 1980s boom in Madrid, the rich got richer and the poor poorer, relative to the rich. The rich went north and west to the parks, hills, mountains, universities, and single family residential suburbs. The poor went to or were trapped in the industrial south and east, the preferred location of most *chabolas* (shanty towns). For example, the average annual individual income in the west was 3.4 million *peseta*, in the north was 3 million, and east and south was 1.5 million as of 1990.[1] Other negative externalities accompanied growth. Duly documented were environmental and infrastructural as well as economic and social impacts. (Assessing the state of the region became a growth industry in itself.) With the sweet came the sour.

The boom peaked around 1990 and 1991. Those were the years of *dame dos* (give me two), referring to Spaniards' shopping slogan while travelling abroad due to new-found wealth and favorable currency exchange rates. The bustling scenario depicted in these pages was the one that Madrid's new regional government faced. Its first regional planning and development efforts proceeding from its 1984 planning law were robust failures. Part of the inadequacy of that law came from its ideation in an earlier period of economic crisis and political instability. Too

---

1    Income figures from *Comunidad de Madrid* (1991b). For other economic and social data see Jesús Leal (1987), Redondo de la Serna (1988), Naredo (1988), Parra Baño (1988), and supporting technical documentation from Promadrid (1993), *Oficina Municipal del Plan* (1993), and *Comunidad de Madrid* (1991b).

many of the old institution's procedures were dragged forward. Now the tables were turned and new ideas were needed.


## An Institution is Born: 1983 to 1996

The Madrid Metropolitan Planning and Coordination Commission (COPLACO), the predecessor to the *Comunidad de Madrid*'s regional planning agency, died a slow and painful death in the 1970s and early 1980s. Its problem, being an entity of central government, was its stubborn refusal to face the music of the democratic decentralization brought on by the citizens' movement of the 1970s and the post-franquist transition. Its rigidity in the face of change was the nail in its coffin. See Chapter 5 for a brief history of COPLACO and a summary description of the citizens' movement.

Was the nail in the coffin for good? Was metropolitan or regional scale planning interred forever? The history of the first years of COPLACO's successor, the *Consejería de Ordenación Territorial, Medio Ambiente y Vivienda* (COTMAV, the Department of Regional Planning, Environment and Housing), seemed to indicate yes. COTMAV seemed to need to learn for itself the limits of technocratic planning that sank COPLACO. In its first years COTMAV was in search of itself.

COPLACO was dissolved in 1983 with the onset of the new regional government the *Comunidad Autónoma de Madrid*. The region was composed of the former Province of Madrid which had 178 municipal corporations, compared to the 27 municipalities within the COPLACO jurisdiction at the time of its demise. (As of 2010 there were 180 municipalities in the region.)

When formed, COTMAV was the third largest department in regional government. It was advised in its policy making and planning review functions by an appointed body, the *Comisión de Urbanismo y Medio Ambiente* (Commission of Urban Planning and Environment). The Commission was to review all regional and local plans, regulations and large scale development projects. It was to pass final review on the lesser plans and projects, reserving final approval to the *Consejero de COTMAV* (department director) for the rest. The Council of Government (regional cabinet) approved regional plans and policy, and could in cases of emergency, intervene in practically any aspect of local planning. Even apart from emergencies, regional government could subrogate local planning when the municipalities did not comply with the law. Shades of COPLACO and prior eras.

The Commission of Urban Planning and Environment was designed to balance multi-interest representation between regional and local government. Its president and vice president were the director and vice director of COTMAV. It had one representative from each regional government department (a total of nine), nine municipal representatives, a representative of the city of Madrid, and four members of "free choice" rounded out the Commission. The free choice members were from prominent interest groups: business, developer, and environmental. This representation was intended to correct the central government's domination of COPLACO. Opening it up to non-government interests was also seen as democratizing. While its meetings were closed to the public, the requirement of preparing reports for its relatively broad membership exerted democratizing and quality control influences on the work of the department. Its existence caused technicians to take into account politics and interest group views, at least those represented on the Commission. While its proceedings were collegial in character, it has not been an important arena for political debate. Decisions usually were made before they reached the Commission. Many saw it as a rubber stamp.

The controversy about 70,000 housing units proposed by the 1993 draft revising the city of Madrid's General Plan illustrates the marginal character of the Commission. One of the biggest recent controversies, it was resolved between the Mayor and the President of the *Comunidad de Madrid*. The conflict revolved around the city's proposal for the housing, which was seen in opposing quarters as neither a planning proposal, a housing proposal, nor one which met any social need. It was simply an operation to build out the last remaining vacant lands, a developers' proposal. Ironically, while settled politically, each side based its arguments on its latest planning policies, which served as a thin cover for the political differences between the conservative (city) and progressive (regional) governments. In 1995 the conservative *Partido Popular* (Popular Party) won the Madrid regional elections. In 1996 the Popular Party won the national elections, ending a four term reign of the socialists and their president Felipe González. Thus in 1996 the conservatives had a lock on all three levels of government in Madrid. The tables had turned.

In addition to its two missions of regional planning and guiding local planning, COTMAV housed the Madrid Regional Housing Institute (IVIMA). The mission of IVIMA was to conduct research, prepare policy, and develop housing. Overall, the department had a large investment budget and the unqualified support of the regional president. It assumed that because it was part of a constitutionally formed and democratically elected government, started with a clean slate, and was led by a seasoned veteran fresh from the then unqualified success of masterminding the revision of the Madrid city plan; it could continue in a superior-subordinate planning style. Soon reality came knocking at the door.

In 1984 COTMAV drafted two laws to carry out its missions which were adopted by the regional government. The first was *Ley 4/1984 del 10 de febrero de 1984, sobre Medidas de Disciplina Urbanística* (Law for Measures for City Planning Practice). It was to guide local planning. It contained detailed land use, development, and building regulations. Its provisions were almost entirely devoted to inspections, infractions, licenses, and fines. Its strict sanctions were a response to a legacy that predominated outside the city of Madrid—one of not controlling development. Another aim of the law was to build the internal capacity of municipalities to plan and control development. As of 1985, most municipalities had not fulfilled their obligation to revise their local plans and regulations as stipulated in the 1980 royal decree. As measures of fulfillment, García Pablos found that 76 of 178 (42 percent) had not started revision, 83 of 178 (50 percent) were in the midst of revision, and 13 of 178 (7 percent) had approved new plans (1985).

COTMAV further kept alive the COPLACO legacy by bringing forward key planning instruments from the prior period, despite their failure in the past. The second law, *Ley 10/1984 de 30 de mayo de* 1984, *sobre Ordenación Territorial de la Comunidad de Madrid* (Law for Territorial Planning), was composed of three figures. They are the *Directrices de Ordenación Territorial* (Regional Planning Guidelines), *Programas Coordinados de Actuación* (Coordinated Action Programs—short term capital programs to coordinate departmental capital budgeting at the regional level), and *Planes de Ordenación del Medio Físico* (Physical Environment Management Plans). The first and the last were brought forward from COPLACO. The former, from the COPLACO *directrices*, and the latter from the Special Plans of the mid 1970s. The investment programs were plucked from the 1956 *Ley del Suelo*, the national planning law. Though the 1984 law provided for these plans, the real story is quite different.

None of these three were ever adopted, despite two attempts at the *directrices*. Draft *directrices* were published in 1985 and again in 1988. One failure seemed to be enough to get the message for the coordinated capital programs, a naive attempt to bring planning theory into executive branch capital budgeting. The failure of the capital programming exercise was due to a lack of political support within regional government at the outset. The new department heads wanted to establish and protect their own turf. No Physical Environment Management Plan was even attempted. The outcomes of the *directrices* and the Physical Environment Management Plan could have been predicted. They were due to the dual reaction to central planning that still permeated the air: municipal claims for autonomy from any higher authority and a general resistance to comprehensive, global planning (COTMAV 1985, Consejería de Política Territorial 1988b, García Pablos 1985).

A content analysis of the *directrices* reveals that COPLACO's ideology still held sway. Not until the failure of adopting *directrices* was overtaken by the success of the political program *Madrid Región Metropolitana* in 1987 was the COPLACO era truly over. The intent of the *directrices* was nothing less than to guide all planning, development, and infrastructure at the regional and local levels. Their content mimicked the failed COPLACO attempts: functional policies for 10 sectors (housing, water, transportation, etc.), policies for 10 *grandes areas*, supramunicipal in size that together covered the entire region, and policies to guide local planning. A technical document that was prepared in about a year, the 1985 draft never got even preliminary approval from the *Comisión de Urbanismo*. It was a defensive document that responded to the problems of the times without presenting a positive image for the future.

Eduardo Mangada, director of regional planning, never sent the document on for approval. Stung by a devastating public criticism by Madrid's city planning director, and trying to cope with a rapidly changing economy that converted Madrid into a boomtown, a vestigial lack of support for comprehensive planning, and an inherently weak document; Mangada regrouped by exerting a greater personal presence in policy formulation and by forming the *Oficina de Planeamiento Territorial* (Office of Territorial Planning) inside his department. He stacked it with many of the best planners Madrid had to offer. Their orders: create policy that would shape the politics that would shape Madrid.

Mangada and the Office of Territorial Planning strategically narrowed their sights on a few key tasks. One was to write the centerpiece re-election campaign platform called *Madrid Región Metropolitana* for the *Federación Socialista Madrileña*, the governing party in regional government. Another was to rethink the region's public intervention strategy. It set about drafting strategies for four zones outside of the city. Finally it continued with the *directrices*. Its work on the second draft of the *directrices* and the zonal strategies was done in parallel, each informing the other. The tide began to turn.

*Madrid Región Metropolitana* helped the socialists' re-election to a new four year term in regional government. The document gave an identity to the new region. Madrid was no longer just the city. According to the document Madrid was also, and now primarily, a metro region. The new identity of the region, according to the platform, was to be "integrated, effective, and equitable". Integrated has several meanings. First was the integration of policy among departments. Territorial planning was now the spatial manifestation of social, economic and cultural policy. The rhetoric and substance of all regional plans since 1987 carry the same message. See, for example, the *Plan Regional de Transportes*, *Plan Regional de Innovación*, *Plan Regional de Calidad*, and the *Pacto de Industria*, among others.

Integration with the European and global economies with new communications and transportation infrastructure was another. An integrated regional territory which worked as a unit, not a scattering of places or a center-periphery opposition. Effective is a code word for competitive, then a new policy catch word, along with strategy. Effective so as to compete in the first rank of the new European and global economies. Equitable means spreading the wealth spatially in the region, to improve the life of the disadvantaged who were disproportionally located in the south and east.

The document also served as a program for the regional planning department. *Madrid Región Metropolitana* became the umbrella for all *Consejería* work. Priority was given to the four zonal strategies because they best fit the new posture of aggressive public intervention. The eastern and southern zonal strategies were the only two adopted and implemented. This was due to the socialist majorities in the zones' town councils. In the east and south the *Consejería* collaborated consensually with the localities, after first applying a little political muscle and promising ample resources and a bright future. This collaborative process is called *concertación*.

The processes used to prepare and adopt the strategies were technical-political ones. They were not open to the public. In most Madrilenean planning of the 1980s and the first half of the 1990s it was hard to draw a line between the technical and the political. Each political effort implied a technical one and vice versa. Technicians acted with political savvy and politicians acted with a technical grasp. Endless debate. "Two steps back and one step forward". "Everything is always on the table for discussion". "The shortest distance between A and B is not always a straight line". "A style particular to Madrid". These are some of the ways that long-time participants put it in interviews. Typically it proceeded along these lines, not necessarily in this order: an idea, from politicians, planners, or past plans, becomes important. The idea was studied by technicians. The technicians agreed on a course of action. It was proposed to the politicians. If they agreed, the technicians took it to technicians in other agencies and governments. If the other technicians agreed, then the politicians negotiated among themselves. In the case of the southern zone's strategy, it was negotiated with each municipality individually. After they agreed separately, the final agreement was negotiated collectively and signed.

*Concertación* did not work for just any matter. A conjunction of other factors had to exist also. In the case of the southern zonal strategy, three factors laid the groundwork for *concertación*. First, a key issue was at stake. It met a confluence of real social, economic, and political needs and demands. Second, there was a continuity of work on the issue over time that gained momentum. The initial idea for a public intervention on a large scale to help the south out of its decline surged from the PAIs in the late 1970s, was on the neighborhood association and city hall agendas of the southern municipalities since then, was picked up in the city of Madrid's 1985 revision of its General Plan, was mentioned in the COPLACO *Directrices* of 1981, and carried forward in the COTMAV draft *Directrices* in 1985; each time with a greater articulation. Third, a clear visual image representing the strategy was prepared by the architect-planners. Their image planted an image in the minds of the actors, moving them to act.

The role of traditional politics is not to be discounted either. The seven southern towns did not have a history of cooperation, much less the resources to make it happen. In this vacuum the *Comunidad de Madrid* took advantage of party discipline to impose its vision of their future. All the municipalities were governed by the same party as the region was except one, which was governed by the then closely related United Left party. It was able to use this strong-handed approach, in part, because the goals of the strategy and the political ideology behind them were shared. This case is described in greater detail in a following section.

In 1988, with the economy recovering and the socialist government at its zenith, the *Consejería* tried once again to adopt *Directrices de Ordenación Territorial*. It picked up the main ideas from its 1985 draft *Directrices*, and packaged them with the relevant materials from *Madrid Región Metropolitana*. In the light of the focus on the zonal strategies and on intensive public intervention to build "pieces of the metropolis", mere guidelines were not as attractive nor as urgent as before. They were never sent to the *Comisión de Urbanismo* for approval. All the bets were on the two leading zonal strategies (Consejería de Política Territorial 1988b).

Such was the import of the zonal strategies and of building pieces of the metropolis that a powerful public development agency, ARPEGIO, S.A., came into being. ARPEGIO was the brainchild of Eduardo Mangada, as were most of its main early projects. It was created in 1988 and made administratively dependent on the *Consejería de Política Territorial*. The main objectives of ARPEGIO's activities were to "endow the Madrid Region with competitive, modern, and effective spaces for economic activities, keeping the insertion of our region among the first regions of Europe in sight" and "placing on the market a potent offering of public land for economic activities that respond to the growth demands of the region" (ARPEGIO 1994, 4). Its mission was to buy land, prepares it for development (infrastructure, utilities, etc.), and develop/co-develop it. The *Gran Sur*, the new name for the southern zonal strategy, was its main project. By the late 1980s ARPEGIO and its *Gran Sur* project became locomotives in the application and implementation of territorial policy.

In spite of and partly because of these successes, in the 1990s the regional planning department became weaker. Paradoxically it weakened in the context of the *giro autonómico*, the central government's increasing cession of powers to the 17 regions making up the nation. Spain's constitution did not conceive a strong federal state as in Germany or the United States of America. Under socialist leadership since 1982, national government sought to decentralize gradually by slowly ceding authority to the regions. This pace quickened in the 1990s due to the increasing clamor from several regions, particularly Catalonia. Since the socialists formed a coalition government with the conservative ruling coalition in Catalonia after the 1993 elections, the regions have been able to exact even more power/autonomy. In 1991, answering critics who decried the excessive power of the *Consejería de Política Territorial*, the regional government split off transportation into its own *consejería*. The *Oficina de Planeamiento Territorial* was abolished. Environmental policy was moved to the *Agencia de Medio Ambiente*. The powerful director resigned, as did his key lieutenants, leaving the *consejería* that remained politically weaker and poorer in leadership, authority, and resources.

In the face of this weakening, the *Consejería* retreated into a phase of institutional consolidation. It began preparing a new law and a regional plan, the centerpiece of the law. The law was intended to direct less and enable more, offering a menu of options to designed to enhance flexibility. In 1994 two drafts of the law were released. It was approved by the executive branch and legisture in 1995.

The *Ley de Medidas de Política Territorial, Suelo y Urbanismo* (Measures of Territorial Policy, Land and City Planning) maintained most of the features of the *Comunidad*'s two 1984 laws, such as regional approval of local plans, regional subrogation of local planning powers when the municipality is deemed not fulfilling its legal obligation, detailed and prescriptive development regulations, stiff sanctions for infractions, limited and circumscribed interest group and citizen participation, and the same approval procedures of local and regional planning instruments (one step in the procedure has been cut out). The law's main thrust was to institutionalize the flexibility created by the *concertación* and *convenio* approach,

**Table 4.1    Precedents for planning figures in the 1995 Regional Planning Law**

| Antecedent | 1984 law | 1995 law |
|---|---|---|
| Directrices Provincial del Ordenación Territorial (COPLACO) | Directrices de Ordenación Territorial | Plan Regional de Estrategia Territorial (includes directrices) |
| Programas de Actuación (1956 Ley del Suelo) | Programas Coordinados de Actuación | Programas Coordinados de Acción Territorial |
| Planes Especiales (COPLACO) | Planes de Ordenación del Medio Físico | Planes de Ordenación del Medio Natural y Rural |

"a way of doing business that was very clear" to all the players during the Mangada era (interview with Ignacio Solana).

It, like the 1984 law it meant to replace, had three figures for regional planning: a *Plan Regional de Estrategia Territorial, Programas Coordinados de Acción Territorial*, and *Planes de Ordenación de Medio Natural y Rural*. Each is drawn from a prior law (see Table 4.1).

The *Plan Regional* combines the old *directrices* with the zonal strategies. The *Programas Coordinados* coordinate infrastructure investments across regional government. The *Planes de Ordenación* are the most direct descendants. The law, in part, institutionalizes experiential gains from the 1980s by giving legal standing to *convenios urbanisticos, concertación*, the zonal strategies (now *Zonas de Interés Regional*, Zones of Regional Interest), and large scale projects—metropolitan pieces—(now *Proyectos de Alcance Regional*, Projects of Regional Significance).

The *Zonas de Interés Regional* are of two types. The first is *Actuación Inmediata*, Immediate Action. The second is *Actuación Deferida*, Deferred Action. They are modeled on the French *Zones d'Aménagement Concerté* and *Zones d'Aménagement Differé*. The aim of the French *Zone d'Aménagement Concerté* is more akin to the Madrid law's *Proyecto de Alcance Regional*, Projects of Regional Significance. In each the public sector acquires land and prepares it for development with infrastructure, utilities, design controls, etc. The aim of both the French and Spanish deferred zones is to freeze the land price and create reserve stocks of land for future development in an effort to prevent speculation from driving up the cost of land.

The law creates two new appointed bodies dependent on the *Consejería*. The *Comisión de Concertación de la Acción Territorial* (Territorial Action Conciliation Commission) is meant to resolve municipal-regional conflicts over *Zonas de Interés Regional* and *Proyectos de Alcance Regional*. The *Consejo de Política Territorial* (Territorial Policy Advisory Board) is convened at the pleasure of the *consejero* (department head). The *Comisión de Urbanismo* (Urban Planning Commission) retains its plan review status.

Yet the law did not merely institutionalize informal yet widely accepted practices of the 1980s. Its new provisions were several. The procedure to prepare *convenios* was now to be a formal public process subject to publication in the government reporter and open to public allegations. Increasing the transparency of the process was an effort to reduce clientelism. The law required half of all new housing to be set aside as *Viviendas de Protección Oficial*, low cost publicly regulated housing. The *Zona de Interés Regional de Actuación Dejerida* (Deferred Action Zones of Regional Interest) allowed for the creation of public land reserves to minimize land price increases due to speculation.

The *Plan Regional de Estrategia Territorial*, the centerpiece of the regional planning law, had been in preparation since the beginning of the 1990s. It subsumed the substantive content of its late 1980s predecessors the zonal strategies and the guidelines for regional planning. Its conception of the region mirrored its precedents back to the 1920s. It posed a regional design perspective with a system of urban settlements and economic activities connected by transportation and communication networks and separated from each other by protected natural and rural spaces. The draft of the plan proposed a five prong strategy: guidelines for regional planning, guidelines for municipal planning, recommendations for coordination, planning for regional public intervention (zones of regional interest), and recommendations for the design of typologizable elements (housing and transportation, for example). The draft regional plan, like its companion the proposed regional planning law, was a cumbersome compilation of many instruments without a clear vision of the region.

This is where the overview ends, in 1996. This descriptive institutional history has several goals. It gives the reader a general background on city planning in Spain, particularly metro planning in Madrid. It provides the baseline data for analysis and theory. It imparts a context for the more detailed case studies later in this chapter. The two cases from the period 1985–1991 document the apogee of Madrid's regional planning. One case is the 1987 re-election campaign platform called *Madrid Región Metropolitana.* The other is the *Gran Sur* (Great South), the "metropolitan piece" that emerged from the southern zonal strategy.

These two detailed cases afford a richer analysis than the institutional description that was presented in this section. The cases will go into the drama of politics, personalities, and other details along with Spanish, European, and international tendencies that influenced Madrid's fortunes. These embellishments were intentionally suppressed in the first reading so institutional features would pop out.

## Madrid Región Metropolitana

To sustain the growth and the quality of life of the region, that is, to solve the problems caused by unequal, rapid growth that came hand in hand with the boom, the planners had to solve multiple simultaneous differential equations, to borrow mathematicians' jargon. The amount of growth outstripped existing infrastructure and services to support it. The pace of growth exceeded the ability of the public and private sectors to provide services and facilities to keep up with the growth. Both spelled lower service levels and quality of life. These were metropolitan problems needing metropolitan solutions. Neither the city of Madrid nor the central government were the appropriate levels of government to attack the problems. Both had their own problems and a sketchy track record at addressing regional concerns. The burden fell on the fledgling regional government.

Madrid had a checkered track record in dealing with metropolitan and regional problems. The relations among the city, regional and central governments (and its predecessor in metropolitan planning COPLACO) provide critical clues to understanding the resolution of metro planning issues. Central city-peripheral town relations and central government (COPLACO)-peripheral town relations were at the crux of these issues. Their ineffective coordination and political conflict in the past prevented solutions to problems faced by the families and residents expelled from the central city due to its renovation and transformation to an advanced services economy. Unable to afford to keep living in the city, they settled in the outskirts, joining immigrants from rural areas attracted by Madrid's economic prosperity. They created urban areas where none existed before. Thus the relations of the center with the periphery came into a dialectic tension.

These relations played out on many stages. Some were political. The popular mayor Tierno Galvan, known affectionately as the "old professor" (he was a university professor), ran a somewhat elitist administration that wanted to control peripheral areas on the city limits. This was nowhere more evident than around the Barajas airport area to the east and the economically troubled area to the south. Though ostensibly a member of the same political affiliation (socialist) that controlled many of the neighboring towns to the east and south, his party, the Popular Socialist Party, merged (some would say it was subsumed by) with the national socialist party (PSOE) in 1978. The PSOE experienced class opposition internally as a result of the merger. This opposition spilled over into metro politics and planning. For example, the 1985 Madrid City General Plan, initiated in 1979 at the start of his tenure, disregarded the periphery of the city at the expense of targeting the historic city center. In the absence of a defined city policy towards the outlying areas, coupled with a hole in national policy towards these areas, the city of Madrid was left to *ad hoc* clashes with surrounding towns and the metropolitan planning agency COPLACO. The clashes between the city and COPLACO carried over to the *Comunidad Autónoma de Madrid* after COPLACO was dissolved in 1982.

The divisions within the socialist party, and the terrain contested among the city, COPLACO/regional government, and the individual municipalities were not only political. They extended into technical areas. City and metropolitan planning were considered by their practitioners as technical exercises. At the same time their leaders and foot soldiers alike knew that all the issues the touched were charged politically. They practiced their craft accordingly. Complicating this matrix of relations were the neighborhood associations, so crucial to Tierno Galvan's election and the preparation of the 1985 city plan. The neighboring suburbs and towns sported these groups as well, and they were equally indispensable to their towns' politics and planning.

Thus there were clashes between institutional powers—city halls and metropolitan/regional governments. There were also battles among interests—an elitist mayor with a popular following against the more left workers and parties in certain neighborhood and outlying areas. Mayor Tierno Galvan was seen as elitist in some quarters because of his scholarly background and demeanor. His former party the *Partido Socialista Popular* was led by intellectuals and professionals who often met for *tertulias* at the *Café Comercial* and other prominent *cafés* around the city.

It should be noted here that the ferment in Madrid that began in the 1960s and peaked in the 1970s was played out in numerous forums. These forums are indispensable in gaining a full understanding of politics and planning in Madrid. The principal one was the urban social movement and its neighborhood base. Another was public discourse and the re-emergence of a civil society. An old Madrid tradition of *tertulias* resumed in cafés, restaurants, and homes. A *tertulia* is an organized yet informal discussion group meeting. The topics run the gamut, focusing on current events and politics, depending on the tertuliants. Cafés and *tertulias*, part of the surging *movida Madrileña*, were also the focus of important political discourse, or more accurately, "prepolitical" discourse (Havel 1985). Many decisions regarding the future democracy were made in these *tertulias*. Madrid in this period became an example of what Habermas referred to as the café societies in various European nations in the eighteenth and nineteenth centuries, which marked the emergence of the public sphere (Habermas 1989).

Getting back to Mayor Tierno Galvan, this view was also due to his administration's aspirations. While he opened up the city to the people, he also saw Madrid as the capital of Europe (as did many of his contemporaries and predecessors). He set in motion or abetted actions that would lead to the coming out of Madrid on the international scene—the football World Cup, the Cultural Capital of Europe, etc.

The Old Professor named as his councilman responsible for city planning Eduardo Mangada, a professional architect-planner who was a communist and an organizer and leader in the citizens' movement. Tierno Galvan delegated all authority to Mangada due to his confidence in him. Mangada had complete control of the planning process to prepare the new City General Plan. Mangada, like many of his key lieutenants, was a committed citizens' movement activist and leader. They were politically leftist professionals who mixed grassroots and elitist orientations. Mangada was to initiate and lead the preparations of the Madrid City Plan (adopted in 1985) until he was selected in 1983 to head the department of Regional Planning, Environment, and Housing in the newly formed regional government.

Enrique Tierno Galvan and his key aides embodied a bundle of contradictions that marked his two terms as mayor. He was a celebrated professor of law and then politics who was also perceived as an aristocrat due to his family ties and international travel and connections. He gave parts of public speeches in Latin and was adored by the masses. His lectures had student followings in the hundreds and occasionally thousands. He was an anarchist who did what he could to end the dictatorship. The mayor who followed him, Juan Barranco, capitalized as best he could on Tierno Galvan's popularity.

To solve the urban growth and planning problems that incided on the metropolitan scale, the *Comunidad de Madrid* called upon its planning department to analyze and solve them. As the economic boom exploded in 1985, the planners struggled to see the growth onslaught for what it was and for what it could bring. The *Comunidad* also called upon its planners to build the new institution of regional government. Planning's dual charge—problem solving and institution building—was a political tactic.

The region was constituted in 1983 and was searching for an identity. Madrid was an odd case of regional identity in that it was manufactured politically, sliced out of the heart of old Castile. Prior to 1983 it had no regional identity. It was cut from whole political-constitutional cloth. In this setting, on the one hand the *Comunidad de Madrid* and the 16 other Spanish regions clamored for increased regional autonomy from the center. On the other hand the regions individually and Spain as a nation were becoming more integrated into the European Union and desired greater incorporation. These factors were present in the minds of the planners and politicians as they struggled to gain an identity for their institution and for their region. Identity turned out to be one handle for solving the problems and building the institution of regional planning simultaneously.

In 1987 regional planning director Eduardo Mangada (an architect by training, as with most Spanish planners) and several colleagues responded to these challenges. They devised a political strategy called *Madrid Región Metropolitana* with four aims: serving as a political election strategy, conferring regional identity, building the institutions of planning and regional government, and crafting a regional planning policy to govern land use and public intervention. This strategy was adopted as the centerpiece of the socialist party's regional re-election campaign platform and slogan. Its rhetoric reflected the globalization of the world economy, Spain's increased incorporation into it; the drive to compete economically at the international level, and Madrid's desire to assert itself as a great European capital. Bolstering the region's (and party's) image on a variety of levels was a key goal of the strategy, a political strategy that chose territorial planning to execute it (Federación Socialista Madrileña 1987).

Another factor entered the fray. Madrid is a leader in Spanish planning.[2] Being looked to for planning solutions colors the posture that Madrid takes to

---

2   Barcelona is another leader and claims some of its own firsts. Its 1859 Plan for the *Eixample* (Expansion) by Ildefons Cerdà, the introduction of zoning in the 1903 plan by the French planner Léon Jaussely, and the emphasis on using urban design scale interventions as a global city planning approach to create pieces of the city by both the Polytechnic

its planning efforts. The culture of leadership coupled with being at the center of power places an extraordinary demand for effectiveness. Yet since the late 1960s until the middle 1980s regional planning had been long on analysis and short on action. COPLACO (*La Comisión de Planeamiento y Coordinación del Area Metropolitana de Madrid*), the predecessor to the *Consejería de Política Territorial* (regional planning department), produced scores of reports and no plans in the last 15 years of its existence, ending in 1983. These efforts were not all for naught. These self-critical documents reflected on the means and objects of planning and were ontological and pedagogical in their nature. They were to influence an entire generation of planners and sow the seeds of the intellectual capital that was to guide metro planning later on. They engaged in what Schön and Rein (1994) called frame reflection. The *Consejería de Política Territorial* itself was unable to implement any of the three figures of regional planning as called for in its enabling legislation: Guidelines for Territorial Planning, Coordinated Action Programs, and Physical Environment Management Plans. This occurred despite having written their enabling law themselves (Comunidad de Madrid 1984a, and interview with Eduardo Mangada). The *Consejería* needed an achievement to legitimate its role in regional affairs, or else suffer the same fate as COPLACO.

The achievement came in the form of the strategy *Madrid Región Metropolitana*, and more specifically the project it impulsed called the *Gran Sur*—the Great South. Apart from its broader political intentions mentioned previously, from a regional planning point of view the strategy has another objective. "The project '*Madrid Región Metropolitana*' has as its basic objective to make the *Comunidad de Madrid* an integrated, efficient and equitable region. The compatibility of equity and efficiency requires in our context correcting the free functioning of the market with regional planning, economic and social policies" (Consejería de Política Territorial 1991, 4, emphasis in original. All translations of Spanish are by this author.). Integrated meant forming a coherent unit of the new territory of the region of Madrid. Equitable meant balancing the long-standing territorial imbalance between the rich north and west with the poor south and southeast. Another clear emphasis was to support the proper working of the regional economy.

The strategy took shape in two ways. First was the overall regional vision, presented in three working documents detailing the specific projects to realize the strategy, and a final document synthesizing it. This vision was carried forward in more depth in the new regional plan *El Plan Regional de Estrategia Territorial*. Second were three "zonal strategies", for the eastern, western and southern sectors of the metro area. The overall and zonal strategies were implemented via three methods. First were regional infrastructure investments. Second were public development projects carried out by ARPEGIO, S.A., a public sector corporation

University of Catalonia's *Laboratorio de Urbanismo* and the City of Barcelona's planning office in the 1970s and 1980s all had repercussions in Spanish planning.

which is administratively part of the *Consejería de Política Territorial*. Third were agreements between regional government and local municipalities to coordinate implementation of the zonal strategies (Consejería de Política Territorial 1991a, 1991b, 1990a, 1990b, 1989a, 1989b, 1988a).

*Madrid Región Metropolitana* was a success. Regional government was easily re-elected to a new four year term. The platform was a key to victory. Its proposition: "govern the region".[3] Governing the region meant first giving it an identity. The title tells all—*Madrid Región Metropolitana*. Madrid was no longer just the city. All of government, spurred by the Department of Territorial Policy (The *Consejería*), strived to create a regional culture—a way of thinking about this new political creature the *Comunidad de Madrid*. This culture has begun to take root. One symbolic yet significant indicator is that at the Real Madrid football matches at home in the Santiago Bernabeu stadium, now along with the mayor of Madrid can routinely be seen the regional government president in the *palco*, the luxury box reserved for the highest ranking dignitaries. Jointly along with regional identity, Mangada sought to establish a "plan culture" at the regional level. A plan culture that would think about and work collectively for the region's future. Linking the two occupied the rest of his tenure.[4]

What enabled the *Consejería de Política Territorial* to proceed confidently was its role in the re-election and the identification of the regional planning program as a "political program" with full political support. Another consequence was the long-sought integration of territorial planning with the departments of transportation and public works. As partial reward for being a prime mover in the re-election, the *Consejería* was enlarged by the addition of the *Consejería de Obras Públicas y Transportes* (Public Works and Transportation). It was now the largest department, with over half the region's budget. The surging real estate and overall economic boom of the go-go years between 1985 and 1992 also played a big part in the new-found confidence.

*Madrid Región Metropolitana* became the umbrella for all regional planning. Priority was given to the zonal strategies because they best fit the new posture of aggressive public intervention the *Consejería* displayed. Realizing them would leave tangible and lasting marks on the region, something unseen in Madrid's planning since the 1940s and 1950s. In contrast to the first years of the new regional government when all the planning was attempted *de golpe* (all in one

---

3   A pleonasm, since the word region stems from the Latin *regere*, to govern.

4   Peter A. Hall found a similar occurrence in France. "The most significant contribution of the French Planning Commission lay not in the manipulation of any economic aggregate, but in its effect on the bureaucratic culture of the state" (Hall 1986, 279). Cohen (1969) reached a similar conclusion in his study of French planning. I would not say that the *most* significant contribution of Mangada's regional planning department was the development and diffusion of a plan culture region-wide, but many observers agree that it was an important contribution.

shot), now the *Consejería* concentrated on a few important things and strived to do them well.

This tactic paid off. It prepared a strategy for each of the four zones of the metropolitan area. It negotiated the strategies with the municipalities in the zones with varying degrees of success. Usually, if the municipal governments were of the same political party as the region (socialist), there was agreement. This occurred in the east (*Corredor de Henares*) and south. In the north and west there was less success. The *Consejería* only published three of the strategies (south, east and west). The regional legislature gave its approval to the southern and eastern ones. The strategies had broad interest group support, notably from unions, commerce, and industry. Thus the eastern and southern strategies had green lights, fitting in perfectly with the spatial equity policy (Consejería de Política Territorial 1988b, 1989a, 1989b, ARPEGIO, SA 1993).

The way the *Consejería* created and sold these strategies illustrates its new approach. It was also the vanguard of a new way of doing government business at all levels in Madrid. The code word was *concertación*. Adopted from France, *concertación* is best understood as a back and forth, interactive, collaborative consensus building process.

The way leaders in the *Consejería* developed the strategies was through one-on-one discussions and negotiations between itself and its municipal partners. The *Consejería* staff or regional politicians approached their local or central government counterparts and interest group representatives.

### *Concertación:* Collaborative Consensus Building

Let's do things differently than we have done up to now; let's talk little and do a lot.
(Angel Fernández de los Ríos 1989 (1868), 20).

Perhaps ironically, Madrilenian planners have done a lot by talking a lot. This is due to *concertación*, and its principal product, the *convenio. Concertación*, a process whose terminology and technology came from France, means collaborative consensus building—coming into concert or mutual agreement via communicative action. A *convenio* is a signed agreement among the participants after they reached accord. A *convenio* has legal standing. Madrid has moved away from what Eduardo Mangada called a plan culture to a *convenio* culture (Mangada 1981, where Mangada quotes Tomás Ramón Fernández in describing a convenio: "a confluence of wills between the Administration and private sector actors").

*Concertación* built on the particularism in Spanish culture and the informal processes so prevalent and effective in Madrid regional planning. *Concertación* has been confirmed as the tool to use to get things done. It was used to reach agreement on important matters, such as large scale projects and capital investments, and multi-year infrastructure programs. It was used when money was on the line and when vital interests were at stake. "If there isn't *concertación*, things don't get done" (interview with Eduardo Mangada).

"Interadministrative *concertación*" was used to effectuate intergovernmental coordination among and within levels. "Social *concertación*" was used between government and interest groups or other social and economic agents. *Concertación* has become more collective. It has spread to such activities as strategy making, conflict resolution, and plan making. The PAIs were primordial efforts at *concertación*. The zonal strategies were collaborative consensus processes. It is being used by national ministries and other departments in Madrid regional government to prepare and implement policy, such has been its implantation into the institutional apparatus and way of acting—structure and agency.

Recent Constitutional Court decisions have ruled that existing law can overrule the *convenio*. This has caused some reluctance to sign *convenios* to conclude the negotiations. For this reason the regional government is modifying its planning law to provide a legal basis for *concertación*, *convenios*, and their structural counterpart the *consorcio* (consortium). The 1992 national planning law and the 1984 regional law did not mention *concertación*, *convenios*, nor *consorcios* (Consejería de Política Territorial 1994a).

*Concertación* was another step in the evolution of the metropolitan planning institution away from acting directly on the territory to acting directly on other agents, who in turn act on the region. This, however, bumped against the prevalent home rule attitude. Therefore the *Comunidad de Madrid* and especially the *Consejería de Política Territorial* were prime movers in an educative form of region wide collective social *concertación* to create a "plan culture" and a "regional culture" so that the sense of working together and the sense of the region as a whole permeates processes and permits *concertación* to work.

*Convenios* substituted for the planning instruments prescribed by law just as *concertación* took the place of planning processes enabled by law. They capitalize on the strengths of the informal processes and endow the institution with flexibility. However there is a dark side to *convenios*, a potential for their abuse. Eduardo Mangada, an architect of the *convenio* scene in Madrid, has warned of abuse. "Disgracefully, the agreement, in many cases, has tried to substitute these administrative figures and has converted into other things, into a barely rigorous horsetrading, sometimes wrongly used, or with negligence on the part of the administrations" (interview with Eduardo Mangada in *Alfoz*, 7, 28 (1989)).

The one-on-one approach to *concertación* in the southern zone was preferred for at least two reasons. First was the sensitivity of the issues at stake. The regional planners did not want to provoke premature real estate speculation in the southern periphery, which would have foreclosed the strategy. The second reason was the novelty of the idea of the *Gran Sur*. Formalized dialogue in standard political arenas could have resulted in posturing and a sterile political debate. Instead of the tradition of a superior level of government publishing a plan which affected and directed municipal interests, the *Comunidad* consulted with the municipalities and other organizations to layout its proposals and co-opt the other parties to it.

**Table 4.2    Population growth in the *Gran Sur* 1970–1991**

| Municipality | 1970 | 1981 | 1991 |
|---|---|---|---|
| Alcorcón | 46,076 | 140,957 | 139,662 |
| Fuenlabrada | 7,369 | 78,096 | 144,723 |
| Getafe | 69,396 | 126,558 | 139,190 |
| Leganés | 56,279 | 163,910 | 171,589 |
| Mostoles | 17,895 | 150,259 | 192,018 |
| Parla | 10,317 | 56,318 | 69,907 |
| Pinto | 9,636 | 18,761 | 22,251 |
| Total Gran Sur | 216,968 | 734,859 | 879,340 |
| Total Region | 3,761,348 | 4,686,895 | 4,947,555 |

*Sources*: National Census of 1970, 1981, 1991; Consejería de Política Territorial 1988a, 6.

In the terms of Erving Goffman, the regional government was creating new frames of reference, new frames of experience. Goffman would have called the southern strategy an "out of frame activity" (1974). The creators of the new frame relied on their power, their command of the issues, familiarity with the territory and the players, their own personal prestige, and the saliency of the issues in establishing their authority in the new frame. They used these factors to their advantage to stake a claim of legitimacy to their bold proposal. Goffman called these attributes used by the principal actors "connectives" (1974, 211). Connectives connect across frames, from the prior, known frame to the new, unknown frame. Healey refers to this phenomena as relational planning (Healey 2007). To anchor these new planning activities in the new frame, the protagonists relied on one-to-one interaction in informal settings. The lack of formality decreased the theatricality that often attends official, formal political settings. The players were not performing for an audience. Instead they were more able to delve to the heart of the matter, into the substantive issues. An account of their *modus operandi* follows.

### *El Gran Sur*

The southern part of the metropolis was for decades a dormitory suburb for central Madrid and a zone for heavy industry. Since the 1940s rural immigrants flooded the southern and southeastern parts of the metro area. The pace picked up in the late 1950s and 1960s as Franco opened up the economy and targeted Madrid for industrial growth. The south was the site of most waste disposal facilities and had few parks. Government always kept it on a low priority. Few improvements were made. Those that were kept the zone peripheral to and dependent on Madrid, such as high rise public housing without services and public transport linked radially to the central city and not transversely among themselves, forcing residents to shop and recreate in Madrid city.

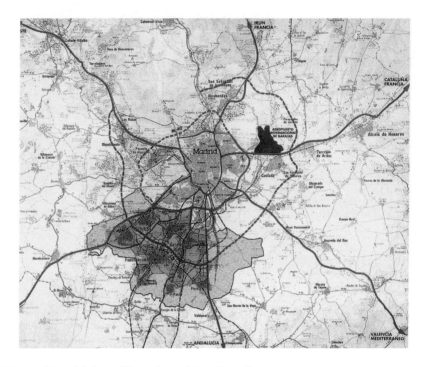

**Figure 4.1    Metropolitan view of the *Gran Sur***

*Source*: *Madrid Gran Sur Metropolitano: Territorio, Desarollo Regional y Medio Ambiente*, 1993, ARPEGIO, SA/Comunidad Autonoma de Madrid.

The seven municipalities comprising the Great South—Alcorcón, Fuenlabrada, Getafe, Leganés, Mostoles, Parla, and Pinto—had grown over 300 percent between 1971 and 1991, from 216,965 to 879,340 people (see Table 4.2). During the 1960s and 1970s much of this explosive growth was housed in medium and highrise superblocks, "vertical slums" to many due to the lack of adequate infrastructure, community facilities, and social services.

Its seven towns were "municipalities adrift" (Arias 1988, 23). They had a weak identity and low self esteem. As it grew in size, the south began to take on a weight of its own, develop its own problematic, and suffer from a poor self image. In the 1980s the municipalities began to compete with each other for new growth in classic "fiscal zoning" fashion. The towns were "dominated by the logic of the real estate market" (Arias 1988, 23).

The towns began to see that going it alone was making their plight worse. They began to see positive results from working together. The challenge was to unite them. How? There were many forces splitting them. Status was but one. Who wanted to be linked with a maligned industrial zone? The city of Alcorcón, for example, identified itself with the high tech west and not the industrial south.

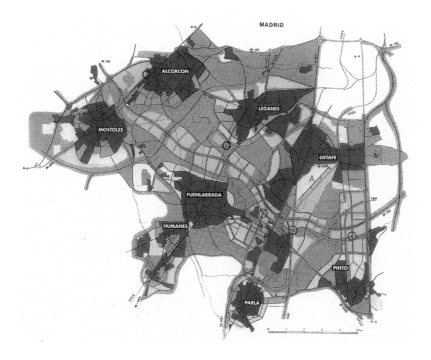

**Figure 4.2     The central area of the *Gran Sur***

Source: *Madrid Gran Sur Metropolitano: Territorio, Desarollo Regional y Medio Ambiente*, 1993, ARPEGIO, SA/Comunidad Autonoma de Madrid.

One key to unity was recognizing that "the south has a metropolitan origin" (Arias 1988, 23). Without the city of Madrid, the south would not exist.

The solution was a push from above, from the regional government. It crafted a strategy for the south. The *Gran Sur* (Great South) project promised to diversify the economy by adding commerce and services to the heavy industry, converting the dormitory suburbs into more self-sufficient communities, cleaning up the environment, and developing regional and local parks.

The *Gran Sur* was a sub-regional piece of the general metropolitan strategy *Madrid Región Metropolitana*. It tried to organize within a single framework all future development. The *Gran Sur* encompassed seven municipalities whose areas total 36,700 hectares—142 square miles (Figure 4.1). It proposed five key spatial elements. First were the existing town centers, for which it strived to "consolidate" and improve their urban quality (Figure 4.2). Second was the M-50 Linear Park, which creates a new east-west axis (part of the circumferential freeway M-50) for large scale mixed use development with an area of 13 million square meters (139 million square feet). Third was the Southern Forest Park, intended to give the south a major environmental face lift. Fourth were Protected Agricultural and

**Figure 4.3     Design image of the *Gran Sur***

*Source*: *Madrid Gran Sur Metropolitano: Territorio, Desarollo Regional y Medio Ambiente*, 1993, ARPEGIO, SA/Comunidad Autonoma de Madrid.

Ranching Zones, with the multiple purposes of protecting farmland, maintaining environmental quality, and managing growth. Finally it proposed regional and local scale infrastructure of all types to fully serve projected growth. The total public investment needed was estimated to be 125 billion *pesetas*, about $1 billion at 1995 exchange rates (ARPEGIO, SA 1993, 12-25).

Most of all, the project gave hope to the residents by placing the area in the spotlight and giving it a new image. It was easy for the planners to sell the idea to the *Consejo de Gobierno* (regional government cabinet), the *Asamblea* (regional legislature), and planners, mayors, and councils in the seven towns because it satisfied many real needs and because it gave a positive image. What was this image? Where was it from?

The overall plan and physical design for the Great South contrasted sharply with the negative social image of the south that prevailed until then (Figure 4.3). Dependent on Madrid for work, pleasure and culture, "the dominant image of the southern region by its inhabitants continues ... with the most stereotypical archetype about the south: poor, uncivilized, conflictive". Yet they also saw themselves and their sub-region as improving, and generally supportive of the changes proposed in the *Gran Sur* project.[5] The new physical design image was effective in persuading the *Consejería de Política Territorial*'s constituency by replacing the negative social image with one perceived to be better.

The *Gran Sur* as it is today began as a mental image of a single person. Félix Arias, director of the *Oficina de Planeamiento Territorial* (Regional Planning Office) in the *Consejería*, came up with the idea in 1986. The image in his mind was simple and clear (see his sketch, Figure 4.4). It occurred to him that for any

---

5    Gabinete de Analisis Sociológico (1993, 69–70). This consulting firm prepared and executed a survey of 1,200 residents, 400 in each of three municipalities of the south: Getafe, Leganés, and Fuenlabrada, with a +/-5 percent confidence interval. It also included nine discussion groups, sometimes referred to as focus groups.

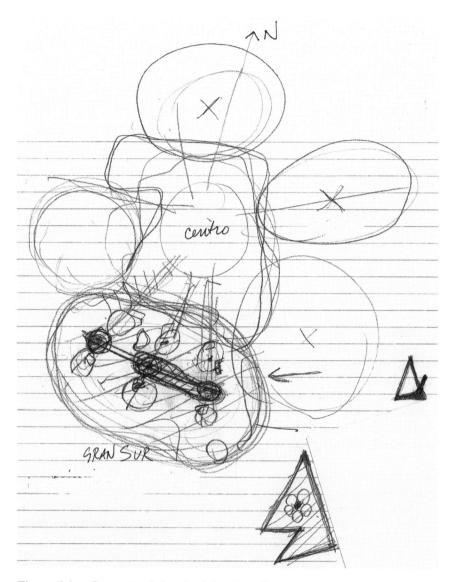

**Figure 4.4    Conceptual sketch of the *Gran Sur***
*Source*: Félix Arias, used with permission.

intervention to have a real impact, it would have to counterbalance the city of Madrid's centrality. The south needed its own identity separate from Madrid. It needed its own transverse axis of communication not linked to downtown. The identity problem was solved in three ways. First, the project was conceived on a grand scale, forging an area of new centrality by combining seven municipalities with over half the area of Madrid city, and nearly one million people. Second was giving it a name, *la Ciudad del Sur*, the City of the South (Arias 1988). Third was to break the dependence on Madrid, expressed physically by the radial connections to the center of Madrid, with a transverse axis that connected the towns in the southern zone among themselves. The transverse axis was to be part of the fifth and outermost beltway M-50 around the city, un-built at the time. It was to follow the flood plain of the *Arroyo Culebro* in an eastwest direction and bisect the seven town sub-regions in half. The city of the south was not just a large scale mixed use development project. It was to be a "strategy that governed the territory".

Instructive is the sequence Arias followed in drawing the image. First the center —the city of Madrid. Second the radial access roads into Madrid. Third the five sub-regions surrounding Madrid. Fourth the seven individual municipalities that make up the *Gran Sur*. Fifth the transverse axis. Last the nodes of new centrality along the transverse axis, where existing radial axes crossed.

The most remarkable aspect of this drawing and the mental image it represents was that it was reproduced exactly in form and sequence in most other interviews regarding the *Gran Sur*. Furthermore drawing the sketch was the first thing that interviewees did when explaining the project. Almost all interview respondents qualified the role of images as "fundamental". This can be attributed to the persuasive power, durability, and widespread acceptance of the image.

To be sure, raw politics and other factors played a decisive role in the evolution of the image of the city of the south into a reality. There was no effective opposition from the conservative or center parties. Their opposition carried very little weight in 1987 and 1988 when the socialists were at their zenith in the region. Six of the seven city councils were controlled by the Socialist Party. The seventh, Pinto, was United Left, then a collaborator of the socialists. The overall political balance was to the left of the moderate socialists in power nationally. In the late 1970s and first half of the 1980s many council members and some mayors and council majorities were communist. Southern politicians who did belong to the socialist party were mainly "Guerristas", followers of Alfonso Guerra, then national vice president and orthodox marxist. These politicians were weaned on the grassroots citizens' movement. The movement experienced many of its ardent moments in the south.

The socialist-controlled regional government promoting the project exerted pressure on the towns to ensure they would agree. Party discipline has a long and important tradition in Madrid. In the words of Eduardo Mangada, "if there is no political agreement there is no strategy". The unions and business groups gave full support to the project because of its positive economic and social spin-offs. The European Union supported the project with Structural Funds.[6] In short, too many forces were pushing the project to fruition.

---

6    European Union Structural Funds are used to equitably develop poorer parts of the continent so they can meet European averages. Funds come from contributions of member states. Structural funds come in four categories and consist of the European Regional Development Fund, which aims to reduce the gaps in development between the

A conventional reading of the emergence of the Great South strategy would use resource dependence as an explanatory model. In this view, as it has been extended to networks of organizations, organizational actors cooperate in a network to gain resources and power (Pfeffer and Salanick 1978). The actors engage pragmatically in mutually beneficial relations in which each is interdependent on the others. This was certainly the case in the *Gran Sur*. The government promoting the project, and more to the point its ruling party at the time, sought to establish itself as a major player in the contentious political scene of the capital city in which the two other players, the city of Madrid and the national government, had enjoyed a see-saw dual hegemony for centuries. The municipalities in the south had much to gain from the massive investments and the promise of a reversal of their plight. Economic interests, particularly the development, financial, and building sectors, stood to gain from the inflow of capital. Unions and organized labor would also benefit, leading to their support. Only environmentalists voiced serious objections. Even their opposition was muted due to the proposal's creation of a forest preserve, a separate regional park, and a range of environmental mitigation measures.

However we would be selling the ambitious *Gran Sur* scheme short if we solely based the explanation on resource dependence or exchange relations theory which claimed only power or political underpinnings. The scope, method, and intent of the *Consejería de Política Territorial* and the entire regional government in realizing this program went further. Drawing on the ideology of social and economic equity, their aim was to pull up the south. Greater parity within the metropolis was the stated goal. The sophisticated use of the image to develop the concept (and not just to sell a ready made package) took the project past the confines of politics and resource dependence.

Furthermore, the movers of the strategy carefully tailored it to a specific area to which they conferred a new politically constructed identity. They aggregated social characteristics of the seven municipalities and combined the findings with widely circulating stereotypes and social images of the area that already existed into a social construction that was used as the target of their policies. Thus they selected and crafted the target population as finely as they did the strategy itself. This can be seen in the surveys and other background data prepared by consultants for ARPEGIO, once it had control of the project *(Gabinete de Analisis Sociologico* 1993, Zarza 1991, ARPEGIO n.d.). One of the key elements of the *Gran Sur's* development was the social construction of the target population. This refers to the cultural characterization or popular image of the persons or groups whose behavior and well-being are affected by public policy. These characterizations are normative and evaluative, portraying groups in positive or negative terms through symbolic language (Schneider and Ingram 1993, 334). In the *Gran Sur* the background data employed in the planning process, along with the survey data collected during the

community's regions, the European Social Fund, which aims at enhancing employment and economic opportunities, a Fisheries Fund, and an Agricultural Fund. Between 1995 and 1999 $175 billion was available through Structural Funds (Rogers 1995).

process consistently referred to the plight of the seven municipalities and their residents and businesses in a negative tone. This set the stage for government intervention to come in and guarantee amelioration.

The social construction was accurate, reflecting the living conditions and not merely an image of low self-esteem. The effectiveness of their social construction was enhanced by the degree to which the image matched actual conditions that plagued the south. This negative image was held by all metro residents, including those of the south, and was reinforced by the characterizations during the strategy's formation and execution.

Schneider and Ingram go on to generalize about how policy makers use this technique:

> The social construction of a target population refers to (1) the recognition of the shared characteristics that distinguish the population as socially meaningful, and (2) the attribution of specific, valence-oriented values, symbols, and images to the characteristics. Social constructions are stereotypes about particular groups of people that have been created by politics, culture, socialization, history, the media, ... Target populations are assumed to have boundaries that are empirically verifiable, indeed, policies create these empirical boundaries (Schneider and Ingram 1993, 335).

Images play a role in this technique. In the *Gran Sur* survey data were reported in the media, reinforcing the lowly stereotype of the south. Before and after images of the south, and before and desired future images were employed to strengthen these perceptions. The existing population (the poor) was reconfigured in the planning process, and new positive images were created to represent them. "A great deal of political maneuvering in the establishment of policy agendas and in the design of policy pertains to the specification of target populations and the type of image that can be created for them" (Schneider and Ingram 1993, 336).

### Evolution of the Image, Evolution of the Project

The *Gran Sur* began as a technical proposal of the regional planning department. It was a "*Comunidad Autónoma de Madrid* project from the start", according to one of the participants. Yet its roots can be traced to several sources. In the mid 1970s COPLACO, the *Consejería*'s predecessor, referred to the south as a unit in its special plans for the metro region (COPLACO 1975, COAM 1976). At the time 14 southern towns initiated a *comarcal* plan. (A *comarca* is a group of municipalities smaller than a region or a province. It is roughly equivalent to an American county, and has less political power and statutory authority.) The *comarcal* plan was never adopted.

Nevertheless a sense of southern identity emerged from political action and debate incubated during discussions about the *comarcal* proposal, COPLACO's study, and especially from the citizens' movement. The movement was spearheaded by the recently organized *Asociaciones de Vecinos*. These neighborhood associations provided important forums for introspection, debate, and presentation of demands to government. Their demands were documented in hundreds of Immediate Action Programs (PAIs) prepared under the direction of COPLACO in the late 1970s for the entire metro area on a neighborhood basis. This movement looked inward, towards their own neighborhoods. It took COPLACO and the regional government to provide the push for a larger vision.

COPLACO carried forward in its 1981 *Directrices Metropolitanas* the emerging integral view of the southern zone. In the early 1980s the city of Madrid's planning office conducted research and prepared proposals for the south as part of its metropolitan scale studies as it was preparing its 1985 general plan. (Paradoxically the Madrid city hall of the mid 1980s was against the regional government's *Gran Sur* proposal despite being of the same political sign. This was due to its pride in its *capitalidad*, the desire for growth to occur within Madrid city limits, and the political opposition between the leaders of the two governments. The city wanted new industrial growth within its boundaries to improve its own problem-ridden southern periphery.) The *Comunidad de Madrid*'s regional planning department picked up this unified vision of the south in its draft *Directrices de Ordenación Territorial* in 1985. By the time the 1988 version of the *Directrices* came out, the *Gran Sur* was a done deed.

In addition to the technical origins, the project had more general referents. It responded to a host of political, social, and economic needs. It stemmed from the ideology of the socialist party and the regional government it ruled.

While principal players were able to draw clear diagrams representing the project's essential image in *ex post facto* interviews, they did not start with a clear image. The *Gran Sur* "was not born with a defined image, at least not very defined", per one regional government representative. In the words of a regional planner, it has "never been a precise image". Rather, the image developed and coalesced throughout the life of the process. The image took shape through a back and forth interaction between external images—drawings, sketches, designs, and plans—and internal mental images. The process produced "an agglomeration of concrete [physical design] images and images in the minds of the participants" in which the mental and physical design images began to resemble each other more closely with each passing step. The process was facilitated by, in the words of a professional planner, a "common language by way of images". This recalls the saying of the ancient scholastics "*pictura est laicorum literature*"—images are the literature of the layman.

There were in fact two types of images at play, both semiotic. One was a language of images of the city. These were internal and external, social and physical. They were captured by such phrases as "*Gran Sur*", "declining industrial zone", "dormitory suburbs", and "vertical slums"; and such illustrations as those in Figures 4.1 to 4.3. The other language has to do with intervention in the city. It became operative only after the new image of the city crystallized in the collective minds' eye and inspired action. The language of intervention was a marketing language: images, numbers, and money. It included sexy renderings and project models, square meters of office space, dwelling units, densities, real estate prices, profit margins, capital investments and the like. In both cases these languages confirm French sociologist Raymond Ledrut's "image as a referent of the city" (Ledrut 1968a, 1973). The elaboration of this idea has benefitted from a discussion with Jesús Leal.

The image was so strong that it lived through several project revisions done by the *Consejería*, ARPEGIO SA, and a variety of consultant teams contracted by them. The project is routinely referred to as a *pieza metropolitana*, a piece of the metropolis. The fact that it was built, a regional design becoming a reality, contributed significantly to improving the image of the *Gran Sur*. It is seen as a continuation of a long planning tradition in Madrid in which each major new plan that was realized endowed the city with a characteristic urban fabric distinct from the prior pieces of the city. Each of these pieces has their own identity. The old city, the expansion, the linear city, and so on; each easily discerned by its inhabitants. "This enables us to postulate a metropolis as a varied accumulation of settlements that are not necessarily socially stratified" (Zarza 1991, 21). In this way the social image of territorial equilibrium, balancing the rich north with the poor south by enriching the latter, matches the physical image, endowing the south with new parks, new areas of centrality for settlement, and a linear axis to consolidate the entire area.

From this reading one should not conclude that there was a single image of the former south, or a single image of a new south, at play. Different residents had different images. For example there were varying images of self-identity. One was of a poor place of immigrants. Another was of a tough place of the *ultrasur*, the violent fans of Madrid's football team. Another was of a hotbed of radical political activism and community civic action. Still another was of a dirty place, heavy industry, abandoned lots, shanty towns, fouled streams. Finally there was the image of a dormitory zone for Madrid's unskilled labor, a commuter population dependent on the big city for work, leisure, and culture.

There were also various images of Madrid. As capital, center, and largest city; that is, its *capitalidad*. It was seen as the source of power, government, hierarchy, central control, and authority. Madrid set the trends for much of the nation. "Madrid, as the capital of Spain, condenses and concentrates the main trends of Spanish society. ... Madrid, under the direct control of central government, was the first victim of centralism" (Castells 1983, 287). Madrid had been seen as a city, although by the late 1980s it was more and more seen as a metropolitan region.

There were also several images of planning. Politicians, professionals (architects, engineers, planners, lawyers), and citizens held views that did not always overlap. There was a latent bias against comprehensive planning by all. The citizens and peripheral towns in the region associated planning with the central government, rigid authority, and hierarchy. Old timers had the *Comisaría* and COPLACO in mind. Planning by projects came into vogue in the 1980s due to the widely admired Madrid city plan and the rebuilding of Barcelona. The new planners took inspiration from locals' grassroots claims, to improve their locales now with real facilities, which competed with older bureaucrats' long term ideas.

The politicians, in turn, sometimes used urban planning for their own purposes, irrespective of time horizons or source of claims. As a result of the two strategic processes initiated by regional government in the late 1980s (Great South and Madrid Metropolitan Region), the images began to change. There was a new image of government. Citizens and town councils could talk to regional government. It was more of a partner than a monolith or suspect enemy. The image of planning itself began to change as well. More strategic and less comprehensive. There was a new focus on process, *concertación*, and *convenios*. There were new images of places (south, metro region) created by planners. Smaller scale projects solving immediate needs through direct intervention rather than land use and regulation (although the latter was still done).

These new images began to replace the prior ones as the parallel processes unfolded. There was not one image, not one truth to the planning activities in Madrid during and after the democratic transition. In the upheaval the perceptions of the situation were angular and splintered instead of direct and whole. Ideas and images were competing and the most powerful and persuasive images won. The development of the new concept and the new images of the Great South closely paralleled the phases of concept formation Lev Vygotsky outlined in his theory (Vygotsky 1962, 59–81).

The Great South project evolved on parallel and interconnected political and technical tracks. As it advanced, the *Consejería de Política Territorial* and later ARPEGIO published a series of documents. Each was the result of a distinct phase of the project's planning and development. Each influenced succeeding phases of the process. This is seen in the succession of names that the project acquired. COPLACO in the 1970s referred to it generically as the "*Zona Sur*". In 1986, when still a staff proposal, it was called the Axis of the *Arroyo Culebro* (the river that flows parallel to the M-50 beltway). The name reflected the intent at the time, to break the domination of Madrid by inserting a transverse axis, the *Arroyo Culebro*. This became shortened to the Axis of the *Culebro*.

As the plan gained acceptance, its image and name took on broader social and political purposes. In 1988 it became known as the City of the South and the Southern Metropolitan Zone. It later was called *Madrid Sur* and *Ciudad Lineal del Sur* (Southern Linear City). After ARPEGIO took over the project in 1991, its name underwent a marketing morphosis from the New Metropolitan South to the Great Metropolitan South to the Great South. Each name represented a broader vision and a clearer image of the project. This happened even as each document became more specific about the project's content. The new shorter names were designed to have a wider marketing appeal. The fact that the name given by a marketing and development agency has stuck while the names given by the planning department have not, and the fact that ARPEGIO's *Gran Sur* documents are in English and Spanish suggest the ascendancy of marketing over planning. In street talk the project took on names such as "*Gran Sur*" and "linear city". The regional government proclaimed 1994 to be "The Year of the South".[7] Even the phone book picks up the term. Its 1995 edition was published in four volumes. The southern zone volume was now called *Madrid Gran Sur.*

The strength of the Great South and its strategy development process has led to its replication in other parts of Madrid's metro area by the *Consejería* and ARPEGIO. To the west, the City of the Image project has been built and promoted by ARPEGIO. The City of the Image is a multi-use zone containing advanced production and education facilities for audiovisual programming and telecommunications technology. To the east, the Barajas airport has likewise been a magnet for a multi-purpose development scheme in which local, regional, and central government actors participated.

## Touch the Future, the Past Will Follow (D'Cuckoo 1994)

Madrid touched the future with new images for the *Gran Sur* and the *Madrid Región Metropolitana.* The regional government, the southern cities, and now the populace at large are following them. The images of the *Gran Sur* project, and here I refer to both mental and design images, were the glue that bound the participants to the process and held the process together. They lubricated political accords because beneficiaries could "see" what they were getting. This was true of the covenant signed in 1988 by the seven municipalities and the president of the regional government that gave the green light to change its status from plan to project. It also enabled the project to be transferred from the *Consejería* to ARPEGIO for execution.

The image also played a role in the seven municipalities' revisions of their own municipal general plans. All agreed to revise their plans to incorporate the *Gran Sur*—a political decision for each. It let their professional staff and/ or consultants develop local pieces of the larger image for inclusion in official planning instruments. It has been strong enough to get the southern suburbs to go out on their own again, to act independently, yet with the power of a positive self identity and a supportive regional framework behind them.

The confidence boost provided by the image is enhanced by real improvements. The new University Carlos III in Getafe (Getafe is now known as the capital of the south), the *polideportivo* (public multi-sport complex), the completion of the M-50 beltway in the south, the opening of a new metro line *Metrosur*, and the opening of new parks (the largest regional park is known as the *Pulmon del Sur* —Lung of the South), among other projects, all have contributed amply to the recovery of the south. The image has been converted to a marketing tool by ARPEGIO, the towns, and real estate development firms.

---

7    For the succession of names, and a history of the project through published sources, see Consejería de Política Territorial 1988, Arias 1988, Zarza 1991, ARPEGIO SA, no date a, ARPEGIO, SA no date (1993), ARPEGIO, SA no date b, Casquiero 1993, 1994.

In the *Gran Sur* images shaped political discourse. According to a politician in one of the southern towns, "the role of the image was fundamental". It was fundamental because the techno-political process used to reach agreement between regional government and the southern municipalities was *ad hoc*. The image substituted for formal processes in holding the *ad hoc* process together. This same politician affirmed that they used "a complicated political negotiation process because there was no formal political instrument" available. Flexible postures were key in opening the door to the accord. The image, as it took shape, was never precise. "The image is not a blueprint, it is not fixed, it is flexible", as a regional government appointee pointed out. At the same time it was being molded, it still possessed a clarity that afforded conviction by core boosters. According to one active participant, "The Mangada team knew exactly what it wanted". This same team let the image acquire a life of its own, a life that animated negotiations to turn the image into a project now being realized.

The *Gran Sur* case illustrates the multiple uses of images to create a new perception of a place, to incite the possibility for change, to be the centerpiece of the strategy for change, and to be the backbone of the document that was negotiated to gain agreement for action. In the Great South, planners ideated a new perception of the zone by creating new physical and rhetorical images to describe it. The new perception replaced the earlier one of a deteriorating south. It was not just a design or a glossy rendering for publicity. It solved several vexing problems that plagued the periphery for decades. Its transverse east-west axis countered the north-south radial links to the center of Madrid. It united the seven independent southern towns into one unit. These aspects conferred on the south an identity of independence and greater self-reliance that replaced its dependent one. The strategy proposed parks, clean rivers, preserved forests and farms, and millions of square feet of productive space: offices, industry, and commerce. The new identity and the solutions offered hope and created the possibility and desire for change.

The *Gran Sur* image had many qualities that led to its acceptance and use. It was simple. It was clear and easy to understand. It gave a positive stamp to a zone fraught with negative ones. It united. It solved many real problems. It was a catalyst for renewal. It served a complex technical solution in an appetizing and digestible plate. Political and fiscal obstacles were overcome, due in large part to the image and consensus about it. The image converted a technical idea into hope that inspired belief. The logistic details fell into place after that. The planners capitalized on a Spanish character trait that former mayor of Madrid Enrique Tierno Galvan captured succinctly. "In Spain it is easy for all of us to agree about an illusion [goal], but it is very hard for us to agree on something practical" (Tierno Galvan 1981, 436). (The Spanish word *ilusión* has no direct translation into English. It refers to anything that motivates, inspires, and instills enthusiasm. It often refers to a general sentiment directed toward some dream one aspires to attain in the future.)

As the strategy and the image co-evolved, the image was converted into the centerpiece of the strategy. It became the focal point for negotiations, along with fixing financial responsibilities among the parties to the agreement. As there was no legal mandate to prepare the strategy, nor was there a legally prescribed process to draft and implement it, the image (and the capital budgets) became the crux of the negotiating document. It served as the link among parties in an *ad hoc* non-formal policy space. It also enabled a core team of initiators and managers in the *Consejería* to take the risk to go forward. They had a comprehensive understanding of the situation: its politics, history, the resources and technical know-how to pull it off, and the weight to bring the right people together to make it happen. They were entrepreneurs. The image represented the product they sold. To a great extent the image became the product.

The image began as an institutional one. It was created by and belonged to the regional government. Then it was shared with and imposed on (some of both) the southern towns. As it became accepted it also belonged to the affected local and central government entities. The image facilitated a high degree of networking in the strategy making process. Its novelty induced levels of planning and strategy innovation in the south that increased as the networking increased. The process was opened to a wider range of participants than the norm, though still technical-political at the core. Only after publicity and concrete results did the *Gran Sur* begin to pertain to the broader public. During the process the image and the project ran the course from idea to strategy to political agreement to project to marketing and publicity.

While the *Gran Sur* image was a new one, the use of images in Madrilenian planning was not. It was an accepted tool, particular to the planning institution, which synthesized a gamut of ideas, history, culture, and technical solutions. Planners took maximum advantage of the content of their institution in exploiting the image. It was the main tool in their repertoire.

At the time of the regional elections in 1995 in which the conservative *Partido Popular* ousted the socialists, the draft *Plan Regional de Estrategia Territorial* was in the same state of disarray as its political patron, the socialist party. In the 1990s in Madrid as in Spain the socialists were split among infighting factions, were on the decline, were losing a positive view for the role of government, and lost leadership. A corollary to the socialist decline and the rise of the right is the questioning of the belief that public intervention is best, paralleling the debates since the 1980s in other western democracies. As a result of these political and economic factors, the draft plan is not approved 15 years hence, and seen as having slim chances for approval by observers.

The dilemma confronting the *Comunidad de Madrid* is how to continue to build the region and the institution of regional government in the face of two tendencies in contra. The first, mentioned above, is the growing conservatism of the society and its politics, leading to calls of increased market relevance and decreased government intervention. The second is giving municipalities more power without losing its own newly earned legitimacy. Both tendencies giving rise to the dilemma have institutional design implications at their base.

In its first years the *Comunidad de Madrid* relied on increasing tax receipts to fund its rapidly growing presence as a new actor on the governmental stage. Not insignificant amounts of these funds came from the national government, to which the European Union added. Yet the regional government cannot rely on this approach to sustain itself as an autonomous institution in the future. This problem surges from the degree of debt of all levels of government, and the degree of uncertainty of government receipts, especially in times of economic crisis. The region is also trying to help the municipalities cope with their own mounting and harder to solve problems that have extra-municipal (regional) sources and solutions. These problems are straining municipal coffers and their capacities to deal with issues beyond their control.

Several essential historical and cultural factors condition responses to these issues. One of them is that municipalities do not have a tradition of cooperation amongst themselves. According to Fernando de Terán, a leading student of Spanish planning, "municipalities have no sense of being part of a whole" (interview 1994). This condition has another dimension, elucidated by Isabel Vilallonga, a former regional legislator and now Madrid city councillor. "The City Halls, which are the most important agents, maintain with the Autonomous Regional Government a relationship of clientelism and submission" (Editors 1991, 76).

This condition was described by Ortega y Gasset in his 1922 work *España Invertebrada*. His thesis: "Spanish society was infected by *particularismo* (meaning both individualism and compartmentalization); in other words, the interest groups of the distinct parts of the nation—Church, Army, Courts, Government, etcetera had primacy over the collective interest".[8] Ortega y Gasset used the term "watertight compartments" to describe his view of *particularismo*, of the absence of the sense of the whole. Other ramifications include political separatism and clientelism, two facts long present in Spanish politics.

This tendency is slowly starting to reverse since the advent of democracy in 1976. Eradicating government corruption is becoming a major political issue. Moreover, government is forming commissions and committees with broader representation. The Madrid Federation of Municipalities, formed in 1980 (mainly to fight COPLACO), has now evolved into a regional advocate and a collective forum to debate regional issues that effect localities.

Another characteristic that has profound, pervasive, and persistent impacts on planning and governing stems from Madrid being capital and center. This characteristic is rigidity, evidenced by deference to authority, importance of tradition, hierarchy, detailed inquisition into subordinates' affairs, and the drawing of sharp distinctions (between center and periphery, for example). This rigidity combined with *particularismo* works against democracy by closing out other views and denying social demands (Elorza 1990).

---

8   Ortega y Gasset (1922). For a contemporary discussion see Abellan (1994). The quote is from Abellan.

"Spain is a thing made by Castile". Jose Ortega y Gasset's famous reference to the power of the center in forming the Spanish state from the warring fiefdoms of a peninsula of remarkable cultural diversity captures facets of this rigidity. The strong resistance to this often brutal centralism has marked Spain's history with bloody civil wars and revolutions. A resistance which is based in part on particularism, and in part on the deeply rooted anarchic nature of the people.

The clash of centralism and individualism is the root of a dilemma of Spanish society. It wants to be free, modern, flexible, a part of Europe. It also wants to be protected, defended, subsidized, and clientelist. "It is the dilemma that every society suffers in the process of converting to a modern and open society" (Pérez-Díaz 1994). Spain converted late to modernism. Spain, like Russia, was a peripheral country that opted for the counter-reformation. These two opposites lead to an uneasy co-existence in political affairs. Their stark contrast causes confusion at best and costly conflict at worst. An example is the 1995 *Ley del Suelo* of the *Comunidad de Madrid*. It mixes both centralism and individualism, sending conflicting messages to policy users. Yet it justly portrays this dilemma in society.

"The Gran Sur is a thing made by Madrid", Ortega y Gasset might have said were he alive today. Centralism and resistance are thus seen in Madrilenean territorial planning. Centralism has been perpetuated in planning laws for generations. It can be seen in its organizations and their hierarchical oversight over local planning and development. It is evident in the models of the city and the region that have been perpetuated over the course of this century. The reaction against the center based on particularism is just as prevalent. A reluctance to prepare plans that are required by the center, and a resistance to adhere to or implement plans that are prepared by the center.

While other cultural traits mark Madrilenian planning, one needs to be highlighted. It is the propensity for informality, open endedness, prolixity, and the belief that every thing is negotiable. These characteristics recognize the chaotic, labyrinthine complexity of planning and politics. The "two steps back for every step forward" and "the shortest route from A to B is not a straight line" views of the world. The wisdom to know that change occurs when there is a confluence of conditions, and not before. The best planning in Madrid has been the fruit of these traits and has let its planners do what they do best, improvise with instinct and perspicacity.

The history of planning in Madrid can be used as a basis for a hypothesis. If future laws, regional or national, continue to be interventionist in local affairs, require hierarchical approval, specify excessive detail in plans and development procedures, and in general restrict creativity and local initiative; then planning will continue to be divorced from the real forces that govern the metropolis. Forces that are structured in interlaced networks, that act through interactive and recursive procedures in less than linear sequences, and that can flexibly adapt to multi-dimensional dynamics in real time.

## *Gran Sur:* From Social Movement to Image Building and Selling

In Madrid, the Great South project signaled a transformation of city planning to marketing to via strategic planning. Throughout the life of the *Gran Sur* project, from its beginnings in the 1970s, planning changed from social movement to image building and selling. The urban grassroots movements of the 1970s pressed political and social demands via planning. Now the institution of regional planning has absorbed these demands into its *modus operandi*. Under the guise of a specially tailored image that satisfied these claims on a large scale, regional government fulfilled its own political project and institution building purposes. As one interested observer put it, the *Gran Sur* is "the crown jewel of the socialist party's planning".

Eduardo Mangada, even more interested as the captain of this effort, baldly exposes the intent of the project and its place in regional politics and institution building. In his own words:

> It seems important the idea of the need to create or recompose a physical image as a support for a political message, as a means of co-opting the commitment of the different interest groups in a territorial project. In the case of Madrid this convenience turned into a necessity for the recently born Regional Government, since, in large measure, Madrid *"Region Metropolitana"* is an artificial act, that is to say a political act. The Autonomous Region appears as cheese stuck in a sandwich between the [Madrid] City Hall and the omnipresent Central Government. Only the invention of a supramunicipal territory, the formulation of a desirable image and the commitment in its construction could give legitimacy and identity to the Regional Government, and awaken the feeling of belonging in the citizens. For this the effort was made to construct a political discourse and invent a new territory, part of which is the piece called *"Gran Sur"* (personal correspondence, July 17, 1994).

As in any complex phenomenon, no one factor, not even the image, made or broke the *Gran Sur*. It resulted from the favorable conjunction of many factors. It was an evolving accumulation of ideas and agreements that not only got the project underway, but changed the way planning was done, building new institutions of regional planning and regional government in the process.


## Nothing New Under the Sun

Similar stories have been told about Barcelona and its remarkable urban transformation since the 1980s and the Thames River Gateway between London and the English Channel since the 1990s. Like Madrid, Barcelona also experienced a massive urban social movement in the 1970s and also used new images of the city—high quality public spaces—which changed the way the city saw itself.

Barcelona's planning accomplishments are now used by the city and by the real estate, commercial, and financial sectors to promote the city internationally. For example, a 1994 exhibit in a prominent city museum of the pre-Olympic urban renovation carried an English title Barcelona New Projects and was a multi-media publicity extravaganza sponsored jointly by the city hall and 20 developers, banks, and other business concerns. The images of the new Barcelona assumed an importance and a role analogous to that of the images for the *Gran Sur* and *Madrid Región Metropolitana* in Madrid.

Barcelona's city hall used planning to revitalize the city. Its process was centered around neighborhood revitalization at first. As preparations for the 1992 Olympics gained steam larger urban and metropolitan scale projects were undertaken. Planning and urban renewal have been and still are cornerstones to city politics, as they are throughout Spain. Planning has also been central to conferring a new identity on the city and building local political institutions in the democratic era.

In 1994 a strategic plan was adopted for the Thames river corridor region between London and the newly opened Channel Tunnel. The planning process took advantage of social and physical images for regional renewal. Its strategy also relies heavily on the image of the Thames Gateway in its marketing. The Thames Gateway Task Force used a collaborative consensus process involving a range of stakeholders to prepare its Thames Gateway Planning Framework Consultation Draft. The role of the image of the renewed river and its connection to Europe via the tunnel smoothed the way for diverse stakeholder and public acceptance of the plan. There is an "extremely striking parallel" between the Gran Sur and the Thames Gateway, states Peter Hall (personal correspondence, December 14, 1994). Madrid, Barcelona, and London are not alone. A front page *Wall Street Journal Europe* headline of August 26, 1994 announced "Image Building: Plan to Remake Berlin has Architects Sniping and Investors Smarting". The image/planning/marketing scenario is being repeated in many metropolises.

Chapter 5

# The Evolution of Madrid's
# Modern Planning Institution

This chapter describes metropolitan planning in Madrid since 1860. It accents the period since the 1960s. This synopsis of the era before 1983 is arranged into four periods. Within each period we place one of the planning episodes indicated in Chapter 1. The first period extends from the 1860 adoption of the *Plan de Ensanche* (Expansion Plan) to 1900, when the expansion area was nearly built out. Toward the end of the century growth began to spill rapidly outside the newly expanded area into the surrounding countryside. The second period goes from 1900 to 1939, the end of the Spanish civil war. This period was fertile in ideas and impotent in practice. Its plans were never implemented, yet some of its ideas were carried forth in the plans of the third period, 1939 to 1960. This was the zenith of Franco's dictatorship. Hierarchical bureaucracy led by technicians was etched into the first national planning law and disseminated throughout Spain. The *Comisaría de Urbanismo* (Commissariat of Urban Planning) was formed to lead the metropolitan planning institution. The last period extends from 1960 to 1983. During this period we can distinguish two sub-periods. The first extended from 1960 to 1975. It opened with the formation of the *Comisaría*'s successor organization, the *Comisión de Planeamiento y Coordinación del Area Metropolitana de Madrid* (COPLACO—Madrid Metropolitan Area Planning and Coordination Commission). This time frame coincided with the twilight of the franquist era. Its fortunes and its images of hierarchy, patriarchy, and loyalty were clearly on the decline. In cafés and behind closed doors *progresistas* (progressive persons) were paving the way for the future. The second sub-period was the transition to democracy from 1975 to 1983. In that period urban grassroots movements blossomed and political parties jockeyed for position. This period closed with the constitutional establishment of 17 autonomous regional governments in a quasi (and increasingly) federal system.

Each of these periods signaled a new epoch in the evolution of Madrid's metropolitan planning institution. The signal of each new period was a new metropolitan (or city) plan. Each new plan led to its adoption by law and the creation of a new planning agency to lead the planning institution. An exception is the second period from 1900–1939, during which no new plans were adopted. As we shall see, it was not due to a lack of initiative or ideas on the part of the planners, but rather a lack of clear images of the future in the plans and firm political support for them.

We must allow that before 1940, Madrid, with a population that just exceeded one million, was not a full-scale metropolis. The plans prior to that date were city and not metropolitan plans. Yet even those planning episodes were aimed at expanding Madrid beyond the borders it had at the time.

The Madrid story tells of the remarkable durability of the institution of metropolitan planning, despite great changes accompanying each period. The institutional structures, processes, and content persisted in the face of the upheavals the changes wrought. The story also tells how the institution actually shaped policy and not merely framed or implemented it. This last point runs counter to the received view in which policy makers, politics, or events play leading roles. We further learn that the institution sought flexibility regardless of its internal character or external situation. Finally we see how images shaped policy and the institution itself.

Madrid's modern planning history reflects, as all histories do, the influence of the times on specific events and vice versa. It reflects the transition of planning as reacting to growth to planning as a symbolic political instrument (Neuman 1995a, 1996). It shows planning as a tool of dominant economic interests to assure the highest and best (most profitable) use of land and to support and maintain property values (Boyer 1983). It reveals the influence of planning ideas imported from abroad, mainly France, Italy, Britain and Belgium (de Terán 1982). It reflects the social function of planning in using regulatory means to propagate certain norms (Crozier 1965, Castells 1971b). It evinces institution building through the application of disciplinary technologies by centralized technocratic apparati to maintain order (Rabinow 1989).

The research presented here confirms for Madrid the theses of the studies cited above which were conducted on other places (with the exception of Neuman and de Terán). Each of the theoretical stances in those studies captures a segment, none the whole. The history presented here is also partial. It tells an episodic institutional story. Its moral is images mold planning and planning builds institutions. This history places the institution itself stage center in a starring role.

## The Expansion of Madrid 1860–1900

This period presents the case of an image for the future of Madrid—the city plan image—and the use of that image to seed the incipient modern city planning movement in Madrid and Spain. The laws that would enact this plan over the ensuing decades were adopted during a turbulent historic era in which many governments rose and fell. The pendulum swung from monarchy to an inchoate democracy back to restoring the monarchy, and then to a republican period. The socio-political environment was unstable. Its repercussions on the growth and politics of Madrid, the capital, were significant.

Madrid's first modern plan for its expansion *(ensanche)* was drafted by the engineer Carlos María de Castro between 1857 and 1859, and adopted by royal decree in 1860. The decree, which set up the Madrid Expansion Commission (*Comisión de Ensanche de Madrid*), was the first in a series of acts during the modern era which placed the central government in charge of Madrid's planning and growth. This act continued a long-standing tradition of royal intervention in Madrid's physical development, extending back at least until King Felipe II of the sixteenth century (Fernández García 1993, 420–421). The royal decree gave ultimate responsibility for the 1860 expansion plan to the Minister of Development Claudio Moyano, once he had heard the considerations of the city and the province of Madrid.

This plan enlarged the city's built up area threefold by imposing a uniform grid of square blocks oriented along the cardinal points of the compass. It guided the city's growth through the onset of the next century. It reacted to recent rapid growth due to the economic, technological, and cultural boom of the 1850s and the immigration it induced from the countryside. It also sought to give relief to the lack of open space, high densities, and unsanitary conditions in the existing city by providing open blocks, wide streets, parks, and sanitation infrastructure in the *ensanche*. The plan also aimed to accommodate projected growth owing to key capital investments recently executed or programmed: the new aqueduct, new rail connections, and roads to distant provincial capitals (Castro 1860).

The 1857 Royal Decree creating the commission to study the expansion project indicated that the expansion project was already given, a "*proyecto contado*". The study was done by Castro, who chaired the commission. It was to fix the limits and the form of the expansion. The expansion was to deal with new growth only, not with the existing city. No interior reform of the historic city was called for. The project of the expansion of Madrid, limiting itself to "fix the lines of the roads and the streets, the parks, walks, and plazas, the plots or floor plans of the principal public buildings, the blocks of houses, their general distribution, and finally the city limits" looked to the future without casting even a glance to its past (*Nombramiento de la Comisión para el estudio del Proyecto de ensanche de Madrid*, Royal Decree of April 8, 1857. (Naming of the Commission for the Study of the Project of the Expansion of Madrid)).

The legal-administrative context for the plan stretches back to 1833. At that time the provincial system was set up to divide the Spanish territory into 49 provinces. The provinces were modeled on French *Departements*. The central government appointed the Civil Governors of the Provinces. The real power resided with the military Captain General, who was superior to the Civil Governor. The Province of Madrid appears in 1833 with the geographic boundaries that it and the autonomous regional government the *Comunidad de Madrid* still have today. In 1845 the Municipal Government Law was adopted. It specified that the crown appoint mayors of towns with populations of 2,000 persons or more, and that the Civil Governor of the province appoint mayors in the smaller towns.

The July 19, 1860 decree approving the *anteproyecto* (draft plan), signed by the queen, re-iterated the three principles by which the plan was to guide growth in three of the decree's nine articles. "Article 3. The principal streets of the new city will be at least 30 meters wide, and the rest 20 or 15 meters, according to their length and importance; Article 4. The number of floors in the private buildings can not exceed three, to wit: bottom, principal, and second; Article 5. The blocks will be distributed so that in each one private gardens occupy as much land as the buildings, giving to them [the buildings] at least two facades" (Fernández García 1993, 421).

This plan left development to private initiative. Its other innovation was to use public intervention to guide growth by funding its supporting infrastructure and by ordering its physical pattern. If left to the private sector alone, the city would grow by "isolated projects at each end of the city, realizing the reform without unity or concert" (*Nombramiento de la Comisión para el estudio del Proyecto de ensanche de Madrid*, Royal Decree of April 8, 1857).

Thus a technician with royal and cabinet level support was able to proceed freely, without interference from disparate interests outside of the technical sphere. Free to an extent. Castro was confined within the limits of the prevailing winds, then monarchic and conservative. With this support he was able to single-handedly project the future form of the city by drawing a two dimensional diagram of the layout of its streets. Hygienic layout according to rational principles preoccupied this engineer. It was not until 1892 that the city adopted *Ley de 26 de julio de 1892, Ley del Ensanche y Extensión* (Law of Expansion and Extension), to regulate the growth planned for in the Castro Plan. In 1895 it passed a companion law for the existing historic city inside the expansion, *Ley de 18 de marzo de 1895, Ley de Saneamiento y Mejora Interior* (Law of Drainage and Interior Improvement). These laws each acted on different parts of the city. They exercised their authority directly on the land itself and its property owners. It did not direct any other agencies.

Castro's plan left an indelible image on the city and its planning. The area of Madrid covered by his expansion was built according to its specifications. Over time, building heights have been increased by additions to the original structures, and by the modifications to the building code allowing taller buildings. The most persistent aspect of the legacy, in both imagery and reality, has been the street layout. Castro's grid is similar to that of Cerdà's 1857 expansion plan for Barcelona. Cerdà and Castro were familiar with each other's work. Cerdà entered the Madrid competition that Castro won. He also graduated from the recently formed Engineering School, the source of Spain's city planners at the time. Castro cited Cerdà's Barcelona expansion plan approvingly in the text of his Madrid plan (Castro 1860b).

The image of the street grid was reproduced frequently in maps and the popular press. The plan in fact directed the city's growth for the remainder of the century and into the early stages of the twentieth. Its precepts were codified into the 1876 and 1892 city ordinances. It directed new growth into virgin land while it disregarded the existing city. Castro's plan did not contain any proposals for the interior of the historic city, located within the perimeter of the fortified walls. The walls were torn down to make room for the city's expansion. As influential as Castro's plan image was, it became subject to a scathing critique by publisher, politician, entrepreneur, and long time Madrid observer Angel Fernández de los Ríos.

In 1868 the city government published a book by Fernández de los Ríos, *El Futuro Madrid* (Fernández de los Ríos 1989). Written while in political exile in Paris, it is not only a plan for the future of Madrid, it is one of the most astute analyses of a city ever recorded. It called for complete reform of the existing city and expansion, both sensitive to existing conditions. Fernández de los Ríos opposed Castro by writing that the expansion should occur not in an abstract grid but consider the geography and ecology. New growth should occur in *cercanías*, garden cities separated from the urb by a green belt and connected by rail to the center.

His vision blended a global view of the city with specific project reforms, and included new institutions and reforms of existing ones. Few if any of the proposals in all the subsequent plans for Madrid cannot be found in his book. While his plan was not adopted officially as city policy, he was appointed to the post of *Concejal* (Councilor or Advisor) in the Presidency of Public Works, which he held for a short term. Proposals from his plan and the book which were realized include placing the *Parque de Buen Retiro* in public hands from the crown, building the *Plaza de Independencia*, founding the *Boletín Municipal de Madrid*, and opening new roads and streets; all marking the capital today (Fernández de los Ríos 1989).

Another chapter in Madrid's planning history deserves a mention here. It is Arturo Soria's *Ciudad Lineal* (Linear City). Soria proposed the *Ciudad Lineal* in 1892. It was a private real estate venture that urbanized the then eastern outskirts. A boulevard five kilometers long with 20-meter-wide single family residential lots along its length, it also had commercial establishments. Lacking large investors, Soria formed the private development corporation *La Companía Madrileña de Urbanización* in 1894 to lure small shareholders. He eventually got 600. Lacking solid financial success, he tried to get it declared a public good, in vain. While a street car line was built out to the linear city, it was denied access to its intended Madrid terminal. As a business proposition it had mixed results. Yet it is considered a high point in Spanish planning history for its radical conception and offering single family dwellings with yards (Anonymous 1911, Conserjería de Política Territorial 1990c, Fernández García 1993, de Terán 1968).

The image of the linear city, a 40-meter-wide road of five kilometers, with single family parcels along its entire length, is firmly established in the Spanish planning pantheon. It attained this status not only for its radical proposal, not only because it based its theory on the importance of transportation and access as a basis for the modern city (as did Castro and Cerdà before him), and not only because of its introduction of the single family home for the masses concept into a society whose masses and middle class resided in apartment buildings. It has retained its luster because of the bold and often-reproduced image of the linear city and its (out of proportion) lots emanating from the main street. The *Ciudad Lineal* is a staple of Madrid history books and of international and European city planning histories. For many years it was often the only citation of Spanish city planning. For Spanish histories of the Lineal City see Collins, G., Flores, C., and Soria y Puig, A. (1968), Maure Rubio (1991), and de Terán 1968).

The Lineal City has maintained its historical importance despite never being institutionalized as part of an official city plan. Its legacy marks the *Gran Sur* proposal of the 1980s put forth by the regional government of Madrid. It lives on as an inspiration of the main road axis of the *Gran Sur* (Highway M 50). It is a modern day linear city extending across six towns. The *Gran Sur* replaced Soria's single family lots with office parks and subdivisions, reflecting contemporary scales and technologies. The project borrows Soria's terminology by calling its main development scheme the *Parque Lineal Sur M 50* (M 50 Southern Linear Park).

**Impotent Images, Impotent Practice: Planning Without Politics 1900–1939**

During this period there were repeated attempts at adapting a plan and creating a new institution to implement it. All the attempts were failures. The plans lacked clarity regarding how to manage new growth in the periphery. They offered no persuasive images of a viable future for the city. Like the prior period, this was a turbulent one politically. Starting out as a republican democracy at the turn of the century, the political pendulum swung back and forth between constitutional monarchy and republican democracy until dictator Primo de Rivera's reign in the 1920s. The period closed with another attempt at democracy in the early 1930s (the second republic) and the divisive civil war of 1936–1939.

As Castro's expansion was built out and peripheral growth increased its impact on the city, four plans were put forth in the first third of the twentieth century. A common feature of these plans was the relative freedom their authors had, engineers and architects all. This freedom came at a political price—their plans were not realized. None were adopted for lack of political support. The lack of explicit political support and the lack of strong, clear images contained in the plans contributed directly to their failure to be implemented. In both these regards they contrasted sharply with the plan for expansion in 1860, which was implemented. Planning in this period was the province of an inner circle of specialists. Their labors did not have political repercussions.

Despite the small staff size of the city planning office and the fact that the plans were neither adopted nor implemented, these designers and their plans did influence planning in the period that followed. During this period a succession of city offices were created to deal with planning issues. Planning began its institutionalization as a government activity in the executive branch around 1900. In 1902 the *Comisión Especial para la reforma del suelo y subsuelo de Madrid* (Special Commission for the reform of the land and underground of Madrid) was created. In 1905 the *Junta Consultativa* (Advisory Board) for city planning was formed. The *Sección de Estudios de Urbanismo de La Dirección de Vías Públicas*

(City Planning Studies Section of the Public Works Directorate) became the first permanent executive staff body for planning in 1907.

The first of the four plans of the era was the 1910 *Proyecto para la Urbanización del extrarradio*. It became known as the Nuñez Granés Plan after its author the engineer Pedro Nuñez Granés. Its proposal dealt with the *extrarradio*, the periphery outside the limits of the *ensanche*. The plan responded to the proliferation of housing construction in the *extrarradio*. Housing starts there exceeded interior (old city and post-1860 expansion) construction in absolute amount and in rate of increase. The plan sought "to put a stop to the anarchy existing in the urbanization of the extrarradio" by means of "a rational plan" (Ayuntamiento de Madrid 1910). It was approved in 1916 but never implemented because the city council did not adopt its implementing law, the *Ley de Urbanización*.

The 1910 Nuñez Granés plan was the first to adumbrate the concept of metropolis in reference to Madrid. His conception of the metropolis, while not as extensive as the common notion today, reflected the problematic of his time. His metropolis's urban form was diffuse and anarchic around the edges. The most pressing question was the *extrarradio*, the outskirts. Yet the urban problematic indicated by the terms metropolis and *extrarradio* was never articulated graphically. Nuñez Granés never drew an image which captured the dilemma of growing up (vertically) versus growing out that was confronting Madrid. The term *extrarradio* itself is vague, connoting "something out there" without specifying what is out there and where it is. Its literal translation is the outer edge of town, the quintessential non-place. The *extrarradio* inspired one author to refer to it as "a belt of miscry that surrounds and infects Madrid" (Ruíz Gimenez 1916, in Fernández García 1993, 587).

It inspired another critic, the architect Amós Salvador, to chastise Nuñez Granés's plan for not presenting a clear vision of the future structure of the city in a "general structural plan" (Salvador y Carreras 1923, quoted in Fernández García 1993, 592). It is with little wonder, then, that Nuñez Granés's plan, which focused on the *extrarradio*, evoked so little attention upon its publication. The plan map's small scale and muted tones were no match for the large scale plan map and bold relief of the grid that Castro inked.

In 1923 the *Junta Consultiva Municipal de Obras* (Municipal Works Advisory Board), put forward another proposal, neither adopted nor implemented. The object of the *Informe Acerca de la Urbanización del Extrarradio* (Report on the Urbanization of the Outskirts) was to formulate an official recommendation to guide the growth of Madrid outside the limits of the 1860 expansion (Nuñez Granés 1924).

One part of this proposal was to separate the outskirts of the city into zones, as put forth in the Proposal for a General Extension Plan for Madrid and its Distribution in Zones (Lopez Sallaberry, Aranda, de Lorite Kramer, and García Cascales 1923). In 1926 Nuñez Granés, then the city's engineer, put forward yet another plan, one which also was neither adopted nor implemented. Its title was the *Plan General de Extensión*. Its objective was similar, to guide growth in the periphery. According to Rueda Laffond, "the fundamental achievement of this new work will result ...

in the supersession of the Extrarradio concept by the suburban nucleus, capable of incorporating the future satellite populations" (Rueda Laffond 1993).

But this achievement never came to pass because this attempt at adopting the plan also failed. It too was plagued by not possessing a clear image of the future of the *extrarradio*. It was not adopted, despite an official declaration of "urgency" and reliance on the legal foundation of the new city code, adopted in 1924–1925. The frustration of the city authorities generated by this series of failed proposals led to the announcement of an international competition. They hoped to cast their net further to lure prestigious international architects in furnishing a more graphically articulated proposal.

In 1928 the *Sección de Urbanismo* (City Planning Section) was formed in city hall. Trying to gain additional support for the 1926 *Plan General de Extensión* proposal and for planning in general, the technicians got the city to sponsor an international competition for a new plan in 1929. The competition was declared void without a winner by the jury because no entry fulfilled all the requirements. But the leading entry and recipient of the largest financial compensation for services rendered was submitted by the architects Secundino Zuazo of Spain and Hans Jansen of Germany.

Their proposal was comprehensive, dealing with traffic, health, housing, industry, neighborhoods, urban redevelopment, the airport, and other issues, in addition to the overall growth and form of the metropolis. It signaled a change in Spanish planning that exists to this day. Architects and not engineers were now the prime movers of plans (Ayuntamiento de Madrid 1929a, 1929b, Zuazo and Jansen 1929–1930). As architects, physical form captured their attention, the same as with the engineers. However they broadened the scope of planning geographically to the entire metropolitan region and substantively to deal with the contradictions that arose from Madrid's emergence as a modern metropolis.

The Zuazo-Jansen proposal's profound impact was largely due to its clarity of concept, its structuring of existing problems and conditions, and its graphic presentation. The first of many positive comments on the proposal is by Editors (1930). Spanish planning and design luminaries Pedro Bidagor, Rafael Moneo, and Fernando de Terán, among others, have noted the strong and clear graphics of Zuazo and Jansen's proposal. In fact, the graphic presentation of Zuazo and Jansen was so strong that their proposal, a mere competition entry, became known as the Zuazo Jansen Plan.

In addition, a tangible imprint it left on the city was furthering the impulse of its northward growth by projecting the boulevard *Paseo de la Castellana* from the existing center. Zuazo was contracted by the city to expand the *Paseo de la Castellana*, Madrid's principal north-south boulevard, to the north. This project expanded into a city plan, and later into a metropolitan framework. His work was incorporated into the 1931 general plan for the city.

It further inspired Pedro Bidagor, a young architect who worked for Zuazo and was later to prepare his own seminal plan for Madrid in the 1940s. Also revealing the power of the Zuazo-Jansen image is the fact that their proposal was cited for its illustrations only. The text to the proposal which was printed in the December 1930 issue of the official journal of the Central Society of Architects, *Arquitectura*, that announced the results of the competition was written by another German, Bonatz, a foreign member of the jury judging the competition. It was another example, along with Castro's plan, of the image taking precedence over text and guiding future planning and actual development. It cemented the reign of the image in Madrilenean planning.

The *Plan General de Extensión* was the last of the plans of this period that was not implemented. It was drafted in 1931 by city architect José de Lorite Kramer. It borrowed most of its content from the Zuazo-Jansen proposal and to a lesser extent the two earlier Nuñez Granés plans. Its main innovation was including a "study for a regional plan" which stretched nearly 50 kilometers from the city center. The frustration of not implementing the prior plans due to the lack of political support, and the recognition of the institutional failings which mirrored that lack of support, led de Lorite Kramer to write with remarkable candor in his *Report on the General Plan* in a section titled "Prior and necessary questions that Madrid City Hall must pose and resolve, without which all technical work will be futile and nothing which is proposed will be realized". He wrote

> I begin my report bringing into evidence with some skepticism which can not surprise, because, excepting small differences in detail, it is the fourth time that the city technical staff poses the question, advises the system, signals the order to follow, and it is not taken into consideration. From this rises my skepticism .
> ... It is so fundamental and of such necessity, above all in current times, the study and publication of a law of City Planning and the creation of a superior Council, without which the city technical staff can not work more than can be expected and in a conditional way (de Lorite Kramer 1932).

Kramer recognized that the totality of the institution is needed to make planning work: content (a plan), process (a law), and structure (a council). Like all architect-planners to follow him and like Castro and Nuñez Granés before him, for de Lorite Kramer the plan came first. It preceded and led to (provided the basis for) the law adopting the plan and the institutional structure. This is not surprising given the bias toward physical form that architects and engineers took to their work. The 1931 plan was approved in 1933 by the national Ministry of Governance within the city limits only. The Municipal Charter prohibited the city corporation from exercising supramunicipal powers. The plan was left, in the main, unrealized because of the political instability during the change from Primo de Rivera's dictatorship to the Second Republic in the early 1930s, the great depression, and the civil war during the rest of the decade. A positive outcome was the founding of the Access and Extrarradio Technical Cabinet in city hall.

In 1939 two plans were completed, one regional and the other municipal. The regional plan was an outgrowth of the 1931 plan's studies for a regional plan. It fed upon extensive theoretical nourishment from the regional planning movement that flourished in the 1920s, suckling principally on ideas generated in Britain (de Terán 1982). It was prepared by the Committee on the Reform, Reconstruction and Sanitation of Madrid, a republican entity formed in 1937 to deal with the recovery after the civil war. Its premise was that Madrid had to grow from the outside in, reversing the tendency of prior plans. It proposed to accomplish that by targeting growth in *nucleos satélites* (peripheral towns) connected to the center and each other, and endowed with a regional system of parks and green spaces (Comité de la Reforma, Reconstrucción y Saneamiento de Madrid 1939). This plan and its municipal counterpart the *Plan General de Ordenación y Extensión de Madrid* by José Paz Maroto were never implemented. They were prepared during the republican rule, in the midst of the civil war, which they lost. Both plans were superseded by the Franco regime and Bidagor's Plan of 1941. Paz Maroto was an entrant in the 1929 competition and the current city architect. Paz Maroto repeated his predecessor de Lorite Kramer's call for a law and an institution to see the plan through (Paz Maroto 1939).

In this period Madrid began to come of age in terms of its technical staff. The city planning staff grew in size and increased in sophistication, as the plans show. The inner circle of professionals, excepting its expansion to architects, remained unbroken. Neither technicians nor politicians expanded the planning institution beyond this group. This constricted conception left no room for competing ideas. Its technical personality was absolute, leading to its marginality. An unstable alliance between politicians and planners prevented them from coming to terms with each other. On the one hand resources were provided for the staff and the plans. On the other hand, these plans were left to collect dust. Two things were clear—no political backing and no clear city plan image, no plan.

### Gran Madrid: High on Hierarchy 1939–1963

This period was one in which a strong new image of the city of Madrid—Great Madrid—and a new plan to realize it led to the formation of a new metropolitan planning organization. It was Madrid's first at the metro scale. These events took place within a societal framework of revolution. General Franco's troops had just won the civil war and the 35-year dictatorship had just assumed power.

No one seemed to learn the "no politics and no image yield no plan adoption and no new institution" formula better than Pedro Bidagor. A clear thinking architect, he became head of the technical staff of the *Junta de Reconstrucción de Madrid* in 1939 at the age of 35. The *Junta* was charged by a 1939 decree with rebuilding the city after a violent civil war to fit the aspirations of a new dictator bent on converting it into a capital worthy of empire. The importance of what Spaniards call *capitalidad*, a word without direct translation, a word that appears repeatedly in this era's plans, can be seen in Generalisimo Francisco Franco's preamble to the 1946 law that adopted Bidagor's plan.

Words of His Excellency the Head of State upon the promulgation of the Law of City Planning of Madrid.

The capital of a nation is the symbol of what the nation is, and the capital of Spain, as it disgracefully was in other times, did not respond to the spirit of our youths, to the sacrifices of so many Spaniards. Thus Madrid has to be a living example for all Spaniards. I have always felt the sadness, on entering Madrid, of contemplating those miserable suburbs, those quarters that surround us, those tin houses that were the survivors of a municipal law more than a half century old. This new law means, therefore, the correction of this sad reality and the possibility that the bordering towns enter into the area of action of the capital so that these entrances that do not correspond to the importance of a great city, disappear.[1]

The first sentence of the first document published by the Junta further displays the primacy of this vision of a "Great Madrid". The *Junta*'s mission was to "plan the city such that it is in condition to be the Capital of Spain" (Junta de Reconstrucción de Madrid 1942). Creating Great Madrid was an obsession for Franco and translated to unqualified political muscle and ample resources for the *Junta* to prepare the plan and implement it with scant concern for social or interest group consensus. Madrid became the physical symbol of falangist ideals.

Called the *Plan General de Ordenación Urbana*, it is better known as the Bidagor Plan after its author. It is the exception to the tendency of plans reacting to economic growth. It reacted to a diseconomy, the destruction of Madrid from Spain's civil war. This plan, drawing freely on the Zuazo-Jansen project (Bidagor worked for Zuazo in the 1930s, as well as the *Junta*'s predecessor, the *Comité de La Reforma, Reconstrucción y Sanitación de Madrid*), was begun in 1939, completed in 1941, and published in 1942. It had direct support from the national government, which took over the planning and reconstruction of the capital. It dealt exclusively with the urban form of the inner metropolitan area. It was not regional in scope. It did not call for any new organization to oversee its realization or processes to carry it out.

A lasting contribution of the plan was the insertion of falangist obsessions with hierarchy into the planning vocabulary and imagery. Land use was classified according to its capacity for development: urban, urban reserve, and rural. Plans were hierarchized according to scale: general (for the entire city), partial (for specific zones), and project (for construction). There existed a hierarchical chain of approval of projects and plans. Some of these principles were taken directly from

---

1   Taken from Gran Madrid, *Boletín Informativo de la Comisaría General para la Ordenación Urbana de Madrid y sus Alrededores*, 1(1), 5 (1948). The use of city planning to project "capitalidad" existed long before Franco. See Alvar Ezquerra (1989, 238–289) and del Corral (1990).

the Italian national planning law of the time, also replete with hierarchy. Bidagor travelled to Berlin, published articles on Berlin and German planning in the *Revista Nacional de Arquitectura* ("Reforma Urbana de Carácter Politico en Berlin") and in *Boletín Gran Madrid*. For more on German and Italian influences on Bidagor and Madrid's planning, see these articles and Fernando de Terán (1982).

A few excerpts from the plan give clues to the role of hierarchy. "The ideas of hierarchy, service and brotherhood which support the regime" (page 3). "The vital principles of the New Spain: Religion, Country and Hierarchy" (page 6). Referring to the monumentality of a conjunction of central government buildings: "the three symbolic buildings of maximum national evocation occupy supreme hierarchy within this conjunction" (page 6) (Junta de Reconstrucción de Madrid 1942). Paramount to this notion of hierarchy was that all was subordinate to Madrid: capital, largest city, and social, cultural, and economic pacesetter.

Equal to hierarchy in importance was the emphasis on "Great Madrid", "Imperial Madrid", its "*capitalidad*" and its monumentality. "It is necessary for Madrid to have accesses of Empire, wide arteries that easily connect the heart of Spain with the rest of the Nation" (Comisaría General de Ordenación Urbana de Madrid y sus Alrededores 1944). "*Capitalidad* as supreme function of the city" (Junta de Reconstrucción de Madrid 1942, 5). In this manner Madrid was identical to Hitler's "Great Berlin" and Mussolini's planning for Rome. These images were to resound throughout the franquist dictatorship, with particular resonance during the first two decades. These were not new images. The image of *capitalidad* drew on centuries of precedents. Even today it can be seen in planning and strategy documents of the national, regional, and city governments. It appears with a frequency and importance that has no parallel in its American counterpart, Washington, D.C. The image of a "Great Madrid" was paramount to Franco.

Institutional mobilization took place in the ensuing years to ensure the plan came to life. In 1944 a law adopting the plan was passed by the national legislature. In 1946 this law was made official by executive decree. The plan applied to the City of Madrid and 28 surrounding municipalities. The law created the 12 member City Planning Commission. Nine of them were highly placed in the central government, including the president of the Commission, the General Commissioner of City Planning. The other three, one provincial and two municipal, were political appointees of the regime. The commission was an instrument of central control, as was its predecessor the *Junta de Reconstrucción de Madrid*. The latter had 15 members, all central government functionaries, save the mayor of Madrid and one other city representative.

The commission was dependent on the *Comisaría de Urbanismo*, an organ of the *Ministerio de la Gobernación*, which was the ministry closest to Franco. This ministry was responsible for the coordination and control of government. An organizational diagram would read as follows:

Head of State
|----Consejo de Ministros
|----(Council of Ministers)
Ministerio de la Gobernación
(Ministry of Governance)
|
Comisaría de Urbanismo
(Commissariat of City Planning)
|----Technical Staff
Comisión de Urbanismo
(City Planning Commission)

The *Comisaría* was a powerful agency that dictated the terms of the plan's implementation. This power emanated from five sources. First, the political authority of a direct line to the *Generalísimo* (Francisco Franco), and his assent to city planning matters. Second, the regulation of all construction in Madrid. Third, the ability by law to mandate the fulfillment of the plan's provisions and to step in and usurp municipal powers when Madrid and its outlying localities did not comply with their obligation to implement the plan. Fourth, the annexation of 13 adjacent municipalities into the city of Madrid. (In 1954 the annexation was complete and Madrid took on its geographic limits it has today. The city grew nearly tenfold in area, from 66 square kilometers to 607. Its population grew by 250,000 as a direct result of the annexations. Not merely a planning strategy, annexation was a political strategy as well. It ensured Madrid was the undisputed capital in all respects. It was now bigger than Barcelona in area and population.) Finally, the capacity of direct public intervention using a vast financial resource base—25 million *pesetas* per year throughout the life of the plan plus the authority to raise unlimited funds using a full gamut of legal instruments—to build roads, public buildings, monuments, and housing. For approximately 10 years, to about 1956, the *Comisaría* used these powers to the fullest.

Projects realized as a result of the plan, such as the completion of the *Paseo de la Castellana*, the construction of highway accesses in a radial hub and spoke pattern into the core of the city, and erecting monumental structures in the center went against the plan's goal of decongestion via decentralization into satellite new towns. The satellite new town effort fell far short of its aims. Nonetheless the plan is a landmark in Spanish planning, widely copied and admired. Its principles served as a basis for Spain's first national planning and land use law. Its principal, Pedro Bidagor, was catapulted into the national limelight for decades.

The post civil war planners continued the tradition of architects planning the city. They perpetuated the technical dominance of the planning institution, once political muscle was assured. The technicians relied heavily on the hierarchical structure set by the 1946 law in performing their tasks. Processes were directive, one way, and applied from above. Testament to the surety planners had regarding its implementation is the plan itself. In none of its 12 chapters are organizations or processes mentioned. The how to do was assumed. It will be done. The what to do was the only concern of the plan. This period saw the rise of the technocratic apparatus, which because of the regime's authority, was able to shunt traditional politics aside. It is difficult to refer to politics in a "no-party state" (Gunther 1980).

The *Comisaría* created two institutional innovations. One was the cycle of preparing a plan, its subsequent adoption by law, and its implementation by a new organization created by the law to specifically and exclusively implement the plan. This cycle became a hallmark of Madrilenean planning. The other was the beginning of the passage from an institution that acted directly on the city (physical intervention by building on the land) to one that in addition to intervening directly on the city, did so indirectly by acting on other agencies of government. These other agencies acted directly on the city, and now their actions were controlled by the *Comisaría* through regulating building permits, mandating local consistency with the plan, annexing adjacent towns, and by subrogating local authority in the case of local failure in plan application.

The law also introduced a hierarchical approval process of local plans and changes to them. All budgets, projects, laws and administrative rules were to go through the Commissioner of City Planning to the Minister of Governance for approval. All partial plans and changes to the plan itself were to go through these two to the Council of Ministers for approval. The Commissioner could modify at will any local plans or actions, prevent them, or ensure they do occur, depending on their degree of conformity with the plan. The official documents concerning the plan's adoption and implementation are: *Ley de 23 de noviembre de 1944*, *Decreto/Ley de 1 de marzo de 1946*, *Comisaría de Urbanismo (1947)*, *Comisaría de Urbanismo (1948)*, *Comisaría de Urbanismo (1955)*.

Rapid rural migration to the capital in the 1950s swamped the capacity to provide housing and basic services for this massive influx. The central government responded in two ways. One was the law of 3 December 1953. This law said that public intervention alone was not enough to fully implement the 1946 plan. The public sector had the will but not the resources. To supplement limited public funds the law expanded the institution to include the private sector in the rebuilding of Madrid. This law gave wide latitude and incentives such as 90 percent tax relief to developers who built according to the plan. The second was the 1957 *Plan de Urgencia Social de Madrid.* This plan called for 70,000 housing units to be constructed. Many houses built under its auspices lacked adequate infrastructure and supporting services. Despite this massive attempt, the overall deficit of housing, infrastructure, and community services continued to accumulate, leading in large part to the urban social movement in the following two decades.

In the meantime, the first national planning law was adopted in 1956 after more than five years of drafts and debates. The *Ley del Suelo y Ordenación Urbana* (The Land and City Planning Law) standardized hierarchical planning for all levels of government for the entire country. A far-reaching and comprehensive law, it drew on the precepts of the Bidagor plan and its implementing law. These include tripartite land classification (urban, urban reserve, rural), tripartite plan classification (general, partial, project), mandate from above, approval and subrogation by higher levels of authority, direct public intervention on the land, and detailed oversight, among others. This is not surprising as Bidagor was the key architect behind the law. It also drew upon planning legislation in Britain, Italy and Belgium (de Terán 1982). Such was its impact that the 1992 *Ley del Suelo* maintained its 40-year-old predecessor's main features, as does the *Comunidad Autónoma de Madrid*'s mid-1990s regional planning law. Thus, as predicted, the plan and the laws it inspired sowed seeds in very fertile soil, "forming a local and national city planning consciousness" (Comisaría General de Ordenación Urbana de Madrid y sus Alredededores 1953). A consciousness from on high, laden with images and realities of hierarchy planted in the 1946 plan.

## The Long Fall: Demise of Technocracy 1963–1983

This period presents a case of a weak image in the 1961 plan that, although it led to the formation of a new organization to lead metropolitan planning, was not strong enough to lead planning through the wreckage that became the dictatorship at the end of its life. The weakness of the image and thus of the plan, and by extension the entire planning program of the new agency COPLACO, left COPLACO lurching in a series of planning and political crises that led to its demise in 1982.

In 1961 the *Comisaría General de Ordenación Urbana de Madrid y sus Alredededores* published the *Plan General de Ordenación Urban del Area Metropolitana de Madrid*, "a weak imitation without conviction of the 1941 plan" according to the architect Rafael Moneo (Moneo 1967). It continued the pattern set in Bidagor's 1946 plan by reacting to rapid growth due to immigration. The influx into Madrid, particularly the southern suburbs, was to continue through the 1960s and 1970s. The plan continued the ineffective decongestion and decentralization policies of its 1946 predecessor and relied on the same conceptual underpinning. Despite being prepared by the same planning agency, it had less political clout as well. The regime had now turned to a strong pro-development stance, with less enthusiasm for supporting an entity whose mission was to regulate urban growth. The *Comisaría* was not near the center of power now that it was in the Ministry of Housing instead of the Ministry of Governance.

The plan aimed to regulate the growth of Madrid. It took its policy guidance from the first national Development Plan, which was issued in 1959 and designated Madrid along with Barcelona and Bilbao as centers for industrial and economic development. The 1959 Economic Stabilization Plan liberalized the tight bureaucratic reins on the economy. It increased the role of the market and continued to open Spain's borders to international trade and aid. It led to the "economic miracle" of the 1960s. The economy grew an average of 6.6 percent a year during that decade, with economic productivity growing an average of 5.9 percent annually. Industrial product grew an average of 9.4 percent a year during the same decade, industrial productivity 7.5 percent. Only Japan matched these figures internationally (Shubert 1990).

The 1961 metro plan presented visions at three scales: regional, metropolitan and city. The region encompassed six provinces out to a radius of 125 kilometers. The metropolis included Madrid and 15 surrounding towns. The two larger scales were treated sketchily and their provisions were never implemented. Nor did they influence planning or development in outer areas. These multiple visions, rather than a single image, diluted the plan's message.

The statutory incapacity of the plan's enforcement outside the city limits, despite the word metropolitan in its title and its preparation by a central government agency, made the 1961 plan a city plan by default. It targeted the *reforma interior* of the downtown and never seriously contemplated the suburbs. This despite the plan's call for decongestion. "In general, it has been determined in favor of decongestion of the commercial area of the historic center". This meant urban renewal in the bulldozer style as part of its proposal for a *Plan Especial del Casco Antiguo* (Special Plan for the Historic Center). This special plan never came to be. The north of the city, the *Paseo de la Castellana*, "the great center of capitalidad", was the locus of growth, mimicking its 1929 and 1946 precursors (Comisaría General de Ordenación Urbana de Madrid y sus Alrededores 1961, 50, 48).

Two geographic axes straddling the city—the *Sierra de Guadarrama* mountains to the northwest for recreation, open space and high quality growth; and the Henares, Jarama, and Tajo river network to the southeast for industry—and the proposed centers of attraction along both of them were to be the means for decongesting the central city. This aim was never achieved, as the metro area increased from 2,342,023 to 3,924,480 people between 1960 and 1981 (Instituto Nacional de Estadísticas, Censos y Padrones (Census and Patterns) 1960, 1981). The metropolitan growth outside of Madrid mostly occurred in six southern suburban towns just outside the city limits, not along the rivers as planned. The plan also picks up an internal contradiction of the 1946 plan: decentralizing in rhetoric and centralizing in reality due to a radiocentric transport system leading to the heart of the city. Madrid city grew from 2,259,931 to 3,188,297 inhabitants between 1960 to 1981 (Instituto Nacional de Estadísticas, Censos y Padrones (Census and Patterns) 1960, 1981).

The 1963 law adopting the plan created two new agencies which replaced the *Comisaría General de Ordenación Urbana de Madrid y sus Alrededores*. One was the *Gerencia de Urbanismo* in the city government, responsible for municipal planning and development review. The law also created the *Comisión de Planeamiento y Coordinación del Area Metropolitana de Madrid*, commonly referred to by its acronym COPLACO. It legally distinguished for the first time municipal and metropolitan planning.

The law specified the composition of COPLACO. The president and two vice presidents were members of central government, as were 13 others. The mayor of Madrid was the other vice president. Two Madrid city council members, two from provincial government, and 8 other town council members outside of Madrid made up the rest. Thus 18 of 29 members and 3 of 4 executive posts were from central government, mostly mid-level technocrats. Its mission was to coordinate planning among and within local, provincial and central government at the metropolitan scale, and to approve local plans and building regulations. It had no funds to invest into public intervention such as infrastructure. The structure and mission of COPLACO point to its true (lack of) power. It was a coordinating technocracy with a weak plan as its bible, no carrots, and weak sticks.

> Throughout the entire period since the approval of the General Plan of 1963, the management of COPLACO has been limited fundamentally to final approvals [of local plans and ordinances] and the control of planning and development infractions, lacking the necessary elements to realize true metropolitan development (Ridruejo Brieva 1978, vol. I page 10).

As COPLACO was in the Ministry of Housing, the coordination method it attempted was top-down control. This model was successfully used in the preceding period when planners were able to rely on political backing. This premise was not to hold in the COPLACO era. This made the promise of acting on other agencies and governments a paper promise. There was little, if any, actual coordination because the technocrats lacked decision making authority and the support of their superiors. Real estate developers, especially those maintaining close ties with the administration, took over the role of the state as the protagonist of development.

Nonetheless COPLACO took another step in the shift away from plans and their implementers acting directly on the city/metropolis/region to acting on other organizations. The law enlarged the institution of metropolitan planning, at least on paper, by incorporating 22 municipalities into an officially designated metro area.[2] The word coordination in the name of the agency signaled this institutional evolution.

In the late 1960s and early 1970s three new realities emerged. These changes marked the beginning of the end of the franquist era and the start of the transition to democracy. They were to have crucial effects on metropolitan planning until the early 1980s. The first was the well-documented citizens' movement. The second was the realization that hierarchical institutions no longer corresponded to political and social realities (owing to the grassroots movement). Lastly, the plan's hub and spoke spatial model of the region was no longer corresponding to actual patterns of growth. COPLACO itself later admitted these failings. As of 1967 "the 1963 plan was already unsuited to the pattern of development, and in 1972 the regulations in force were essentially distinct from the original plan" (COPLACO 1979a).

COPLACO's relations with municipalities see-sawed from bad to worse, depending on the mismatch between its big brother approach and municipal and

---

2　The original law, Ley 121/1963 de 2 de diciembre, sobre el Area Metropolitana provided for 22 municipalities, including Madrid. One year later Las Rozas was added for a total of 23. In 1982, the last full year of COPLACO's existence, Alcalá de Henares, Fuenlabrada, Móstoles, and Parla were added for a total of 27.

citizen claims for local autonomy. The following quotation assessed not only COPLACO's reality in the 1960s, it turned out to be prophetic for the 1970s.

> Really, the fundamental reflection that this [1961] plan posits is its possibility of effective application. If the 1941 plan could not be implemented with a theoretically omnipotent public sector, today with the intricate tangle of oligarchic interests created around land use and private construction, it will be difficult to make a plan a practical reality, including one as timid as the one of 1961, without changing a series of structural assumptions that would make possible authentic planning in Spain, that is not reduced to a series of technical calculations of indicative forecasts (Simancas and Elizalde 1969, 21).

These realities plummeted COPLACO into a crisis it was never to recover from.

In this context COPLACO was continually buffeted by events. It cast about for a safe anchorage but never found one. Absent a valid plan and leadership on the inside, absent political direction from its patron, or absent support from its constituency on the outside, it had no other choice but to react to major events with short term solutions.

Its first reaction was in 1972. It responded to the accumulated hopscotch peripheral growth that rendered the 1963 plan obsolete. It also reacted to new guidance from the third National Development Plan. The Council of Ministers Decree of 29 December 1971 charged COPLACO to prepare new planning guidelines for the region to replace the 1963 plan. It was to be called an *Esquema Director* instead of a plan. Imported from France, where it was called a *Schema Directeur* (Directive Scheme), it was more general and less specific, more permissive and less directive than the plan it was to replace. Supporting theory, according to the document, came from English speaking planners and scholars: Peter Hall, John Friedmann, Lloyd Rodwin, and Albert Hirschman.

The *Avance del Esquema Director* was prepared by a newly hired planning team in six months. Completed in mid-1972 and written "without consulting any official agency", much less interest groups and citizens, it received a cool reception from the Council of Ministers in October of that year (interview with Ramón Fernández Durán). The *Diagnostico*—analysis of existing conditions—occupied 5 months and three weeks. The proposals were written in the last week, and the plan map was drawn overnight the last night. Nonetheless the document is impressive, four volumes bound in leather (COPLACO 1972).

The Commission sent it back to the technical team for revision. Mid-level technical working groups were formed. A team of American planning consultants was hired in 1973 to prepare the next draft. At the end of the year the consultants completed the first phase and had contract in hand to complete the revision in the next phase. It was to be signed December 20, 1973. That day the president was assassinated by ETA (Basque Separatist) terrorists. It never saw the light of day again. The fortunes of the plan followed those of the president, Franco's chosen successor.

The *Avance* (Draft) was abstract, full of matrices, criteria, and objectives. It was a product of "systems planning". It divided the region into three levels: region, subregion and municipality. It proposed to "distribute human settlements so as to be integrated with the natural environment" (p. 357). Its regional view was a schematic regional design, with centers for settlement, transport and communications routes, and environmentally protected areas between them. The proposal was too schematic. It did not represent a lucid, unequivocal image for the future of the metropolis. In any event it was over-shadowed by the preponderance of analytical data, quantitative objectives, numerical criteria, and mathematical matrices. Mostly it was overshadowed by indifference from a pro-development regime that was about to fall.

COPLACO advanced its institutional intentions in the *Esquema Director.* It proposed a new and more powerful agency to control development. It proposed to expand its jurisdiction geographically, a law to implement the scheme, and the ceding of all territorial planning powers from all other agencies and governments, whether central, provincial or municipal, to the new agency. Finally it proposed that COPLACO be the new agency. A dream that never came true.

In 1972, reacting to another decree spurred by the National Development Plan, COPLACO began a market-driven urban development scheme to build 40,000 dwellings. *Concursos de urbanismo concertado* (competitions for consensual planning) were convoked to develop specific sites. Developers submitted bids on proposed projects and negotiated these bids with COPLACO.[3] This form of clientelism usually resulted in higher densities than plans and zoning allowed, yielding higher profits for the developers. This experiment was abandoned in Madrid in 1975 for lack of good planning results, and more to the point, lack of investment capital due to the severe economic crisis. *Urbanismo concertado* was highly criticized in the mid 1970s. Carlos Tomé and Alfredo Velasco called it "urbanicidio concertado" (consensual urbanicide or urban suicide) because COPLACO was seen to negotiate away public control over land to the benefit of private developers in exchange for them building infrastructure and providing services (Tomé and Velasco quoted in Castells (1977a). See also Fernández Rodríguez (1974)). *Urbanismo concertado* reappeared on the national scene in the 1975 revision to the national planning law as *Programas de Actuación Urbanísticos.*

## The Big Break: Cries of Democracy 1975–1983

On the heels of the *Esquema Director* and *urbanismo concertado* failures, COPLACO opted for a more realistic route. In 1974 it began preparing four

---

3   See Decreto 2432/1972 de 18 de agosto de 1972, sobre Bases para concursos de ejecución de urbanizaciones en Madrid. This decree implemented article 22 of the revised text of the Ley del Plan del Desarrollo Económico y Social, Decreto 1541/1972 de 15 de junio de 1972.

"Special Plans". The special plans were functional plans for transportation, environment, infrastructure, and large commercial centers. They were technical documents prepared by staff, taking guidance from the 1972 *Avance del Esquema Director* and the *Directices de Planeamiento Territorial* from the national economic development plan (COPLACO 1975a, 1975b, 1975c, 1976). These plans were prepared in short periods, usually less than one year. For the first time COPLACO brought to the plan drafting table pertinent government agencies. These four special plans were approved, yet none had any effect on the other entities they were intended to coordinate.

Agencies able to intervene in regional development because of their capital investment capacity, such as the *Dirección General de Carreteras* (highways) and the *Dirección General de Infraestructuras* (infrastructures) wrote their own plans and invested in accordance with their plans, not COPLACO's. These two examples are especially revealing since they are part of the Ministry of Public Works and Planning, the same that housed COPLACO as of 1977. For criticisms of the Special Plans see Colegio Oficial de Arquitectos de Madrid (COAM) (1976) and J.R.S. (1976).

At least one of the special plans, for transportation, was written to justify projects underway or programmed. This *ex post facto* planning, along with the intent to write a *Plan Director Territorial de Coordinación* (PDTC) piecemeal, by sectors, was roundly criticized by observers and participants. (The PDTC was modeled on the recent *Plan Directeur* for the region of Paris.) The 1975 revision to the national planning law called for the PDTC to be prepared before the *Planes Especiales*, the latter implementing the former.

In 1976 COPLACO mounted its second attempt at a comprehensive regional planning instrument in four years. In response to a provision in the 1975 changes to the national planning law, it embarked on a set of *Normas Subsidiarias y Complementarias Provinciales*. It lowered its sights from the larger region to the smaller province, and from an *Esquema Director* to *Normas* (guidelines), which have lesser legal standing. The guidelines never left the drafting boards. In the upheaval following Franco's death and the surging prominence of the neighborhood based citizens' movement, a radically new strategy was COPLACO's only hope.

In 1978 COPLACO changed course. Seeing that without the iron hand of authority brittle hierarchies crumble, it encouraged municipalities to prepare their own plans, subject to COPLACO approval. This reversed prior policy by which COPLACO wrote local plans or hired consultants to do so. COPLACO hired a new technical director, Fernando de Terán, to steer the ship. Staff director for metropolitan planning Félix Arias, a leader in the citizens' movement and organizer of several neighborhood associations, put forth the *Programa de Actuación Inmediata* (PAIs—Immediate Action Programs). Based directly on the metropolitan-wide *movimiento ciudadano* (there were hundreds of *asociaciones de vecinos*—neighborhood associations), PAIs were street level, neighborhood by neighborhood planning inventories and short to medium term action programs.

While this is not the place to elaborate fully on the urban social movement that transformed Madrid in the 1970s, a few comments on its effects on urban policy, politics, and planning are in order. The movement was made up of over 100 voluntary civic groups called *asociaciones de vecinos* (neighbors associations). The groups were vehicles for social and political representation on the basis of territory. The neighborhood was the base unit and the city and the metro region were aggregate units represented by umbrella organizations constituted by the leaders of the individual neighbors associations. The movement itself married the three—policy, politics, and planning—at the grassroots level. It redefined the model of urban development and official urban policy. As a movement it had several defining social characteristics. It was an inter-class movement involving the participation of a wide range of social classes and not just the middle, working, or popular classes. It worked as the social base of the city, integrating a wide range of actors and interests. It was a social force responsible for the mobilizations that led to political, social, and cultural change.

The movement's demands on government were, like the movement itself, multidimensional. The neighbors associations demanded direct participation in politics and government. They demanded redevelopment of shanty towns through public programs, rehabilitation and redevelopment of public housing, preservation of the historic city center, change in urban policy so redevelopment would not displace families and residents from buildings that were torn down or renovated, improvement of urban services and community facilities, and the decentralization and democratization of planning and local government. By and large, the associations and the entire movement achieved their aims. This synopsis is adapted from Castells (1981, 1983) and from personal interviews by the author.

The citizens' movement had an internal dynamic that was its source of strength as a movement and its effectiveness in pressing demands and getting them satisfied. At the same time, the internal dynamic was the font of its ultimate downfall. This dynamic involved the movement's leaders efforts to defend the movement's autonomy against political partisan control. At the height of the movement in the mid to late 1970s numerous political parties of all stripes were jockeying to fill the vacuum left by the death of Franco. Into this mix was added the role of the professionals in advising the neighbors associations and giving to the associations both technical data and legitimacy in their dealings with the government administration. These professionals were planners, architects, lawyers, engineers, economists, and related occupations; all oriented toward improving the urban predicament. Many of the movement leaders and advisors served dual if not multiple roles. They were activists, organizers, professionals, politicians, and bureaucrats. Multiple allegiances led to severe role strain in some cases, with adverse effects on the movement and the individuals. Mainly, however, the multiple roles added a depth and richness to the cause and the debate. It helped resolve the complex and inter-related phenomena they attempted to deal with.

The movement's aim of replacing the dictatorship with direct democratic participation in urban planning and local government had a political origin. Yet the multiple roles that many of its leaders and activists attempted to carry off led to a series of contradictions which provoked an internal crisis that eventually led to its diminished stature. This came to a head after the first democratic local elections in 40 years, in 1979, when the "Citizen Movement fell apart, unable to absorb the contradiction between its political origins and its autonomous stand as a social movement" (Castells 1983, 236).

The citizens' movement provided a new direction and new impetus for city planning for both the city of Madrid and COPLACO, as well as for the surrounding towns in the inner metropolitan ring. The city was to start a process to prepare and adopt a new General Plan in 1979, at the height of the movement and in the wake of the local elections. The plan was based on the data, goals, and demands of the movement. Many of the professionals and leaders in the city planning department, its outside consultants, along with the city councilor responsible for planning, the architect Eduardo Mangada, were movement activists and leaders, or otherwise had close affiliation and sympathy with it. As the plan was based on the ideology of the movement, it focused inwardly, on the city and its historic center. Thus it did not engage the city's periphery in a substantial manner, nor its metropolitan area. This stance of neglect for the metro area, coupled with the oppositional relations between city hall and the metro (later regional) planning agency and government (see Chapter 4) led to a crisis in metropolitan planning that was to topple COPLACO. This occurred despite its cooperation with the neighborhood associations and the development of the PAI methodology, and despite the 1981 law that mandated that COPLACO's plan be compiled from the bottom up, aggregating municipal general plans into a composite metropolitan plan.

The PAIs became the only success in the 20-year history of COPLACO because they fulfilled the social, political, and economic demands of their claimants, the neighbors associations. The social demands were for services and utilities to serve their houses and communities, more and better housing, and urban renewal (but not of the bulldozer brand). The political demands were for participation in democratic politics. The economic needs were for jobs in the midst of a crisis. The PAIs were a qualitative shift from top-down to bottom-up planning. This turnabout was the only way forward as COPLACO was facing its maximum local opposition. The PAI effort was aided by the political parties and the neighborhood associations. The PAIs also served as the base for the 1979–1985 revision of the Madrid General Plan, for the revision of local plans by towns outside of Madrid, for COPLACO's last effort at a comprehensive regional guide, and for its successor agency's first shots at the same (COPLACO 1979b). There were hundreds of volumes of data collected in the PAIs. A very partial listing is presented here to provide a sense of their monumentality. Most were compiled by consulting firms, usually composed of sociologists or planners, with the aid of the neighborhood associations.

> Programa de Actuación Inmediata (PAI) de los barrios 101–117 [neighborhoods 101–117 of Madrid], 71 volumes, 1979.
> PAI Chamartin [a neighborhood of Madrid], 41 volumes, 1979.

PAI de los barrios 34 and 35 [neighborhoods of Ibiza and Jerónimo, Madrid], 20 volumes, 1979.
PAI Suroeste I [municipality of Pinto], 9 volumes, 1979.
PAI Suroeste [municipality of Getafe], 17 volumes, 1979.
PAI Suroeste [municipality of Alcorcón], 17 volumes, 1979.
PAI Suroeste [municipality of Leganés], 15 volumes, 1979.

Clientelism in Madrid's planning process referred to a one-on-one relation between government and an interest to the exclusion of others. An example of an institutional skirmish with clientelism was the decree for *urbanismo concertado* during the tenure of COPLACO between 1972 and 1975. In *urbanismo concertado* the administration negotiated away the "public prerogative [to control land use for the public interest] to the benefit of private developers in exchange for public facilities and services" (Castells 1981, 218). Another example, though usually not seen from this point of view, was the *Programas de Actuación Inmediatas* (PAIs) of COPLACO from 1978 to 1980. In them the administration negotiated directly with neighborhood leaders to build up a planning database and determine planning programs, to the exclusion of other interests. The planners and movement leaders assumed that a wide range of interests were represented. This assumption was often but not always satisfied (Castells 1983). Based on the experience and data gained from preparing the PAIs, in the early 1980s the *Oficina Municipal del Plan* of the city of Madrid negotiated the provisions of the new general plan (adopted in 1985) directly with real estate developers, to the exclusion of other interests (interview with Félix Arias). The extra-legal (not meaning illegal, but rather a procedure not enabled by law) one-on-one method of clientelism does not occur in an open forum or arena. It was shielded from public scrutiny behind closed bureaucratic doors.

COPLACO published a report on the state of metropolitan planning in 1980. On the heels of the bottom-up PAIs, the report brought to a head an ongoing reflection of how to proceed with metropolitan scale planning in concert with the municipalities, which had just tasted savory bites of self-determination in the first local democratic elections (1979). But the report did not lessen the incipient tension between the towns and COPLACO. The municipalities wanted in (COPLACO 1980).

Only one response could soothe the tensions. Royal Decree/Law 11/1980 of 26 September 1980 divested COPLACO of its authority to prepare local plans and returned that authority to local government. Up to then the powers to prepare and revise them were retained by COPLACO. Even after the landmark decree, COPLACO still retained the power to approve local plans. The decree incorporated the spirit of the grassroots movement by stipulating that the new General Plan for the metro area will be composed of the sum of the local plans. COPLACO was to provide *Directrices de Planeamiento Territoriales* (Regional Planning Guidelines) to guide the towns in their own plan making.

One year later COPLACO issued the *Directrices Metropolitanas*, as they came to be known. The guidelines were based on the PAIs and the mountain of studies prepared in the 1970s. It began to take into account the emerging reality of the region: the concentration of high level services in the city center, continued sprawl, globalization of the economy, flexible specialization of manufacturing and services, environmental degradation, and the increasing socio-spatial disparity between the north and south of Madrid. The directives introduced a major policy shift that was incorporated by COPLACO's successor in metro planning, the regional government and its *Consejería de Política Territorial:* social equity and its spatial manifestations. This policy proposed six main strategies: protect the historic center, decentralize the metropolis, integrate modes of transport, protect the environment, improve industrial areas, and provide housing with adequate utilities and services by matching infrastructure and service capacity to the housing supply (COPLACO 1981). The document dedicates much space in its beginning to explain the guidelines. The term *directrices* appeared for the first time at this level, although the 1975 revision to the national planning law allows for "*grandes directrices de la ordenación del territorio*" in the National Plan; a plan that has yet to be prepared. According to a former staff member, COPLACO wrote the *directrices* to their taste, owing to a relative political autonomy. It had no real power after the 1980 decree and saw its imminent demise. It thus was emboldened to drop old proposals such as a new airport and insert new ones such as social equity.

The *directrices* were never implemented. The transition to the new regional government in 1983 made the document moot *vis-a-vis* its legal standing. Most of the municipalities, who were supposed to amend their local plans in accordance with the *directrices*, waited for the new regional government to form and provide its own planning guidance. The COPLACO *directrices* did, however, influence the content of the first attempt of its successor in drafting its own.

The COPLACO era was a dismal rerun of the first third of the twentieth century. Impotent in practice and ideas. Only two COPLACO contributions went on to shape future planning. These were the PAIs and the socio-spatial equity policy. Significantly, both contributions (successes) were home-grown rather than imported. Few of its plans were ever approved, and none were implemented. This was because throughout the roller coaster of the 1970s, COPLACO's actions often ran counter to prevailing winds. It tried to compensate by short-sighted reactions to past events and failures without regard to the stampede just over each horizon. A stampede that crushed the hopes of COPLACO and left its own imprint on the metroscape and its institutions.

COPLACO's main problems were four. First, its top-down structure and composition led to a "permanent antagonism" between it and the municipalities from the start. Next, its lack of institutional savvy in sailing the turbulent seas of the transition from dictatorship to democracy was directly tied to its fortunes. It was also constantly out of phase with the dynamics of society that should have served as its rudder (PAIs and the 1981 *Directrices* being notable exceptions). Lastly,

COPLACO floundered back and forth between its views of the spatial structure of the region, and its approach to relating with its constituents. It maintained no clear vision or intergovernmental posture, two necessities for a coordination agency. All of this led to, in the terms of its technical director in the late 1970s, a "spectacular disparity" between real regional development and its planning (de Terán 1982, 574). He goes on to say "The case of Madrid clearly shows that we are dealing with the end of an era in which one could not continue to ignore some invalidating contradictions" (1982, 576). These contradictions marked the limits of technocratic planning, a style that paralyzed COPLACO throughout its life. Its rigidity in the face of massive change was the nail in its coffin.

# Chapter 6
# Urban Planning and Images

This chapter is a bridge between the preceding empirical Chapters (4 and 5) and the theoretical exegesis in Chapters 7 and 8. It synthesizes insights from the selected episodes of the evolution of the metropolitan planning institution in Madrid. It also serves as an analytical platform on which to base the theory of institutional evolution.

This chapter is organized in three sections. The first has to do with the planning process as it has evolved. The stress is on the interplay between the technical and political facets of planning. The second section analyzes how the structure of the planning institution has evolved. City plan images have been one source of the structure. The persistence of some of the structural (administrative) features is remarkable, given the spectacular divergence among political regime types in the last century alone. The last section looks at the thematic content of the metro planning institution passed from generation to generation, from episode to episode. The themes have been drawn from the main texts of Spanish planning practice— the plans themselves. We spotlight the *city plan image* of the plan documents, and the encapsulation of thematic content of the metropolitan planning institution in the plans and their physical design images.

## Planning Processes

> There is a desire for political confrontation. Each party wants to show it won't give in to the other. It is simple, raw politics. (Fernando de Terán, interview 1994).

In the nation's capital, politics casts a long shadow on daily affairs. How can planning hope to emerge from the shadow of raw politics? This becomes harder when party politics is the prime fact of political life in Madrid. It is harder still when party politics center on personalities.

Planning in Madrid is deeply implanted in politics, a sign of its importance. Politics is deeply imbedded in metropolitan planning, a sign of its maturity. This is so because both are highly interventionist. The public sector intervenes decisively in development. It does not just regulate land or construction, though it is also highly interventionist in those arenas. Public intervention is an act of political will. It needs continual political support.

To analyze the highly politicized planning process, we identify four features that typify it in metropolitan Madrid. They are particularism, informality, a technical-political alliance, and the explicit recognition that planning is political. Their combination identifies a style of planning unique to Madrid. *Concertación* (collaborative consensus building) is another key element of the Madrid planning style. See Chapter 4 for a discussion of its influence on and role in Madrilenean planning.

## Particularism

Particularism stems from a Spanish character trait. It refers to strong self-identification, tight group identity, clear boundaries among groups, us-them relations, and a cellular conception of society, among other things. Its planning and political ramifications in Madrid have included clientelism, hierarchy, imposed collective subjectivity, a low degree of inter-subjectivity, a control over or power over relation with the "other", a divide and conquer approach to power, strong home rule, and to a certain degree, a special type of corporatism.

The term corporatism has not usually been applied to comprehensive urban, metropolitan, or regional planning because there are too many policy fields and competing interests at stake. In certain sub-areas of planning such as housing or transportation, we can see in Madrid a special type of corporatism where unions, for example, are accorded a special role in the policy arena.

## Informality

Informal in this context does not mean casual. Rather it refers to *ad hoc* or extra-legal processes that are outside statutorily prescribed planning forums and arenas. Informal processes are not legally prescribed or enabled, nor are they legally prohibited. Informal planning in Madrid was typically interactive, a back and forth intercourse. Listening was as important as talking. Feedback was an important element. Informal processes were more likely than formal ones to be spontaneous, improvisational, and creative. They came more from the heart than the code. It was an important business style in Madrid that can be highly formalized. (Distinguishing formal and informal can be risky and misleading. To an extent it is arbitrary. All formal process have elements of informal ones and can be informalized, and vice versa. Many informal processes can occur within a formal one, such as the multi-year preparation of a plan.)

In Madrid informality was proper to meals, *tertulias*, conferences, social gatherings, cafés and bars, breaks in formal proceedings, and real time communications mediated by technology (internet, phone, electronic mail, fax, video, and the like). It occurred while networking. Informal processes built intersubjective understandings among their participants. The *Gran Sur* is an example of a project that grew from informal roots, involving continual discussion over the years in a vast array of settings. As the project took shape discussions and negotiations took place between the regional planners and central, regional, and municipal agencies, many outside of formal forums and arenas. Other examples are COPLACO's PAIs, *urbanismo concertado*, (even though its negotiations were formalized and occurred within a formal framework), and the zonal strategies of the *Consejería de Política Territorial* in the 1980s.

The role of informal processes based on particularism suggests why the centuries old heritage of hierarchy overtook the gains of bottom-up citizens' movement. As Robert Putnam points out in his 20 years of research in an another Mediterranean culture (Italy) in which informality also is an accepted mode of conducting affairs, "Informal norms and culture change more slowly than formal rules and tend to remold these formal rules, so that the external imposition of a common set of formal rules will lead to widely divergent outcomes" (1993, 180). This implies a need for greater flexibility in the formal rules that appear in the planning codes.

Informal processes, along with images (see Chapter 7) helped bind hierarchical structures that otherwise connected only vertically by formal structures and procedures. They were a thread of continuity through ongoing discussions. They were background music into which formal discussions receded. Dialogue returned to official arenas with greater coherence. The story continually unfolded informally. Informality allowed interlocutors to map ahead without being constrained by or committed to formal policy processes. In Madrid they have proven to be important and successful in many phases of planning—early on to create trust or reach understanding as well as later on to reach agreement, prepare plans, and implement them.

*Technical-Political Process*

> It is hard to draw the line between the politicians and the planners. (Francisco López, interview 1994).

In the 1980s the *Consejería de Política Territorial*'s planners—who freely referred to themselves as technicians—no longer operated in a political vacuum, as did their counterparts at the beginning of the twentieth century. Nor did they operate in an arena where technicians exert complete control with unconditional political backing, as in the middle of the twentieth century. Planning is now technical-political. In the 1980s planners and politicians worked together, sometimes in tandem, other times in parallel. Each political act implied a technical act and vice versa. Their interaction lowered the fences between them and diminished the distinctions between their roles.

Far from politics corrupting planning or hiding planning in its shadow, in the democratic era their union has had largely beneficial effects. It raised the level of debate and policy. It gave more legitimacy to plans and planning by leavening technical proposals with representative democracy. It reflected the high status of planning as a profession, and its high priority in public policy.

As the institution of regional planning evolved, how did planners and politicians gain mutual respect and trust? How did their two spheres merge for the betterment of each? The best outcomes resulted from processes built on prior experience. Failures occurred when one or more of the following three conditions applied. First, lack of political support. Second, political support was out of step with prevailing social and economic conditions. Finally, foreign technologies (ideas, practices, instruments) were imported and misapplied out of context.

The merger of technicians and politicians came at a price. One cost was the exclusion, by and large, of other members of the planning institution, as we have more broadly conceived it in Chapters 2 and 3. They included social and economic actors, civic groups and neighborhood associations, ecologists, unions, and so forth. Madrid city and regional planning in the late 1980s and early 1990s had almost no place for individual citizens acting on their own behalf. This was most apparent in the production of policy. Individuals and organized groups could only react to strategies and plans. They were not proactive partners in the formulation stages. Once the data was collected, the diagnosis made, and the draft plan or strategy formulated, then the public was able to respond. They did so at public hearings or attending exhibits of the plan in museum settings. Experts presented the plan or strategy, then individuals and organizational representatives asked questions or made suggestions. Another option was to write letters to the agency or political representatives.

Another cost (or benefit) of the technical-political process was the degree to which political parties condition the professionals. Each party was associated with an agenda that includes a planning component, although the two principal parties have become more alike recently. For example the socialists were known for affordable public housing, public transportation, and public intervention. The conservative Popular Party was known for market solutions to housing, favoring cars, and real estate developer intervention.

Limiting processes to technical-political input in part allowed for a rather straight trajectory—continuity—in the development of planning thought and policy.

Circumscribing planning to technical and political actors precluded the chance of obtaining the full benefit from the diversifying and democratizing influences of other actors. It also strained representative democracy. (For a rich development of this point see Pitkin 1967.) The exclusion of others from city and metropolitan planning in the late 1980s and early 1990s, particularly citizens and interest groups, was routinely explained in interviews conducted by the author as a non-issue. The elected officials are responsible for representing them. Or the planners know what is best. Regarding citizen and community organization participation, one high level planner averred "it is not very useful. It is not needed. The technicians know what is needed". He was not alone in expressing this sentiment. Indeed, this comment was rather common, particularly among those with much experience in the citizens' movement of the 1970s. They believed that deep immersion into the heart of the barrio 20 years ago sufficed.

The technical-political monolith at the same time accounted for the flip side of continuity—intransigence. The story of planning processes in Madrid unveiled the role of institutional momentum in maintaining this continuity/intransigence in spite of many societal and political upheavals along its path.

The predominantly technical-political nature of planning was a style of policy making particular to Madrid. It was not pluralist, grassroots, corporatist, or clientelist in the strict senses of these terms. The technical-political alliance also dealt with the inherent tension between the short term, election-to-election caricature of politicians and the long term preoccupations of planners. Planning focuses on the big picture, the longer view. Since the citizens' movement, there has been more balance between global, comprehensive, long term approaches and local, particular, short term actions. This shift responded to the influence of direct participation and the constant failures of comprehensive planning. In general, the politicians dominated when technicians were not politically powerful. An example is the 1900–1939 period. The technicians dominated when they had full and explicit political support that gave them free reign. This occurred in the Castro and Bidagor eras. In the dual technical and political void of the 1960s and much of the 1970s the populace rose to fill it. Only in the 1980s and 1990s did the technical-political alliance become more balanced.

**Planning is Political**

> If there isn't political agreement, there isn't a strategy. (Eduardo Mangada, interview 1994).

It is tempting to leave it at that. It is, in a way, that simple. Of course, politics is anything but simple. Two facts have governed Madrid's political life. Parties have dominated politics, and political personalities have dominated parties (Giner 1984, Linz 1981).

The party dominance of politics and the party's conditioning of technical planning staff had two outcomes in the intergovernmental sphere. When the political parties on each side of the negotiating table were the same, agreements were common. When they were opposing parties, agreements were rare. An exception to the former was the disagreements regarding the urban periphery (particularly the southern periphery) in the late 1970s and early 1980s between the city of Madrid and COPLACO (metropolitan planning agency). An exception to the latter rule occurred when big issues with lots of political symbolism and popular visibility are at stake. Examples included the three main events in Spain in 1992—the Expo in Seville, the Cultural Capital of Europe in Madrid, and the Olympics in Barcelona. In those cases partisan differences were set aside.

In Madrid an issue that transcended political partisanship was the historic city center. The three administrations (local, regional, and national) reached agreement on the financing of an ambitious revitalization plan in 1993. The center of the city had been deteriorating steadily for two decades. The national, regional, and local administrations agreed on the urgent need to reverse the decline. Each level of government made very public its commitment to finance one-third of the costs. While the president was the first to back it at the national level and has promised over $100 million over five years, the two other levels were hard pressed to fulfill more than rhetorical or symbolic obligations due to their fiscal constraints. As of April 1995 the final agreement obligating financial support had not been signed, pending resolution of local and regional financial problems and upcoming elections.

What made this agreement striking is that the conservative-controlled city hall and socialist-controlled regional and national governments agreed. This underscored the importance of the historic center city on the political landscape. Another battle was to embroil these protagonists in an intimately related issue at the same time (1992–1995) was the revision of the Madrid city General Plan. The regional government had the statutory obligation to approve the city plan. The city had a Popular Party (conservative) mayor and council majority.

The revision to the *Plan General de Madrid* of 1985 began in earnest in 1992 when the city hall set up the *Oficina Municipal del Plan* to prepare the revision. To appreciate why the city undertook revising the plan, let us look at local politics. Under no legal mandate to revise a plan adopted merely seven years ago, the *Partido Popular* was looking to reply to criticisms of the lack of an urban agenda and to strengthen their support among the real estate and business communities. In a city with a history of important contributions by the planning profession to its growth, a city in which planning issues dominated politics and civic life in the democratic era, the present city regime sought to make its mark on Madrid using the most powerful and symbolic tool in its planning kit—a new city plan. All the preparatory documents and the 1993 draft began with an elaborate rationale for the need of the new plan. The rationale is notable for its attack on the prior plan.

City government mounted a large scale technical and public relations campaigns to back the political thrust. The *Oficina Municipal del Plan*, whose only purpose was to revise the 1985 plan, has 100 full time employees and scores of paid consultants. Expenditures since its inception to the end of 1994 were three billion *pesetas*, about $23 million. Public relations, under the guise of public participation, got ample promotion and has generally been qualified by non-*Partido Popular* participants and observers as a marketing campaign (Neuman 1994). An entire issue of the journal *Alfoz* was dedicated to the revision of the general plan. Many of its articles affirm these comments. It should be noted that *Alfoz* was published by the socialist regional government.

Nevertheless, at the end of the six month public comment period 27,160 suggestions were received in the form of 4,097 distinct documents (Oficina Municipal del Plan 1994). Their tone, apart from claims of property owners regarding their parcels of land, suggested that the draft plan was an instrument to advance the incumbent conservative's agenda. It was typically referred to in the press and the corridors of planning as the "*Partido Popular* plan". This moniker not only reflected the lack of political consensus. It also revealed its use as a political symbol to further city hall's ambitions.

In this climate the controversy surrounding the 70,000 housing units proposed by the 1993 draft plan was resolved between the mayor and the president of the *Comunidad.* The conflict revolved around the city's proposal for housing, which was seen in opposing quarters as neither a planning proposal, nor a housing proposal, nor one which met any social need. It was simply a developer's proposal to build out the last remaining vacant lands in the city. The controversy had to be settled at the highest levels. The matter was resolved by the region dictating that it would accept half of the housing units. It was in a position to dictate because the law provided for regional approval of local plans. The resolution did not satisfy either party. It was a zero-sum, win-lose proposition in which the breakdown in negotiations led the regional government to mandate a resolution. According to one manager in the city planning office, "City Hall does not know how to negotiate with the *Comundidad de Madrid* and vice-versa".

Political platforms also played prominent roles, because parties were known for them in addition to being known for their leaders. But personalities stood out, reflecting an emphasis on individuals at the expense of institutions. Joaquin Leguina, then president of the *Comunidad de Madrid* referred to a "hyper-leadership" syndrome in his party (interview in *El País*, February 1, 1994). Pacts negotiated by individuals count more than documents required by law, such as plans and programs. That is why so many agreements became known by the name of their protagonist. The *Plan Felipe* was an inter-administration public works program negotiated in the late 1970s and named for Spain's president Felipe Gonzalez. The 1977 *Pactos de Moncloa* was a corporatist accord among unions, business, and government laying the basic societal groundwork for the new democracy, named for the presidential palace in which they were ratified. The *Plan Borrell* was another inter-administration public works program of the 1990s, named after the then-Minister of Public Works Josep Borrell. Corollaries to this are the sense of everything being negotiable and seemingly omnipresent custom of trading favors and even outright corruption. Political and financial corruption scandals occupied a major place in the media and became a consuming worry on the political panorama in Spain.

The personal, almost private nature of Spanish and Madrilenean politics, a politics by force of personality, is changing slowly and steadily. Laws are assuming more importance in the institution of government. Also, individual negotiations, clientelism, and corporatism (such as they exist) are shifting to collective negotiations among larger groups. The realization that policy issues are interconnected among sectors and levels of government has led to more integrative and inclusive approaches. Some are beginning to see a need for opening up political processes more to capture the diversity of Spanish culture. How far these ideas get bound up in the political ethos and power structures—how much they become institutionalized—is for now an open question.

## Legal-Administrative Structure of Madrid's Metropolitan Planning Institution

The framework supporting the structure of the institution of metropolitan planning in Madrid is a legal one. The national and regional planning laws are the two cornerstones. The current versions of both get their foundation from the 1956 national statute. The 1956 law contains some provisions adapted from other countries' statutes. However it is primarily based on the 1946 law for Madrid and the plan that the 1946 law adopted. This plan itself is an updated version of the 1929 Zuazo-Jansen proposal. We find that the institutional structure is rooted in images of urban form that extend back several generations.

The 1956 law is the "law of threes". It provides for three categories of land— urban, urban reserve, and rural. It provides for three scales of plans—general plans, partial plans and special plans. There are three means for implementation— expropriation, compensation, and cooperation. Plans were prepared at three levels of government—provincial, *comarcal*, and local. (A *comarca* is a group of municipalities smaller than a province.) The law provided for a National Plan, which has never been prepared. The rule of threes also applies to the 1984 regional law and its 1995 revision. The 1956 law drew support from the 1942 Italian law that had a three level plan hierarchy: general coordination plans, general regulatory plans and partial regulatory plans.

Rooting the institution in images has had consequences. Tracing the planning institution's genealogy back we see that the images are of urban form contained in plans. The urban form images underlying Madrid's metropolitan planning institution were born when the modern movement of architecture (and its effects on city planning) reigned almost unchallenged on the continent. This hints at the sources of rigidity in the current institutional structure. This is not the place to go into depth on the Bauhaus, the International Congress of Modern Architecture, its Athens Charter, and their repercussions on planning and actual urban form. What interests us is their impacts on the institutions of city and metropolitan planning in Madrid.

Plans have historically driven the structure of the Madrid planning institution. The organizations and procedures were devised afterwards, to implement and revise the plans. In Madrid, the plan is the heart of the institution. The plan carries much weight in public policy and is laden with political symbolism. The plan matters and is treated as such. This has been particularly true for the city, and for the region during the Mangada era.

The modern movement of the twentieth century is perhaps best known for simplicity and pureness of architectonic form. It is the structural manifestation of abstract rationality. It provides an ideal. An ideal institutional structure is also what the 1956 planning law aimed for. "The institution of an ideal organization is a basic condition for the attainment of the proposed ends of ... city planning", according to section 7 of the introduction of the *Ley de 12 de mayo de 1956 sobre Régimen de Suelo y Ordenación Urbana*.

The clean organizational lines of the "national planning system" (it was not yet an institution) provided clear cut distinctions among levels of governments, types of plans, and categories of land. Its straight line, one way processes left no doubt as to who was in charge and that each lower level in the hierarchy was to fulfill the aims of the superior. It normalized and boxed activities for maximum control. Its vertical orientation gave little notice to horizontal processes within an individual level of government (among departments, say) or within a geographic area (among municipalities, say). Thus this modernist inspired law mimicked the vertical thrust of modern architecture, whose skyscraper was its crowning achievement.

The author of the law, Pedro Bidagor, was an exemplary modernist architect. He was schooled and trained in the 1920s and 1930s, the zenith of the modern movement. He also was steeped in fascist architecture and planning. He maintained ties with Berlin and Rome and published favorable assessments of their city plans. He breathed in the spirit of the age and exhaled it fully into Spain's first national planning law. This law provided for planning at all levels, not only the state. It paid close attention to municipal planning, land use, and the development and construction of real property.

The successors to the 1956 law have encumbered this ideal with added bureaucratic detail, legal requirements, and minuscule specifications; clouding its prior clarity. Tweaked and expanded, but not changed in its essence.

Hierarchy remains the main characteristic of the planning institution's structure. A hierarchy is vertical, top-down, one-way, directive, and rigid. A hierarchy is not horizontal, bottom-up, two-way, with feedback, and flexible. The national law permitted some openings in its vertical structures for relations among members at the same level. Yet it sent a contradictory message. For example, prior to uniting the Ministries of Public Works and Housing in 1977 there were four entities attending to national planning issues in central government, each of a different rank. The four, the Council of Ministers, the Council of City Planning, the National City Planning Commission, and the General Directorship for City Planning, Architecture and Housing, were designed for horizontal coordination. Yet the law specified that the arrangement among them be hierarchical. The coordination problems this vertical-horizontal mixup engendered were evident in the incapacity of COPLACO. Though COPLACO was an agency of central government designed expressly for policy integration *vis-à-vis* Madrid, it did not achieve it.[1]

---

1    Article 208 of the 1976 revised text of the 1975 law, unchanged from the 1956 version, reads: "One. The city planning Agencies of the Ministry of Housing exercise their respective functions in a hierarchical order. Two. The city planning Agencies can delegate to the immediately inferior level, for a determined and renewable time period, the exercise of the functions it considers convenient for the greater effectiveness of services. Three. Any superior Agency can also inquire into the affairs that belong to its hierarchical inferiors and revise their actions".

The structure of the national planning system affords little autonomy to lower levels on the hierarchy. The detailed and directive structure leaves small margins for creativity and discretion. Each higher level can prepare, modify, approve, or suspend the plans of a lower level, or direct the lower level. An upper level can delegate, though this is rare. It is far more usual for the hierarchy to direct downward. Even delegation is a form of one-way direction. (I direct you to do it your way, as long as you meet my criteria.) The law provides no opportunity for feedback from lower levels, nor from non-governmental agents.

The composition (membership) of the planning institution has been purely governmental. Within government, the executive branch has exercised the lion's share of the work. The courts have had limited influence, although they have been pivotal when they have intervened. Elected bodies have wielded differing degrees of control, depending on the regime in power and the level of government. Nationally, the franquist legislature was obedient to the regime, essentially a rubber stamp for executive branch programs. The democratic legislature has spent its time on planning issues revising the national planning law and funding infrastructure and renewal programs. It also directed the executive branch in developing programs that comply with European Union criteria and receive European Union structural funds. Regionally the legislature of the *Comunidad de Madrid* has also maintained a supervisory posture, passing/revising laws and setting budgets, in addition to being involved in big disputes.

In short, technicians prepared the work, bureaucrats and/or politicians approved it. The 1992 and 1975 revisions to the national planning law, and the 1956 original, did not provide for interest group or citizen involvement. An exception was to allow them to provide written comments on proposed plans and to attend public hearings, once the plan has been released for public comment. Historical accounts make no mention of non-governmental participation (see Table 6.1).

Prior to the current democratic period the main players in the planning game were the nation and the municipalities. The go-between provinces acted as partial referees for the towns, controlled as they were from above. There was little planning at any intermediate geographic scale. The smallest intermediate polity, *comarcas*, had no planning powers. Metropolitan areas, except for Madrid and later Barcelona, were not statutorily enabled to conduct spatial planning. Provinces had some authority by law but little political punch and less fiscal bite. Regions did not yet exist. In any case provincial governments and metropolitan agencies were appointed by the center. *Mancomunidades* (voluntary consortia of adjoining municipalities) were authorized by law and could have been formed to collectively exercise planning powers. None were.

In 1975 the national planning law was amended for the first time. The revision attempted to loosen up the middle level structure to facilitate metro and regional planning. The changes provided for a *Plan Director Territorial de Coordinación*. This plan was intended to establish "guidelines for territorial planning". The guidelines did not have the same legal force as the binding land

**Table 6.1 Structure of the Spanish National Planning System**

| Law: | 1956 | 1975 | 1992 |
|---|---|---|---|
| **Organizational structure** | | | |
| | **National** | **National** | **National** |
| | Comisión Nacional de Urbanismo | Ministry of Housing | Ministry of Housing |
| | Dirección General de Arquitectura y Urbanismo | Dirección General de Urbanismo | |
| | **Provincial** | **Provincial** | **Provincial** |
| | Consejo Provincial de Urbanismo, Arquitectura y Vivienda* | Abolished | Region adopt their own structure |
| | Comisión Provincial de Arquitectura y Urbanismo | Comisión Provincial de Arquitectura y Urbanismo** | |
| | **Municipal** | **Municipal** | **Municipal** |
| | Unspecified | Gerencia de Urbanismo | Gerencia de Urbanismo |
| **Instrumental structure** | | | |
| | Plan Nacional de Urbanismo | Plan Nacional de Urbanismo | Plan Nacional de Urbanismo |
| | Plan Provincial | Replaced by PDTC*** | PDTC for Region |
| | Plan Comarcal | | |
| | Plan General Municipal | Plan General Municipal | Plan General Municipal |
| | Normas Subsidiarias y Complementarias | Normas Subsidiarias y Complementarias | Normas Subsidiarias y Complementarias |
| | Plan Parcial | Plan Parcial | Plan Parcial |
| | Plan Especial | Plan Especial | Plan Especial |
| | Proyectos de Urbanización | Proyectos de Urbanización | Proyectos de Urbanización |

**Table 6.1 (continued)**

| Law: | 1956 | 1975 | 1992 |
|---|---|---|---|
| | | Programas de Actuación Urbanística | Programas de Actuación Urbanística |
| | | Estudios de Detalle | Estudios de Detalle |
| | | | Catálogos |
| **Plan approval hierarchy** | | | |
| | Higher level can delegate to lower level | Higher level can delegate to lower | Dependent on law of regional government |
| | Higher level can subrogate any power from or direct lower level | Same as 1956 | Same as 1956 |
| | Consejo de Ministros approves Plan Nacional | Consejo de Ministros approves Plan Nacional | Consejo de Ministros determines who approves Plan Nacional |
| | Comisión National de Urbanismo approves Provincial Capitals' plans, general plans of towns > 50,000 population | Same as 1956 | Local government approves remainder |
| | Comisión Provincial de Urbanismo approves remainder of plans | Same as 1956 | |
| **Plan implementation** | | | |
| | Compensation | Same | Same |
| | Cooperation | Same | Same |
| | Expropriation | Same | Same |
| | Poligonos | Same | Same |

**Table 6.1 (continued)**

| Law: | 1956 | 1975 | 1992 |
|---|---|---|---|
| | Programas de Actuatión (5 year capital program) | Programas de Actuación Urbanística (4 year development plan) | Programas de Actuación Urbanística (4 year development plan) |
| Land use category | Urban | Urban | Urban |
| Land use category | Urban Reserve | Urbanization | Urbanization |
| Land use category | Rural | Non-Urbanization | Non-Urbanization |

*Notes*: * Presided by Minister of Housing's Provincial Delegate; ** Presided by Civil Governor (Central Government Appointee); *** PDTC is the Plan Director Territorial de Coordinación. It can be prepared at the comarcal, provincial, and supra-provincial scales.

use classifications found in the general plans did. The entity to prepare the *Plan Director* was not specified. It could be prepared at the *comarcal*, provincial, and supra-provincial scales. It was to be binding on national government ministries' territorial policies. Municipalities had one year to revise their plans to conform to it. No *Planes Directores* were ever prepared. Everyone awaited the shakeout of the transition to democracy and the upcoming regions and their planning laws in order to take stock of this change.

Up to 1995 the national planning structure has been based largely on *Madrilenian* and imported structures from the middle of the last century. Since the middle of the century Madrid's metropolitan planning institution has slowly loosened this rigidity. In the late 1970s the bottom-up citizens' movement did temporarily invert the processes and ideological content of the planning institution. It did not change its legal-administrative structure, however.

A consequence of not taking advantage of the open door to change the structure that the citizens' movement afforded has been the gradual reversion of the institution to its more rigid past. As the leaders of the citizens' movement, who went on to become planning and political leaders, lost their influence through the passage of time, their ideology and the substantive content of the policies adopted during their tenure has been lost as well. Part of this loss can be attributed to the move to the right that Spanish politics has been undergoing. The rigid structure has also imposed its logic on planning and governing processes. The grassroots approach of the citizens' movement has been subsumed by the institution's techno-political process, which is itself constrained by the bureaucracy. The citizens' movement itself has become institutionalized. The neighborhood associations and their regional federation are now simply another interest for the process to cope with (see Table 6.2).

History does not reveal a rush to take advantage of the few structural chances for cross-wise interaction in Madrilenian planning. This was aggravated by a free floating attitude of hierarchy and loyalty that permeated planning affairs

**Table 6.2    Structure of the Madrid Metropolitan Planning Institution**

| | 1946 | 1963 |
|---|---|---|
| Name | Comisaría General de Ordinación Urbana de Madrid y sus Alrededores | Comisión de Planeamiento y Coordinación del Area Metropolitano de Madrid (COPLACO) |
| Plan name | Plan General de Ordenación Urbana de Madrid y sus Alrededores | Plan General de Ordenación Urbana del Area Metropolitano de Madrid |
| Membership in governing organization | 17 total<br>9 central government | 30 total<br>19 central government<br>3 regional utilities*<br>1 civil governor*<br>1 provincial president*<br>4 Madrid city<br>2 other city mayors |
| Planning tools | Partial Plans<br><br>Zoning<br><br>Annexation<br><br>Mancomunidades<br><br>Urban Limit Lines<br><br>Infrastructure and Development Projects<br><br>Mandatory Compliance of Local Planning | Esquema Director 1972<br><br>Urbanismo Concertado<br><br>Plan Director Territorial<br><br>Directrices Provinciales<br><br>Programas de Actuación Inmediata (PAI)<br><br>Directrices Metropolitanas 1981<br><br>Special Plans 1975–1976 |
| **Inter-administrative structure** | | |
| | Congress approves Plan<br><br>Council of Ministers approves changes to plan, partial plan<br><br>Ministry of Governance** approves laws, regulations, municipal budgets<br><br>National City Planning Commission approves local partial plans and projects<br><br>Municipalities prepare, higher level approves | Ministers approve Plan<br><br>Ministry of Housing*** approves changes to plan<br><br>COPLACO approves partial plans, urbanization projects, urban action programs<br><br>Municipalities prepare planning instruments for higher level approval |

|  | 1983 | 1995 |
|---|---|---|
| Name | Comisión de Urbanismo y Medio Ambiente**** | Comisión de Urbanismo |
| Plan name | Directrices de Ordenacion Territorial (never adopted) | Plan Regional de Estrategia Territorial |
| Membership in governing organization | 26 total<br><br>12 regional government<br>1 mayor of Madrid<br>9 other municipal<br>4 interest group reps | Comisión de Urbanismo same as 1983<br><br>Consejo de Política Territorial (Advisory)<br><br>Comisión de Concertación de la Acción Territorial |
| Planning tools | Coordinated Capital Facilities Programs | Coordinated Capital Facilities Action Programs |
|  | Physical Environment Management Plans | Natural and Rural Environ. Management Plans |
|  | Zonal Strategies | Zones of Regional Interest |
|  | Subregional Urban Action Programs | Projects of Regional Significance |
|  | Public Development Corporations (ARPEGIO) | Public Development Corporations |
|  | *Convenios, Consorcios* |  |
| **Interadministrative structure** | | |
|  | Regional Assembly approves budget, laws | Same as 1983 |
|  | Council of Government approves regional planning instruments, local plans | Same as 1983 |
|  | City Planning Commission provisionally approves regional planning instruments, local plans for cities < 50,000 | Same as 1983 |
|  | *Consejería de Política Territorial* provisionally approves local plans for cities > 50,000***** | Same as 1983 |

*Note*: * Appointed by and dependent upon central government; ** After 1957, Ministry of Housing; *** After 1977, Ministry of Public Works and Urbanism. **** After 1988 Comisión de Urbanismo; ***** Before 1987 Consejería de Ordenación Territorial, Medio Ambiente y Vivienda.

regardless of what the law said or which political regime was in power. (Again, the exception is the citizens' movement.) The escape valves to the top-heavy hierarchy were informal processes in which extensive networking dissolves boundaries both up and down. As nature abhors a vacuum, Madrid's planning institutions instinctively abhorred rigidity if they sought to stay alive. The health of metro planning in Madrid was a testament to the flexible relief that improvised informal interactions gave and still give. Madrid's planners would have appreciated Clifford Geertz's observation that "Argument grows oblique, and language with it, because the more orderly and straightforward a particular course looks the more it seems ill-advised" (Geertz 1983, 6).

Personal friendships and constant social contact during and after work were important. The roles of key individuals also mattered. Leaders took the initiative to break down formalities. The line separating this collegial networking from favoritism, clientelism, corruption, and worse has tripped up many Spanish politicians and bureaucrats. Daily media accounts have catapulted the issue to a national obsession by the middle of the 1990s, continuing on to this day.

As the idealized structures became increasingly irrelevant, even while their hierarchical geometries were transmitted from generation to generation, the networks that described the patterns of informal relations together with the images that kept those networks together, prevented the legal structure from toppling altogether.

### Images and Plans: Encapsuling the Thematic Content of the Planning Institution

> From the president to the porter of the last apartment house believe in the need to restore the city center. (José María de la Riva, interview 1994).[2]

Certain things are understood, are recognized as given in Madrilenian planning. These things led planners to proceed with surety, without the need for extensive debate and negotiation. They transcend quarrels among political parties. A persistent example in Madrid that has spanned centuries is the historic city center. What is it that puts the center in a special category in the collective psyche and fixes it at or near the top of the political agenda generation after generation? That is, how did the historic core of the city get to be the core of politics and planning? How has it taken its place among other issues to collectively make up the substantive content (agenda) that government pays attention to?

One could read *El Futuro Madrid* and be done with it. Since then there has been little that any plan for Madrid has added that Angel Fernández de los Ríos's astonishing, and astonishingly contemporary, 1868 book has not said better. It took over a century, until the 1985 Madrid General Plan, for a document to afford such a detailed account of the city and offer a coherent set of proposals to

---

2    De la Riva was a Madrid City Councillor and Secretary General of the Socialist Party in city hall.

improve the city center. But his book went beyond the center, and went beyond the city itself. Its clear and rich view of the unity of the city and its region, combined with its project-by-project plan to improve the city has not been equalled in Spain. Two contenders have fallen short. Barcelona's remarkable transformation of the 1980s targeted the city, especially the historic center, in favor of the entire metropolis. Madrid's 1985 General Plan, highly touted and imitated, has at the same time received ample criticism. The critics contend it narrowly conceived the city in urban design terms, was a project plan, lacked a comprehensive view, emphasized the recovery of the existing city at the expense of looking outward or to the future, did not anticipate the rapid growth that practically made it obsolete before it was adopted, and did not incorporate economic realities. Yet each book and each plan is the product of its time and each generation writes its own history. And so it has been with Madrilenian planning. It is a notably consistent history in terms of thematic content.

The most persistent themes for Madrid have highlighted its centrality, its *capitalidad*, and its economic growth. In the city plans these themes have been recorded in plan diagrams and maps, in city and regional designs, in specific urban design projects, and in textual rhetoric. The most persistent strategies to attain the visions are renovating the city center in all its incarnations (*casco antiguo, centro historico* and *almendra* (almond—within the first beltway)), accessing the center using a radial pattern of roads and rail, decongesting the center, growing to the north, satellite towns, and green belts; all packaged in a regional design of settlements connected by transport networks and buffered by natural environs.

Recent thematic innovations include European integration and economic competitiveness (high speed trains, airport expansion, metropolitan mobility, advanced technology, global city), ring roads, integrated transport systems, socio-spatial equity, and coordinating housing and community facilities construction.

The fountain of these innovations were the "catch up" impulses from the change to democracy: joining the European Union and catching up to the levels of its neighbors, addressing the claims of the grassroots social movement, and catching up on ground lost during the franquist era. This mind shift can be shown another way. Before the current democratic reforms, the society looked inward. Madrid was the center of Spain, of (a former) empire. Accesses led *into* the city. Since the transition, the view has been outward, making external two-way links. Madrid aspires to global cityhood, as the 1993 *Plan Estrategico de Madrid* of Promadrid, the *Nuevo Plan General* of *la Casa de la Villa* (Madrid city hall), the 1991 *Madrid Región Metropolitana*, and the draft 1994 *Plan Regional de Estrategia Territorial* (never adopted, due to the change in regional government from socialist to conservative in 1995) of the *Comunidad de Madrid* leave no doubt.

These persistent visions and recent innovations have been expressed in Madrid planning culture in documents called plans. Recently, mainly in the regional government, they have been expressed as strategies, or strategic plans. The city government of Madrid, for example, completed a strategic planning process in 1993. It published a strategic plan titled the *Plan Estratégico de Madrid.* Prepared by an international management consulting firm, it was not legally binding and has had relatively little impact on city growth, by the accounts of most observers.

Metropolitan and regional plans and strategies in Madrid have at their core a physical design of what the form of the metropolis should be in the future. They are normative statements and explicitly so. Spatial designs and territorial models have been the *sine qua non* of Madrilenian planners. No surprise, as they have been architects by training, almost to a one. Typically plans presented a single, static view of the future. Proposals for smaller areas and sectoral (functional) policies accompanied the vision. The views ranged from provincial and regional to national and European in scope, some with visions for several scales. They reacted to growth and its impacts, assuming a defensive posture. Some planners combined defensive reactions and positive images of the future, such as Fernández de los Ríos, Zuazo, Bidagor, and Mangada.

The plans with the greatest impact on the city and its environs, and with the greatest impact on Spanish urbanism, are those that presented the clearest and most persuasive image of the future and had the strongest political backing. All the plans that met these two criteria drank from Fernández de los Ríos's fountain: "The base of the reform of the city is in some general and other local measures" (Fernández de los Ríos 1989, 73).

All plans, regardless of their content, expressed societal forces. The prevailing winds of their times blew some forces into the eye of the storm, other forces into its fury, and still others out of the storm's path. A hallmark of the most famous plans is their integrated vision and clarity of graphic presentation. Ones that stood out are the Plan Castro (1860), Zuazo and Jansen's proposal (1929), the Bidagor Plan (1941), *Plan General* (1985), and the *Gran Sur* (1989). Their clarity masked internal contradictions just as the confusing and incoherent plans underscored them. In the end, all fit this description:

> Rather than urban policy, such as an all-coherent and articulated one, it can be more correct to speak of various and diverse policies, supposedly complementary, but also contradictory, the consequence of a State whose apparatus is contradictory at the core and whose different levels do not constitute a complete monolith nor are coordinated in the measure which could be supposed as a result of an authoritarian State of the dominant class. Within those policies only some are explicit, directed at urban objectives, and formulated to that end, in laws or agreements. Others, however, can be classified as "implicit", in principle not directed at those objectives or never formalized as such, even though they do bring about action from the Administration more important that than those that are derived from an "explicit" policy, like a plan (Leira, Gago and Solana 1976, 136).

Remove their bias against Franco's dictatorship endemic to post-franquist planners and one has a lens *à propos* to view any modern era plan for Madrid.

Table 6.3 shows the continuity of 10 selected planning themes over the last 135 years, spanning 12 plans and visions.

**Table 6.3    Plan content continuity 1860–1994**

| Plan | *Capitalidad* | Urban renewal | Zoning | Radial accesses | Expansion |
|------|------------|---------------|--------|-----------------|-----------|
| 1860 Castro Ensanche | x | | | x | x |
| 1868 Futuro Madrid | x | x | | x | |
| 1909 Nuñez Granés | x | | | x | |
| 1929 Zuazo-Jansen | x | x | x | x | x |
| 1931 Lorite Kramer | | | x | x | x |
| 1939 Paz Maroto | | x | | x | |
| 1939 Regional CRRSM | | x | x | x | |
| 1941 Bidagor | x | x | x | x | x |
| 1963 Metropolitan | x | x | x | x | |
| 1985 Madrid City | x | x | x | | |
| 1993 Madrid City | x | x | x | x | PAUs |
| 1994 Comunidad de Madrid | x | x | | | Zonas de Interés Regional |

| | Develop north | Decongestion | Satellite new towns | Ring road | Green belt |
|------|---------------|--------------|---------------------|-----------|------------|
| 1860 Castro Ensanche | x | | | x | |
| 1868 Futuro Madrid | | x | x | x | x |
| 1909 Nuñez Granés | x | x | x | | partial |
| 1929 Zuazo-Jansen | x | x | x | x | x |
| 1931 Lorite Kramer | x | x | | x | greenways |
| 1939 Paz Maroto | x | x | x | x | |
| 1939 Regional CRRSM | | x | x | x | |
| 1941 Bidagor | x | x | x | x | x |
| 1963 Metropolitan | x | x | | x | partial |
| 1985 Madrid City | | | | x | |
| 1993 Madrid City | x | | | x | |
| 1994 Comunidad de Madrid | x | Areas of new centrality, ZIRs, PACs | x | x | |

## The Image Rules Thematic Content

> There are images in the nooks of books that are more alive than many men and
> women ... There are metaphors that are more real than the people that walk the
> street. (Pessoa 1984, 50)

A special place has to be set aside for the image. The image was at the heart of
plan making and institution building in Madrid. A good image was able to present
a range of ideas in ways that words were not. Planning images embodied more
than just a technical-political proposal for the future of Madrid or a part of it. They
captured the social context around the proposal and infused it into the image, thus
making it legible by its "constituency". According to Jung, "The term 'image' is
intended to express not only the form of the activity taking place, but the typical
situation in which the activity is released" (1986, 106). An image is a package that
includes not just what we see in our mind's eye. Activities and settings are also
attached to it. Images are not isolated forms.

Several examples in Madrid highlight the importance of images and their
multiple purposes. First was the use of the image of a grid street pattern to create
the first city plan for Madrid (Castro's plan of 1860). This plan along with a
similar one to expand Barcelona (Cerdà's plan of 1859) established the institution
of modern city planning in Spain. These plans, Cerdà's pioneering 1867 book
*General Theory of Urbanization*, and Fernández de los Ríos's *El Futuro Madrid*
of 1868 set the standard for practice and marked out the field of debate.

## The Plan Image and the Metropolitan Region

The plan image also was used by planners to represent changing perceptions of
Madrid and its metro region. This image was by definition at the heart of the
content of the institution of metropolitan planning there. The changes to this image
over time further represent the changes to the planning institution.

Perhaps the first to use an image of Madrid as an urban region was Angel
Fernández de los Ríos. While criticizing the state of the city and praising its
surrounds, he put forth a positive image of a region not subordinate to the center.
One in which the outskirts and the city formed an interdependent whole. He called
the new part of the region outside the city limits *las cercanías* (1989 (1868),
225–268). *Cercanía* is literally and poorly translated as neighborhoods or vicinity.
Fernández de los Ríos expanded the meaning of this word in a magisterial chapter
to mean an interconnected set of settlements that enable the old city to grow into a
new regional one without destroying the old center or the environs in the process.
Planning would have to wait until Patrick Geddes and Ian McHarg to see another
thinker with such a complete regional vision.

Fernández de los Ríos's vision was not attained in his lifetime. Subsequent
generations have tried to retrofit parts of his vision, perhaps unknowingly, on a

sprawling metropolis that was too far gone to be reshaped according to his *dicta.* Nonetheless each generation of planners postulated its versions of the expanding city-region. Most continued the line of thinking of their predecessors, principally "quality" growth to the north, industry to the south and east, keeping the region center-based with transportation radiating to the periphery. An important exception to this pattern was the international airport to the east.

This line of thinking (thematic content of the planning institution) can be seen in the regional plans of the twentieth century summarized in Chapter 5. The first two of them, the 1931 Madrid city plan (never adopted) and the 1939 Madrid Regional Plan (never implemented) were the first official government representations of Madrid as a region.

In 1941 the *Junta de la Reconstrucción* published its metropolitan plan (adopted 1946 and implemented). It keyed on the immediate metro area, while its two predecessors opted for a wider regional portrait. The 1963 metropolitan plan presented three regional perspectives of Madrid, muddling the image of the region in the process. The images in this sequence of plans from 1931 to 1963 built up an institutional archive for metropolitan planning, a depository for its thematic content.

A change to this thematic trajectory was proffered by the *Comunidad de Madrid* in the 1980s. Creating a plan culture and a regional culture were central to its political and planning programs. It also changed the image of the region to an "equitable and integrated region". Redistributing wealth to the south and seeing the larger metropolitan region as a whole were its hallmarks. A major part of the effort was putting Madrid in a bigger geographic context. It strived to be a great European capital. The new image identified Madrid as an important "Euro-region". This approach put it in a class with Barcelona, Milan, Rome, Bonn, and Amsterdam; below the world cities of London and Paris. Competing for regional status, international capital, and tourists was the aspiration. The image, via planning that was used as a marketing tool, sold it.

Over this century the role of the planners was to create the image. The planners used design-based plans and strategies to build successive incarnations of the metropolitan planning institution—the Bidagor plan and its *Comisaría*, the 1961 plan and COPLACO, *Madrid Región Metropolitana* and the *Consejería.* The planners used the image to catalyze planning processes, and to attain agreement as well. As the processes recurred over decades and generations the planners built up the intellectual heritage of their institution, its doctrine.

# Chapter 7
# Continuity and Change: The Dialectic of Institutional Evolution

The questions that guided this research were few. What is an institution? How does it evolve over time? What effect does an institution have on public policy? And how has government used planning to design and build new institutions and reform existing ones? Above all else, the answers in the case of metropolitan planning in Madrid tell us that the institution subsumed, or perhaps better said, integrated many factors shaping policy formerly held to be separate and extra-institutional. Before the rise of the new institutionalism, factors that shaped policy such as interests, power, agents, and political parties were less grounded in organizations and institutions. They were attributed more to individual actors and disembodied concepts. Prior formulations relegated the institution to intervening status variable, at best. The more integrated view of planning, policy making, and politics—in a word, governing—that is advanced in this research has provided a powerful optic to see relations that were hidden by other analytic means. It has taken us further back in time to see shaping tendencies, has enabled us to understand current events better, and has let us predict the future with greater confidence. The institution matters.

As these research findings demonstrate, the institution of metropolitan planning in Madrid has grown as the metropolis itself has. Until 1939 the institution was strictly a technical one. It involved a few technician-designers with varying degrees of support from city hall. Its city was treated architectonically. How was it built? What was its physical form to be in the future? The answer was in the grand plan from the hand of the master city builder. All the plans up till then literally were signed by their creators with a florid swirl of the pen. Between 1860 and 1900 these technicians were engineers and had royal and political backing. From 1900 to 1939 the engineers gave way to architects. They lost their political patronage, weakening the institution to the point of almost total marginality.

After the civil war ended in 1939 the institution expanded its geographic reach to encompass adjacent suburbs. It stretched its organizational tentacles to outlying city halls, the provincial government, and state ministries. Architects still controlled the drawing boards, churning out images of a Great Madrid. Central government now directed the act, with the locus of power shifting from the city to the state. The technical-political marriage was consummated, leading to aggressive direct public intervention on the cityscape.

In the 1960s the institution was split into two. The city became responsible for its own planning, and COPLACO was responsible for the metropolitan area. After this split the institution was never able to find a balance of power among the city of Madrid, the other municipalities, the state, and COPLACO itself. Metropolitan planning nearly died, as city planning nearly did in the 1920s. In the 1970s the citizens' movement temporarily broke the grasp that the government was trying to maintain. In reality the masses plugged a massive hole. Government was on the brink of collapse. The severe economic crisis due to the 1973 oil shock brought the private sector to the verge as well. Citizens swept in to fill the void left by the central government's gradual withdrawal of support from COPLACO, leaving it nearly powerless by the late 1970s. An active civil society expanded the institution into the fullest expression in its history. The neighborhood associations incorporated a wide array of interests and participants, inverting the top-down process along the way. Manuel Castells referred to the "apparent mystery [that a] civil society so shunned by the state took its revenge by developing such a prolific social tissue that the Political institutions became increasingly obsolete" (1983, 215).

This grassroots expansion of the metropolitan planning institution was short lived as a new actor, regional government, appeared on the scene. It replaced citizen action with a techno-political approach to policy making. Once again the institution was closed off from public involvement, in the main. The new regional government expanded its size to 179 municipalities. It loosened the techno-political process somewhat by inventing a consensus-based negotiations process (*concertación*) among levels of government, and with developers. The regional government was in a phase of consolidation in the early 1990s, attempting to institutionalize the experiments of the 1980s by adopting a new law for regional planning. This law was to codify the recent shift from plan-based to process-based planning. The law's language also aims to move away from purely governmental to more collective processes.

Despite these and other shifts the institution has exhibited remarkable continuity. It has remained tied to a technical-political process. Its laws hold fast to a rigid structure of hierarchical relations among members of the institution. Legal procedures remain detailed and riddled with prescriptive mandates from "superior" to "inferior" levels of government with little room for feedback. It continues to seek institutional flexibility using informal means. Its policies mainly are expressed in and focus on physical form. The plans carry forward similar goals from generation to generation. Individual citizens have little say about the future of their metropolitan region, except in an institutionally controlled environment in which they may react to highly developed proposals.

Where does this continuity come from? Why haven't dramatic political events like the grassroots movement or the dictatorship had greater effects? Why haven't a variety of economic crises, each with its own causes and character, put more than a dent in the institutional body? How is a putatively rigid institution able to absorb these shocks and stay intact?

Part of the answer is the continuous debate the guild of planners and politicians maintain regarding the nature of their metropolis, the cities that make it up, and the planning and governing institutions. Some of their debate has centered around fundamental issues. What is metropolitan or regional planning? Is it city planning scaled up? The aggregate of local planning? The aggregate of sectoral (functional) planning? The aggregate of planning for metropolitan pieces? Some or all of these? Is it a plan, strategy, policy, or set of guidelines? Is it mandated from above, built from below, crafted interactively back and forth? These debates were, and are, not just academic. They are reflected in official documents and press accounts. It is a living and lively debate carried on in the spirit of praxis.

Another source of institutional continuity is the strength of the images created by planners and found in city plans. These images were sometimes expressed in physical designs, sometimes in words. They played multiple roles in the institution. They provided a seed that sprouted into debate. Images guided debate and debate molded images in a dialectic. Well-constructed images based on cultural archetypes shaped policy, as in the *Gran Sur* and *Gran Madrid.* They also were central to overall political strategy such as *Madrid Región Metropolitana.* They helped to build the *Consejería de Política Territorial* and the *Comunidad de Madrid* and the *Comisaría General de Ordenación Urbana* before it. A well-defined image exposed with clarity and coherence, just as it masked with simplicity and unity. In policy making just as in institution building images had two faces. They were misused as well as used.

In addition to the intermediate reflections on the planning process, the image's influence on the institution, and the legal-administrative structure in the previous chapter, the principal findings are grouped under five themes in the rest of this chapter. One finding is the durability of some aspects of Madrid's planning institution. It has preserved certain structural, processual, and substantive features in the face of massive changes in society. The second finding is the role the institution played in maintaining this continuity over time. Third, we find that the institution in and of itself shaped policy. That is, we can trace the sources of policy—its thematic content, its processes of making, and its status in public life—to the institution, in large part. Other sources of policy are cultural. Still others can be traced to individuals and their ideas. The dual nature of structure and agency as developed in social theory reveals that institutional factors are enacted in agency and action, and that individual and cultural factors are channeled through the institution (Bourdieu 1977, Giddens 1984).[1] Fourth, institutions seek flexibility in order to survive. Finally, the role images play in structuring (in the Giddensian sense) the institution. Interpreting in this way makes the most sense in winding one's way through the institutional labyrinth. It helps us see the dialectic between stability and change. It also points to key parameters for institutional design.

---

1   Sewell (1992) and Emirbayer and Goodwin (1994) make important criticism to Bourdieu's and Giddens's theories, particularly as they apply to the relation of agency and the institution.

**Institutional Continuity**

To start, it would mislead to say that nothing has changed. The two leading events marking Madrid in this century led to the most lasting institutional innovations. Both were crises. The civil war opened the door for Franco and all that followed. The *Junta de Reconstrucción*, its 1941 plan, and its 1946 successor organization the *Comisaría General de Ordenación Urbana* spawned the 1956 national planning and land use law that cast a long shadow on following generations. The second event was the transition to democracy and the grassroots movement that surged from the crisis in the twilight of the franquist era. It toppled COPLACO and opened the door to regional government. The citizens' movement and the socialist party put equity on the public policy map alongside economic growth. The insertion of Spain into the European and world communities came on the heels of democratic reform. The view outward brought new ideas, needs, demands, and resources into the institution, changing it in the process.

Yet even these ruptures were built on the back of the institution as it existed before. Pedro Bidagor appropriated most of the ideas for the 1941 plan from Zuazo and Jansen's proposal and dressed it in falangist garb. The grassroots movement used a new process and new actors to press many of the same claims that COPLACO and the *Comisaría* had attempted yet failed to satisfy. The European Union's drive toward European scale territorial equity pushed the institution further and faster along its own economic development, infrastructure, and socio-spatial equity paths.

The real strength of the institution can be seen as it absorbed its opposite, the *movimiento ciudadano*, the citizens' movement. The citizens' movement was its opposite in structure. Hundreds of small neighborhood associations were loosely networked across the metro area. Each association itself was organized at the street level. Together they formed a horizontal semi-lattice with strong nodes and loose links among the nodes. Vertical invertebration only came from the small umbrella organization of the movements neighborhood associations, the *Federación Regional de Asociaciones de Vecinos* (Regional Federation of Neighbors Associations). The movement was the opposite of the institution in process. The grassroots communicated via bottom-up information gathering and sharing. It was making claims, not mandating by law. It was working from the outside in, citizens making demands on the government. The movement was its opposite in the substance of its demands. The citizens clamored for street specific and neighborhood specific improvements to abate pressing deficiencies rather than long term and comprehensive metropolitan plans. The citizens demanded better living conditions, social justice, equity, direct participation in government, and democracy. In sum, a fascist bureaucracy met a radical, activist and organized citizenry.

While the citizens' movement did shape planning for a time in the 1970s, and even left its imprint on the 1985 Madrid City General Plan and the regional government's twin strategies in the 1980s, as of this writing the citizens' movement as morphed into neighborhood associations has become just one more interest among others in planning and political processes. The movement has lost much of its representational force and practically all of its mobilizing force in urban planning.

In short, bureaucracy won. The citizens' movement was absorbed and dissipated. Former movement leaders led the institution of regional planning built in the aftermath. They also occupied political posts. The bottom-up structure was dissipated as it ran up against a monolith in theory and a behemoth in fact. Its democratic processes were absorbed into the techno-political innards of regional planning. Its content was directly absorbed with little modification. Data from the PAIs, the *Asociaciones de Vecinos*, and their umbrella group the *Federación Regional* were central to the 1985 Madrid Plan and the various 1980s efforts of COPLACO and the *Consejería*. The ideology of the movement, social equity penetrating all planning and public policy, remains a cornerstone. Attention is now given to short and medium term local problems as well as long term and comprehensive ones. These have been important contributions. Yet nearly 20 years after the uprising of citizens little else has persevered. The institution has reverted to using exclusionary processes in bureaucracies that serve economic development interests, now enlightened by the principle of equity. Some of the movement's former leaders are now mostly union leaders, bureaucrats, planners, mayors, or council members caught up in the day to day, having wizened and lost the activism of the bygone age.

The superior mass and momentum of the institution was able to absorb, deflect, or dissipate much of the grassroots energy after 1980. The *Asociaciones de Vecinos* have become institutionalized themselves. They played the planning game according to rules they did not create, instead of creating the turf on which planning is played out. They have their own bureaucracy that is getting out of touch with its local members as its staff increases in size and develops its own policies, procedures, and structures. The neighborhood associations and their regional federation have become just another interest competing among many in the policy arena, instead of defining the arena themselves. The *Asociaciones* and their *Federación* painted themselves into this single interest corner by perpetuating the myth that only they could represent the citizens. In the mid-1990s the neighborhood associations and their regional federation had a structure composed of weaker nodes, stronger links, and even stronger central coordination and control than the citizens groups of the 1970s. Local planning issues no longer dominated their agendas. Quality of life and social services issues occupied more of their energies. The movement has been co-opted.

Some investigators' preliminary assessments accorded the movement a reshaping of city and metropolitan government institutions (Castells 1983). As outlined above, this reshaping was partial. While the movement did have important positive consequences, a telling example of how it was sidestepped occurred just after the zenith of the movement, in the early 1980s. When Madrid began to revise its General Plan, the *Oficina Municipal del Plan* negotiated one-on-one with the land owners and real estate developers to try to set the plan's land use zones. It favored this quasi-corporatist interest-based approach (shades of *urbanismo concertado)* over a bottom-up sociopolitical approach that would have based the land use categories on democratic consent obtained in concert with the neighborhood associations (interview with Félix Arias, manager in the *Oficina Municipal del Plan* in the early 1980s, 1994).

The citizens' movement declined drastically after the democratic municipal elections of 1979. Enrique Tierno Galvan, Madrid's mayor in the early 1980s, gave limited support to the movement. The radical left political ideology that fueled the movement was dulled as its leaders moved into formal seats of power, tempered by electoral politics and daily demands. The neighborhood organizations first appeared in Madrid in the mid 1960s. They were a form of opposition to the regime. Despite the demise of the dictatorship, many of the urban and social ills persist (though transformed over time). The citizens' movement has attempted to perpetuate itself in order to continue the battle to solve these problems. *The Asociaciones de Vecinos* continue today, though less active, less influential, and less involved in planning. They are even less involved with institution building except for their own. In contrast, Barcelona's neighborhood associations, which also had their own citizens' movement in the 1970s, existed for generations prior to the 1970s grassroots experience. They played key roles in city planning and development throughout the 1980s and 1990s, though they are less influential in the twenty-first century.

Our interviews revealed that the attitude of insiders in the city and regional planning agencies toward the neighborhood associations was mixed, indicating a decline in its status. According to a member of the city plan revision technical staff, who significantly was an organizer of individual neighborhoods and a prime mover in the entire citizens' movement, "we [planners] know what needs to be done. We came from the citizens' movement. We came up with the PAIs and the plan's analytical base. It was a type of despotism [on our part]. We had a lot of firepower and political power" (interview with Félix Arias 1994). While the words and their tone may seem extreme, a less jarring sense was shared by other movement cadres who turned into professional bureaucrats. Thus even those who came from the movement and were thrust into positions of authority because of it were among the first to turn away.

This attitude persists today, albeit in a toned down version. The affirmations of a top level appointee in regional government are representative. "There is no union or neighborhood association participation in the preparation of plans. It isn't useful. It isn't needed. The technicians know what needs to be done". These attitudes underscore the absent tradition of civic debate outside of and parallel to the formal and informal techno-political processes.

There were practical reasons why the citizens' movement was specific to its time and has not persisted. It was a historical moment that enabled a society exhibiting a low degree of participation and associationism, and which cannot accurately be called a civil society, to change its tack when Franco died and democracy erupted. There is a large and ongoing debate on this topic. For a pro-civil society argument see Pérez Diaz (1993). For a more critical view, see Elorza (1990). Leading Spanish thinkers, politicians, and writers have broached this subject with regularity, a favorite theme of favorite sons. See Pi i Margall (1982) and Ortega y Gasset (1922).

Many citizen demands were translated directly into political action, such as strikes, protests, and demonstrations. Many citizen claims were satisfied with government response. Action and satisfaction oiled the gears for more demands and protests, a self-reinforcing cycle (virtuous circle). Or so it would have seemed.

Even though the grassroots movement was a success in its time, and its leaders and ideology were infused into planning and governing for a while, it was not enough to transform it into a permanent social tissue we may call an active civil society. The prior institution with nary a new physique marched on.

An analysis of the contrast between Barcelona and Madrid shows the critical difference that an active civic culture and a history of associationism in the bourgeois public sphere made in transforming the planning institutions. (The term bourgeois public sphere comes from Habermas (1989)). First noting the cities' similarities will put their differences in starker relief. Both had strong citizen movements in the 1970s, with similar aim and means. The movement transformed planning and the city in both Madrid and Barcelona. In both, city planning figured high on the political agenda and was practiced in a highly interventionist manner.

This being said, the two cities have numerous historical, cultural, and political differences. One that bears heavily on the evolution of the institutions of planning (whether city, metro, or strategic) is that Barcelona has a long tradition of civic activism, a mature and active civil society, and a history of cooperation between and voluntarism in the private and public sectors (Borja 1977, Giner 1994). Barcelona's neighborhood associations existed for generations prior to the citizens' movement while Madrid's formed in its midst. Barcelona's were sown into the fabric of civic society (Vázquez Montalbán 1992, Kaplan 1992). Barcelona's planning institutions, as part of this civic fabric, were more prone to transformation by it. Planning in Barcelona in the 1980s and 1990s continued to be citizen-based, participative, and open to a wider range of interests. Barcelona's citizens' movement was strengthened by the tradition of civil society, giving it deeper penetration into the latter. It was further strengthened by the history of neighborhood associations' involvement in public affairs. The movement not only transformed planning temporarily, as it did in Madrid. It transformed the *institution* of city planning, and its metropolitan and strategic counterparts as well. For metropolitan planning in Barcelona during that period, see Serratosa (1979) and Area Metropolitana de Barcelona (1991, 1995).

Their processes are more inclusive and participative, and their structures more cooperative and networked. These characteristics persist even as the individual neighborhood associations and their city and regional federations have descended from their 1970s zenith, as they did in Madrid. In summary, the existence of a civil society and its reinforcement of the movement spelled the difference between Madrid and Barcelona *vis-à-vis* planning.

Another example of the difference civil society has played in planning in the two cities is their recent forays into strategic planning. The strategic planning process that Barcelona undertook in the late 1980s and the early 1990s is an outcome of this civic culture. For a time it was widely imitated in Spain and Europe. Its main claim to success is that it has strengthened civil society even further and gotten a broad consensus on several pressing issues. It was able to succeed and be touted abroad because it tapped into this civic reservoir. Madrid, on the other hand, has not seen its strategic planning process imitated, nor has it had import on the political scene. Observers indicated that Madrid initiated its strategic plan because Barcelona was preparing its own.

Returning to our analysis of Madrid, two factors contribute to the continuity of its metropolitan planning institution. One is its centuries old tradition of hierarchy and its consequences that are central in its structuring. The second is the nature of institutions in general. Their structuration, according to Giddens, builds on their individual members' and society's values over time in an interactive process in which the institution evolves, develops, and matures through the actions of its members. The reverse also occurs. The institution imprints its characteristics, forming multiple, overlapping, simultaneous and iterative loops that perpetuate one another. A virtuous circle. People institute institutions and institutions institutionalize.

The long tradition of hierarchy in Spain stems back at least to the Hapsburg monarchy (1561 to 1700). It was intensified by the Bourbon kings (1700 to 1868), from whom provinces and the hierarchy they entailed were imported. Planning in Madrid was to become increasingly hierarchical until the end of the franquist era. It continued to import planning structures and instruments from France, which in parallel to Spain also was refining its own central apparati. The imports included the techniques of *concertation* (*concertación* in Spanish), *expropriation* (*expropriación* in Spanish), *urbanisme concerte* (*urbanismo concertado*), *activite urgent* (*actuación urgente*), *directives* (*directrices*), the Parisian *Schema Directeur* (*Esquema Director*) and the Parisian regional *Plan Directeur* (*Plan Director Territorial de Coordinación*). Thus planning institutions had impacts across borders as well as across time.

To what extent did becoming dependent on imports prolong the propensity for hierarchy? Did importing retard innovation and so perpetuate hierarchy? To what extent did imports and the very process of their importation stifle local ingenuity in creating locally appropriate planning tools?

It was relatively easy for Spain and Madrid to import from France because both countries had highly developed centralized systems of government. Angel Fernández de los Ríos wrote that Spain imported hierarchy from the court of Versailles. He referred to "France, the typical country of exaggerated centralization" (1868, 10). According to Castells, another Spaniard who spent important formative years in France, "Madrid, as the capital of Spain, condenses and concentrates the main trends of Spanish society ... Madrid, under direct control of central government, was the first victim of centralism" (1983, 287). Spain also imported during the

Franco years the *Piani Territoriali di Coordinamento* from Italy. They were given the name of Planes *Directores Territoriales de Coordinación* in Spain, combining the French and Italian terminology (Neuman 1994).

Spain also exported hierarchy. The most lasting export was known as the Law of the Indies. This law was actually a compilation of laws and decrees. Issued by King Felipe II in 1573, it governed the establishment of towns in Spain's new world colonies. It imposed by royal decree a uniform square grid layout of streets that served as the entire city plan. Hundreds of cities and towns were built according to its precepts.

In 1513 the first Spanish royal orders appeared regarding city planning for the new world, issued by king Ferdinand, presumably to build Panama. They were used by Cortés in the founding of Mexico City. (Cortés arrived in 1519 at Tenochtitlan and started building after he defeated the Aztecs.) These royal orders were made more specific in 1523. On July 13, 1573 king Felipe II issued a "comprehensive compilation", expanding on and incorporating prior decrees. The Law of the Indies was a set of 148 ordinances on city planning, ranging from site selection to political organization. (Crouch, Garr and Mundigo 1982).

But the institution did not maintain itself by perpetuating administrative structures alone. It needed something else to keep it together. The deeply rooted ethos of hierarchy accounted for structural rigidity and institutional durability more than actual structure itself. The rigid mentality prevails even today and pervades the institution like an ether, keeping it suspended in time and space (Elorza 1990). Unlike real ether, this ethos does not vaporize. It has been part of the culture for centuries. Yet even it is not the lone factor holding the institution together.

The real glue that held the structure together was a composite of images and informal processes. Images perpetuated planning ideology and doctrine across generations. The role of images and informal processes as glue (cohering logic) and their prominence within the institution were directly related. Their importance has increased over time. The informal processes responded to, were escapes from, and worked together with the formal structures and processes in a multilectic. The informal processes filled in the cracks of the rigid structures, much as glue cements structural materials. The informal processes, along with the thematic content as depicted in images, plans, and ideology structured (read as a verb) the institution far more than the law that constituted it. Images and informal processes were the main ingredients that agents relied on in the structuration of Madrid's metropolitan planning institutions. Images were the stock tools of the trade of architects, the leaders of the institution. Informal processes are second nature to Madrilenians. It is what they do best. So too are images and informal processes their institution's nature.

## Institutional Self-Reproduction: Same as it Ever Was

Why does an institution have one form at a given point in time? Given the range of options available and the host of events that influence it, why is there no other outcome? Because the institution itself dictates its form. The institution is most responsible for its reproduction.

Institutional reproduction is nearly a pleonasm. Attempts to explain it would border on tautology, given a Giddensian view of structuration, a Bourdieusian view of the *habitus*, and Weberian and Foucauldian views of institutional effects on its members and society. How can we talk sensibly about the very real effect an institution has on maintaining itself?

In Madrid one clue to how the institution maintained itself is found in the way it defined itself. It was a techno-political governing institution that held a self-referential posture towards its mission. It maintained this posture over time by restricting membership to professional planners, architects, and politicians, with the significant exception of the citizens' movement and in restricted cases development interests engaged in *concertación*. It did not share its power outside of its boundaries. Planning in Madrid was a turf issue. Power asserted itself through institutional forms and was used to maintain the institution. The institution itself was a power structure that continually reasserted itself through its own reproduction.

A battle in Madrid exemplified how the metro planning institution conserves itself through its narrow self-definition. The battle was a classic turf issue that involved its very future. The power struggle culminated in 1991. It involved the size and power of the *Consejería de Política Territorial*. Some opponents judged it to be too big. Over half the region's budget was concentrated in one of its 10 departments. The struggle was largely read as a power move against its boss. Some felt he had more power than the regional president. The outcome: the *Consejería* was split into two *Consejerías*, *Política Territorial* and *Transportes*. The debate surrounding the split was strictly technical-political. The debate took place in the same informal forums in which policy is usually debated, using the same informal methods. The arena in which it was resolved was political, in the regional legislature. The institution adjusted internal fences to keep itself healthy. Alternate conflict resolution paths, whether inside or outside of the institution's bounds, were not available because of its limited self-definition.

Since 1939 planning has been used as a political strategy to build the institution of metropolitan, and later regional government. This strategy was successful with the *Comisaría General de Ordenación Urbana* from 1946 to 1963 and the *Comunidad de Madrid*'s *Consejería de Política Territorial* from 1986 to 1991. Even the citizens' movement's use of planning played a key role in building democratic institutions in the transition. Some of COPLACO's experiments were efforts at institution building, though unsuccessful.

The use of city planning in this way, as an intentional political strategy of institution building, is rare. It is noteworthy that this strategy spanned the ups and downs of the dictatorship through the urban social movement to democracy; three different socio-political phenomena. The consistent use of planning regardless of the nature of the political regime invested it with a level of importance that boosted its already high status and priority on the political agenda and in the minds of citizens. It also served as an important link in the chain of continuity.

Part of the collective unconscious of the metropolitan planning institution was wrapped up in the endeavor of building government. It projected this unconsciousness on all of its activities and transformed into a collective, conscious attitude. "Governing the region" is a slogan that emanated from the planning department. It is inconceivable that it would have come from another department. It is even more telling that it did not come from the legislature, cabinet, or presidency. The continuing political project of creating a metropolitan/regional institution in the space between the city and the state animated politics and served as a communion spanning political ideologies.

## Institutions Shape Policy

> I understand something about labyrinths. It's not for nothing that I am a great grandson of one Ts'ui Pen, governor of Yunan ... scholar in astronomy, astrology and in the untiring interpretation of canonical books, chess player, famous poet and calligrapher: he gave it all up to create a book and a labyrinth. (Jorge Luís Borges, *The Garden of Forked Paths*, 1971, 106, 109).

The labyrinth is a metaphor and fact that captures the inevitability of institutional self-perpetuation. As a metaphoric image one can see getting lost in the complex maze. Even insiders, not to mention those outside of the institutional maze, can get stuck in a corner without finding the exit. Think of intergovernmental coordination, implementation, or the adoption of a bold measure.

Another image of the labyrinth suggests how an institution determines its own policies. A labyrinth's design (structure) specifies the path taken once inside (process). There is but one entrance and one exit. Understanding the structure will lead to the exit. The labyrinth therefore dictates the path and the exit. In institutional terms the entry is always fixed by history. In Madrid's planning institution the formal and informal processes are fixed by law and tradition. There is only one outcome (plan, policy, strategy, let's say) that the institution specifies. Only institutional redesign can change the path (processes), structure, and exit (outcomes). Chandler's research found that in the United States in the 19th and 20th centuries the invisible hand of the market was replaced by the visible hand of corporate planning in creating the institution of the capitalist corporation. (Chandler 1977).

Like Alfred Chandler's relation of structure and strategy, in which structure shaped strategy, in Madrid planning institutions shaped policy (Chandler 1977, 1990). They did not merely frame it or implement it. Thinking about policy in this way lets us see its sources. The continuity over time of the institution's substantive content was at the heart of the way it shapes policy. Ideas became fixtures. Ideas that began informally around the water cooler, in the library or cafeteria, over a phone call, or at a meeting or conference. Ideas inspired images which blossomed into plans and policies. Once policy overcame institutional inertia and was assumed by its members, it became accepted as part of their ideological repertoire. It became institutional doctrine. A vivid example of this in Madrid was the co-evolution of the *Gran Sur* and *Madrid Región Metropolitana.* An earlier instance was the Zuazo-Jansen proposal that was transformed into the Bidagor Plan, itself the base for the *Comisaría General de Ordenación Urbana* and the 1956 national planning law.

## Institutions Seek Flexibility

Flexibility has been and will remain the key pre-occupation of the architects of Madrid's metropolitan planning institution in the foreseeable future. Despite the rhetoric devoted to flexibility in past planning documents, which was ample during the COPLACO and early *Consejería* years, and can be read in the 1994 draft of the regional planning law; the institution continued to be partly dysfunctional, largely owing to its rigidity (Consejería de Política Territorial 1994). Insufficient authority/ power to solve planning problems at the local level and a lack of adaptability to changing circumstances were two conditions that nurtured dysfunction.

What were the signs of rigidity? The legal structure vested disproportionate power at the top and insufficient power at the "street" level. The administrative structure limited occasions for two-way communication and feedback, damping the learning curve. Legal procedures were typically one-way, mandatory, and overly specific. They left insufficient room to maneuver for operating agents. The technicians dominated the day to day, resulting in a double blindness: to other disciplines and other interests. Party discipline resulted in ideological blindness.

Yet each of these legal-administrative prescriptions had an informal or extra-institutional counterpart that acted as an escape valve to counterbalance rigidity. Informal horizontal networks formed around power nodes, making flexible connections among members. Real estate developers and the market as a whole stepped into the power vacuum at lower levels of the hierarchy and asserted their own muscle, countering the formal power at the institution's vertices. *Concertación* and other *ad hoc* processes superseded or ran parallel with formal mechanisms. Political pacts and technical agreements on large scale projects, action programs, and capital budgets largely supplanted long term plans and strategies.

Even party discipline was not monolithic. Factions within parties and the strong role the opposition plays stimulate debate and prevent hegemony. For example the socialist party, the party which governed the region and the nation in the early 1990s, counted *guerristas* (ideological purists), *renovadores* (renovators), *turbo-renovadores*, *integristas* (those who want to reconcile factions), *leguinistas* (those loyal to the regional president), and *felipistas* (those loyal to the national president). Rigidity, as much an ideological imprint as a structural fact, is a cultural attribute that made it difficult to reconcile these factions.

Problems arose when the real processes and structures were out of step with the ones specified by law. The formative years of the *Consejería de Política Territorial* in the early 1980s, or COPLACO throughout most of its life, were testament to the mismatch between paper rigidity and extant flexibility. The real institution was an organic collectivity that was chaotic, inconsistent, and in constant search of power. The *Consejería* in the early 1980s found that real power was in politics and in real estate development. It quickly abandoned the three figures of its 1984 law—Regional Planning Guidelines, Coordinated Action Programs, and Physical Environment Management Plans—because they were not linked to the real powers shaping the region. There was no political buy-in to support their preparation and adoption. They were irredeemably linked to less than successful efforts of a past life that were wanting to be forgotten.

The *Consejería* quickly learned from its errors and adjusted to political realities via *Madrid Región Metropolitana* and development realities via the four zonal strategies. Where political and economic realities coincided with institutional efforts, as in the *Gran Sur*, the *Consejería* achieved its greatest success.

This rapid adaption was due to the *Consejería*'s director assessing the need to change to a new way of doing business. The new approach was more subtle and sophisticated. He made the shift from a sequential and functional analytical planning and implementation model to a contextual and co-evolutionary one. The *Consejería* began to act on other governments via consent and coordination rather than only intervene directly in land development. The department also acted on other agencies (mostly municipalities) through the extensive support of municipal planning by its *Dirección General de Urbanismo*. The department still intervenes directly, through its housing agency IVIMA (public housing) and ARPEGIO, S.A. It also controls some infrastructure development. The *Consejería* was still looking for a balance between acting directly and indirectly, between regulating and developing on the first instance and policy making and coordinating on the other. It is a question of when to hold power, when to share it, and when to delegate.

The term "power structure" hints at the source and locus of power. In Madrid the power structure has been long cast in center-periphery opposition. The center has been the state. The center acted directly on land by building infrastructure and monumental projects, or less directly through regulation and coordination. Since 1983 the region has been another center of power. These centers held their power cards close to their chest. Even during the height of the grassroots movement COPLACO did not divest statutory power to the municipalities, except when ordered to do so by decree. In general, the center's tight grip on the reigns of power was deeply imbedded. It is not only a product of an obsessed dictatorship. It can be seen in the 1994 bill for the new regional planning law. Its rhetoric emphasizes flexibility and increased local responsibility and authority. Yet it keeps and even strengthens punitive sanctions for local non-compliance. It maintains regional approval of local plans and the ability to step in and take over local planning. In so doing it perpetuates a long tradition.

A real challenge of flexibility was to allow for an ongoing political debate by civil society which permitted an evolving conception of the public good. On a more practical level the challenge to all levels of government was to administer the public good. In the face of rising pressure for a type of flexibility that places more control over development in private hands (the *Partido Popular* position), up to 1995 the socialist response had been to regulate development and sanction infractions even more strongly. This has kept rigidity locked into place.

Another model of flexibility that Madrid's regional government experimented with contrasted with the *laissez faire* market-based model advocated by the conservatives. This model seeks flexibility via recursive interactive processes. So far it has tested this model (*concertación*) more in implementing rather than making plans and strategies (this despite our selection of the Great South and Madrid Metropolitan Region as case studies). It has not yet sought a sustainable model of *concertación* that matches the actual structure and function of the territory.

Not finding this match in the past has ultimately led to downfall, whether that of a regime (Franco), an institution (COPLACO), a process (*urbanismo concertado* or *Programas de Actuación Coordinados*), or a plan (any COPLACO one, the *Consejería's Directrices*). The recurring mismatches of the last several decades have been presaged by Rafael Moneo. If the city/region is to opt for a decentralized model of growth, "this will not be achieved strictly by physical urban planning, but by measures authentically decentralizing, those which would oblige a well-diversified structure of governance" (Moneo 1967, 93).

**The Image and the Institution**

In the evolution of urban planning in Madrid the image played a pivotal role. The image of the city (and later the metropolis) has been used in each plan since 1860 to posit an identity for Madrid that was larger than and different from its prior self. These plans' identity-changing images rose from the crux of crises and reached for new ways of seeing the future. These same images have been used to create the institutions that have governed these new Madrids: the Madrid of the late 19th century that expanded beyond its old city walls, the Madrid that rose phoenix-like from the ashes of the civil war, the metropolis of COPLACO, and the metropolitan region of Madrid in the current democratic era.

Notable in these transformations has been the role of planning. Planners have created images in the forms of plan maps and physical designs. They often designed the planning processes to convert these images into reality. They wielded strong influence on the laws that codified the plans and structured the institution. Thus planners have jumped the traditional gap between planning and politics by shaping political debate through their images. They have become institutional designers in addition to their usual role as city designers. In the early 1980s the top planners in the *Comunidad de Madrid* tried to design the new institution of regional planning before first inventing a new image for the region. They did not succeed. Only later when they returned to the proven formula did they achieve their aim. This formula is create a new image for the place (first), prepare a plan (second) in such a way that it inspires its adoption by law (third) which specifies a new institution to carry out the plan and govern the newly created territory (last).

Saying an image has been central to creating or reforming an institution borders on simplification. In the three cases in which the image was the driving force (Castro, Bidagor, and Mangada eras), however, an inspiring vision captured the essence of what the institution could stand for. Structuration of the institution over time by knowledgeable agents still occurred. The image became integral to structuration when it captured or created salient mental images in the minds of agents that corresponded to features they wanted the institution to possess.

The image that transformed urban planning institutions in Madrid did not stand alone. It was bound to a policy narrative in a set of complex diagnostic, analytic, and prescriptive documents called the plan. (Contemporary equivalents to the plan have been called strategies and frameworks.) Successful Madrilenian plans built on the past, responded to the demands of the existing scene, and imparted a picture of what tomorrow could bring. Plans themselves have become institutions in their own right. The plans touched the future. The past followed, in the form of a changed institution.

In Madrid the string of events typically followed a three step cycle. First the plan, in response to a crisis or a tangle of problems. Second the law to adopt the plan. Third the formation of an institution created by the law to realize the plan. In this way the image/plan led to the institution. This occurred with Castro's *ensanche* (expansion) in the 19th century. It was drafted in 1859, adopted in 1860, and institutionalized in 1892 by the Law of the Expansion.

A plan-law-institution sequence that brought image-led structuration into bold relief is the Bidagor Plan of the post civil war period. Published in 1942, adopted by law in 1944, and institutionalized by decree in 1946 that created the City Planning Commissariat for Madrid and its Environs. This was the first supra-municipal planning institution. The plan presented a crystalline image of the new Madrid. It was based on the 1929 Zuazo-Jansen scheme widely regarded because it "distinguishes itself, above all, for the clarity which it planned" the growth of Madrid (Moneo 1967).

In 1961 a new metropolitan plan was prepared, adopted by law in 1963, and institutionalized by a 1964 decree which created the 1946 Commissariat's follow-ons, COPLACO and Madrid's city planning department the *Gerencia de Urbanismo*.

The most recent instances of strategy-led institution building were the strategies of the *Consejería de Política Territorial* for the *Gran Sur* and *Madrid Región Metropolitana*. They were responsible in large measure for the consecration of the *Consejería* and the entire *Comunidad de Madrid*, a region artificially carved out of the center of Castile. The images provided regional and sub-regional identities where none or negative ones existed beforehand. They rallied the region around new organizations of governance and invested them with meaning.

Episodes where plans did not result in new or altered institutions support the thesis of image-led institutional formation by offering counter examples. None of the four plans written between 1900 and 1931 were sufficiently clear and inspiring to be adopted or implemented. They did not spark the creation of new institutions, despite pleas by their drafters to do so. Their images were weak. They did not compel.

COPLACO's 1972 *Esquema Director* proposed an "organization of coordination, management and control" to implement the document, explicitly recognizing Madrid's pattern of plans preceding organizations. Yet the document, an intellectual product of its time, contained not one image of the future of the metropolis. Instead it was replete with text, criteria, matrices, systems diagrams, objectives, formulas, processes, and methodological appendices. A corresponding change in the planning institution did not occur.

Even the *Consejería*, prior to its late 1980s accomplishments, failed in its first attempt to build itself into a viable organization. Its 1984 law specified three instruments, each a type of plan. None were ever adopted. None contained images of the region's future. The planning director and his director of regional policy realized this fault, and the error of adopting a law first without a plan. As they were later called to consult to other regions, or to address conferences, they advised "write plans first, before writing laws, to gain experience". A candid and public self-criticism which they were later to heed as they crafted Madrid's zonal strategies and *Madrid Región Metropolitana* (interview with Félix Arias 1994).

These institution building processes rely on the mutual interplay of mental (internal) and design (external) images. While non-image factors also make a difference, the way images work is perhaps best expressed by a visionary who was also adroit at institutional intricacies—Angel Fernández de los Ríos: "It is necessary to detach oneself from the point of view which accustoms one to live in a town [as opposed to a city]. It is necessary to coldly look at and analyze the current local conditions of Madrid, not restraining the courage due to the pressure of traditional ideas that keep one accustomed to look at as invariable that which is found under the patronage of determinant institutions ... keeping in mind first the plan [image] of the city" (1989, 18).

This exhortation portrayed a booming Madrid on the cusp of becoming a real city, leaving behind for good its life as a mere town. He signaled the institution's part in maintaining fixed ideas about the past (a town) and the role of the plan in changing those ideas (to a city). As in much else, he was prophetic in this regard.

Images were at the heart of the dialectic of institutional evolution. Images had the dual capacity to sustain an institution across time and space, and to provoke changes to it. On the one hand the image encapsulated the norms of the institution. It was the picture that institutional agents saw in their minds' eyes that carried the essence of what the institution meant to them. It let them perpetuate traditions effortlessly, so ingrained the image. On the other hand it was this very same image of the institution that needed to be shattered and replaced (by another image) in order to change the institution.

# Chapter 8
# Prolegomena to a Theory of Institutional Evolution

Flow sport athletes must know their medium to ride it. Radical use of the medium comes from radical knowledge. In most cases it is intuitive knowledge gained from experience, not reason. Knowledge and practice lead to mastery. In practitioners' jargon (surfers, sailors, soarers, snowboarders) they become one with the wave.

Recognizing the limits of analogy we can look at planning, policy, and politics and their medium the institution in a similar way. Waves, like the seas and skies they surge from, have life cycles (wave cycles). Institutions, like the societies and cultures they surge from, also have life cycles. They are created, they exist, and die. Institutions rise and fall, and do so at varying rhythms and moments in their lifetime. They amplify and attenuate individuals' proclivities at one end of the scale and societal and cultural tendencies at the other end. Institutions are alive just as the humans that give them life. How are they sustained during their lives? What role does planning play in sustaining public institutions, namely government? What role does planning play in opening government to civil society through enlightened governance?

Talcott Parsons concludes "Prolegomena to a Theory of Social Institutions" with the plea "the theory of social institutions must be concerned with the dynamics of institutional change". One of the two "fundamental problems" he associates with institutional change is "structural change". Structural change "will be concerned with the process by which exiting value systems change and new elements come in" (Parsons 1990, 333). This is central to the questions we have investigated in this research. We have found that new political regimes inject their values into the institutional machinery conveniently packaged in an image. In Madrid the city plan is a meaningful document that is an effective instrument of urban policy. Its contents, at least on the rhetorical level, are known to all. For example, the 1985 Madrid General Plan's slogan "*Recuperar Madrid*" (Recover Madrid) was widely cited and quoted. The meaning of *recuperar* has more to do with restore than with the narrow interpretation of the term recover implies. The slogan captured essence of the city plan's intent in tangible imagery. *Recuperar* caught the new ethic of redirecting attention to the existing city, especially to the center. The *Consejería*'s twin strategies Great South and Madrid Metropolitan Region infused, via their imagery, the socialist party's values of social equity and equitable spatial distribution of growth into the planning vocabulary. Franco's Great Madrid imposed falangist values of nationalism, patriarchy, hierarchy, and *capitalidad* on a city eager to heal its wounds after a bloody civil war. As publicists and agents know too well, it is the image that sells. Madrid's planners learned this lesson early.

James Coleman's commentary on Parson's Prolegomena, "Social Institutions and Social Theory" opens with a sentence that flatly asserts "little headway has been made since 1934 when he [Parsons] submitted the paper for publication to the Journal of Social Philosophy" (Coleman 1990, 333). Ignoring for the moment that Coleman disregarded empirical and theoretical advances from the new institutionalism and other sources, our research has addressed Parson's call for a theory concerned with the dynamics of institutional change. Our dependent variable is institutional change. Using this prism to refract the institution has afforded a unique vantage on two elements that tend to be absent from institutional research. One element is the image, and thematic content more broadly. The other is the entire institutional life cycle. Let us recap how leading theories have handled these two elements.

Social theorist Anthony Giddens devised a concept of structuration to explain the constitution of society and its institutions. Yet his theory did not consider the moral or thematic content of institutions (Giddens 1984). Despite his use of cognitive approaches to come to terms with his perspective, it lacked an analysis of the way images shape cognition and structuration. Nor did his theory address institutional creation or demise—two critical points in the life cycle. Analysts who considered the rise and fall of institutions usually did so on a grand scale: nations, societies, empires, and civilizations. Others addressed the small scale, a practice, group, or "mere" organization (opposed to a full-fledged institution with history, traditions, moral content). In the middle range, where the majority of the institutions that encompass and impinge on daily life are found, Elinor Ostrom stands out with her work on the evolution and performance of a single type of institution, those dealing with common pool resources (Ostrom 1990, Ostrom, et al. 2002, Dolšak and Ostrom 2003).

A complete theory of institutional dynamics needs to consider the entire life cycle and the mode of institutional development and change throughout the life cycle. At one extreme is structuration, the incremental evolution from the ground up. Recursive behavior patterns inscribe meaning and substance into enduring institutions. In turn the institutions encode and imprint their own meanings and behaviors on individuals, reflecting the duality of institutional ontology. In this mode institutional development, individual agent behavior is aggregated in an iterative and cumulative process, and the institution is an emergent outcome of their actions. There is no outside force intentionally designing the institution. There are no visible hands that shape and frame incremental structuration.

At the other end of the spectrum from structuration as a mode of institutional development is revolution and radical change. Societal unrest sweeps in a new institution and topples the old one. In between revolution and structuration we find various incremental approaches combining routine maintenance and planned change. This research on public institutions has highlighted one category in this middle range, institutional design. The creation of public institutions from "scratch" and the reform and redesign of existing ones follows a design approach, constituting it with members, structures, and processes. Legislators, ministers, judges, functionaries, and a constructed category of "others" called citizens make up the membership of governing institutions. The category of citizen, as viewed from the pulpit of democratic government, embodies the contradiction of being outsiders to the very system that they constitute and that putatively serves them ("of the people, by the people, for the people"). The term citizen is usually tacked on last, as an afterthought, if at all, to the list of interests to be dealt with by government or by governance, as evidenced by typical official documents and pronouncements. Executive, legislative, and judicial branches at various levels of government (municipality, province, region) constitute the official governing institution. Processes to administer justice, create policy, protect rights, support social and economic endeavors, and so on are also designed up-front. Rarely do designers ponder the institution's content, thematic, moral, or otherwise. Even the archetype for the design of a government, the US Constitution, left the Bill of Rights until later, as amendments to the adopted Constitution. The premise of institutional design is to construct a broad framework to govern society based on *a priori* notions and assumptions, and hope that society would behave according to their designs and the assumptions behind them (Knight 1996).

Our theory favors a life cycle approach. Life cycle theory spans the gaps among incrementalist structuration, radical revolt, and institutional design, while incorporating the two end points of creation and demise. It is an empirically derived theory that critically confronts several dichotomies that have clouded institutional theory. In the words of Ruth Lane it is a concrete theory (Lane 1990).

One such dichotomy is the structuration-design debate. Another is the micro-macro controversy of the sources of influence on institutional development. Still another is the modernist-postmodernist and structuralist-poststructuralist macrologue in which the "post" proponent of each pair attempts to reveal the domination and subjugation inherent in long standing institutions and social structures. They do this while erecting formidable intellectual structures of their own. They counterpoise other types of structure, networks and flows to name two examples, and lack of rational structure, such as chaos and fuzziness. These exhibit more subtlety and less clarity, and therefore are more insidious technologies of cooptation, subversion, adherence, and domination. They are dangerous because institutions have latched on to their efficacy and transformed them into instruments of power.

While these dichotomies address important issues, they are false debates. To go beyond them we must move beyond the dialectical imagination and the dichotomies dialectic represents. We must go beyond the enantidroma that spans the twin towers of thesis and antithesis, namely the bridge named synthesis. Synthesis sometimes weaves together strands that don't belong together. Experience, including institutional experience, teems with chaos, surprise, disjuncture, fragments, and rough edges. These and other destabilizing and destructuring elements that pervade our lives are bumps and potholes in the road that a well constructed, and even a well deconstructed synthesis, cannot pave over.

Reality is angular and splintered, not centered and coherent. To understand reality and not merely subject it to any one mode of perception, we must peer deep inside and outside of phenomena, over, under, around, and through them. To construct a theory that accurately reflects observed experience and enables contextual prediction, we need to go beyond thick description. Nor is critical theory, an analytical mode that was *à la mode*, our method. Much of critical theory was a stylized variation on the Frankfurt original that has been sublimated by an idealized over-reliance on communicative action, to the neglect of strategic and other modes of action. Critical theory also neglected non-discursive modes of communication such as those reliant on imagery. Moreover, critical approaches and criticism in general dissect their object in the image of the critic or critical theorist, and thus subjectify the object. This imposes an intellectual yoke that suits the vicissitude of the analyst. The words of Nobel Prize for Literature winner John Steinbeck are on point. "In ... criticism the critic has no choice but to make over the victim of his attention into something the size and shape of himself" (Steinbeck 1962, 76–77).

Our life cycle theory takes into account these considerations. We start by offering a life cycle typology of institutional transformation comprised of four variables: change, stimulus for change, image constituting the institution, and outcome of the transformation. The typology is built from our empirical analysis of the evolution of Madrid's modern city and metropolitan planning institution. A more generalized typology is then induced from the empirical one. The remainder of the chapter explores the image and how it has co-evolved with the institution under study. It then examines image sources and how images are used in both the structuration and design of institutions. The exposition concludes with an inter-relation of the image with the life cycle. Our exposition suggests the dual nature of the image-institution relation: images sustain, and institutions maintain their constituting image(s). We close the chapter with a reflection on the theory and its import for city planning.

## The Institutional Life Cycle: Evidence from Five Episodes in the Evolution of the Madrilenean Metropolitan Planning Institution

Our explanatory model of institutional transformation has identified four variables (see Table 8.1). The first variable is the type of institutional change. We have identified five types of change. One type is creation. It may be constituted by an act of political will and institutional design (1946 *Comisaría General de Ordenación Urbana* and 1983 *Comunidad Autónoma de Madrid*). It may be created by a revolution or social movement (1939 *Junta de Reconstrucción*, 1970s *Movimiento Ciudadano*). Change may be through gradual evolution (1950s *Comisaría*, 1960s COPLACO). Or change may occur by reform, a non-incremental jump (1860 Castro plan, 1980s *Consejería de Política Territorial* strategies). The fourth

**Table 8.1    Institutional transformation in Madrid's city and metropolitan planning**

| Type of change and exemplary episode | Stimulus for change | Change to constituting image | Outcome of change |
|---|---|---|---|
| Demise: Planned or unplanned | External threat, internal neglect | No image, loss of image | Extinction |
| 1982 COPLACO | Citizens' movement and democracy | Dictatorship to democracy | COPLACO Abolished |
| Degeneration/ destructuring | Internal neglect, external threat | Loss of faith in existing image | Atrophy, decline |
| 1970s COPLACO | Struggle to maintain central control | Hierarchy gave way to social movement | Ineffective planning |
| Evolution: Incremental change | Marginal improvements | Maintain existing image | Stability within existing societal framework |
| 1960s COPLACO | Efficiency, efficacy | | |
| 1950s COMISARÍA | Expand area of control | | |
| Reform: Major intended change | New norms and criteria | New image co-exists/competes with existing image | Change intended to preserve stability within existing societal condition |
| 1963 COPLACO | Economic development | Metropolitan Area | Division of city and metro area |
| 1980s CONSEJERÍA | Social equity | Madrid Metropolitan Region, Great South, Plan culture | Revived regional planning |
| Creation: Constituted by design, social movement, revolt | New world view, new perception of existing conditions | | |
| 1940s BIGADOR GRAN MADRID | Dictatorship, hierarchy, central control | *Gran Madrid, Capitalidad* | *Comisaría General de Ordenación Urbana* |
| Citizens' movement | Democracy, local control | Grassroots activism | Neighborhood Associations |

type of change is degradation or destructuring (1970s COPLACO, *Comisión de Planificación y Coordinación del Area Metropolitana de Madrid*). Finally there is demise, which can be planned or be the result of "natural" extinction (1963 *Comisaría* and 1982 COPLACO, respectively).

The second variable is the stimulus for and source of the change. They vary according to the type of change. In the cases of creation and radical change, the stimuli are a new world view and/or a new societal frame. The source of the stimuli is usually external to the institution (civil war leading to the 1946 *Comisaría* plan, the citizens' movement leading to the transition to democracy in the 1970s). For incremental evolutionary change, stimuli include marginal improvement of the institution, expansion, greater efficiency, and greater efficacy. Their sources are more likely to be internal to the institution. For a major reform, stimuli come from emergent or new norms in society. An example is the goal of equity in the strategies of the regional government in the 1980s. In the stage of destructuring or degeneration, the stimuli include neglect and intentional destructuring (re-engineering). The sources for both reform and degradation may be internal, external, or both. An example is COPLACO's struggle to maintain hierarchy and central control over local planning and development in the face of the citizens' movement. Lastly, in the case of demise, the stimulus is usually an external threat (1980s COPLACO).

The variable "change to the constituting image" also varies according to the type of change, resulting in five different values. To form or create an institution, one needs a new constitutional image (1940s *Gran Madrid*, 1970s grassroots democracy and direct participation). To change an institution incrementally (gradual evolution), the image needs to be maintained, yet improved or polished. The *Comisaría*'s annexation program of the 1950s that implemented the *Gran Madrid* vision is one example. Another is the several plans of the 1900–1939 period, none of which were adopted. Each had its own vision of the metro area outside the city: *extrarradio*, satellite towns, zoning. None had substantial persuasive powers. Nonetheless, a weak and variable image of the metropolitan fringe was a constant during this time. To reform an institution, a new or emergent image first co-exists and then competes with the existing constitutional image. If the reform is completed, new image(s) displace the old one. The *Consejería*'s *Gran Sur*, *Madrid Región Metropolitana*, "plan culture", and "regional culture" are examples of new images. In a destructuring institution there is a loss of faith in the existing image, or several weak images vie to be the constitutional image. The COPLACO fight with the neighbors associations from 1970 until the 1979 PAIs exemplifies this instance. Finally there is demise, when the constitutional image becomes obsolete, undesirable, replaced, or otherwise is lost, destroyed, or overthrown. The *coup de grace* of COPLACO in 1982 is a case in point.

The last variable is the outcome of institutional change. This variable, like the others, varies across five parameters, depending on the type of change. For creation, the new institution either replaces an old one which has been divested of legitimacy or it is formed *de novo*. Examples include the downfall of the dictatorship in 1975 and its replacement by democracy, and the 1936–1939 civil war which brought the downfall of the second republic and its replacement by a dictatorship. For incremental change the outcome is a stable institution within the existing societal frame. For reform, the outcome is a major transformation intended to preserve the stability and continuity of the institution and the stability of overall society within a set of new societal conditions or new perceptions of existing conditions. Continuity and stability are the intended results. An unsuccessful reform could lead to institutional and possibly social instability. An interesting case with one set of short term consequences and another set of long term consequences is the split of the *Comisaría* into the *Gerencia de Urbanismo* (city planning agency) and COPLACO (metro planning agency). The *Gerencia* remained stable, evolving and growing until it was transformed in 2004 to the *Area de Urbanismo, Vivienda, e Infraestructuras*. COPLACO survived in the short run (though ineffective) and became a casualty in the long run. For the case of institutional degeneration, the outcome was atrophy and decline. This characterized the downward slide of COPLACO in the 1970s until the PAI strategy. For demise, the outcome is extinction. The example is the dissolution of COPLACO in 1982.

An episode by episode exegesis of institutional transformation in Madrid as displayed in Table 8.1 (p. 163) follows.

Castro's 1860 expansion outside the city walls illustrates the creation of a new institution. The plan responded to major changes Spain was undergoing. Rapid economic growth brought by a new form of production, industrialization, along with an explosion of technical and cultural innovation, and huge rural in-migration permanently altered the profile of Madrid. It unleashed a new logic that called for a new way to accommodate urban growth. Castro's plan provided a new image and the basis of a new reality for the city. It included a square grid of wide streets, and later uniform building and hygiene codes. The village of Madrid became a modern city. The plan enabled the city to grow in an ordered and stable fashion, preserving societal order and traditions while responding to new conditions.

Planning in the first third of the twentieth century typified gradual evolution. The plans for the city (it was not yet a metropolis) and its planning office within city government evolved slowly and incrementally. The new ideas or visions for the city which emerged in this period competed for primacy until Zuazo's and Jansen's definitive proposal. Nevertheless, due to an extremely unstable political environment during the latter two decades of this period, an effective planning institution would have to wait to be reborn. Thus for nearly 40 years the institution was effectively dormant. It remained a small technical staff with scarcely any import in urban affairs. Despite many shifts in types of national government, Castro's scheme essentially maintained its guiding hand on city growth. Spill-over growth outside Castro's limits were essentially uncontrolled.

Franco's and Bidagor's *Gran Madrid* was a case of revolt. The revolution consummating the 1936 to 1939 civil war resulted in the falange's victory and ascent to power. It precipitated a radical change in society from republican democracy (albeit short lived) to a tyranny that effectively closed its borders to the world. It attempted to sustain an almost exclusively domestic economy. The new image was one of absolute power, paternal patronage, and supreme hierarchy. A Grand Madrid as capital of a (lost) empire. Its national and local governments were replaced, and a new metropolitan institution was created.

COPLACO's fortune was a story of institutional demise brought about by disregarding the new social and political realities by the political leadership. This gradually weakened the organization to the point of near irrelevance. The end came at the hands of the radical urban social movement that rendered its bureaucracy meaningless, until the PAIs. By then it was too late. The entire metropolis lost faith in COPLACO's vision and what the organization stood for. COPLACO was incapacitated and unable to remake itself. The new image for the future came from the outside. The new image was never absorbed by the crumbling institution, leading to its abolition.

The transition to regional government in the 1980s was a case of the demise of one institution (COPLACO) and the reform of another, the regional government *Consejería*. The stimulus at that time was the change from autocratic rule to democracy prompted by Franco's death in 1975. The new images of democracy, Madrid as a metro region, and the Great South at first co-existed and then replaced the prior images of autarky, Madrid as capital city, and a southern periphery adrift. The shift to democracy brought about changes to the system that preserved some broad features such as a market economy and a nation-state with autonomous borders. It also changed local and regional politics and created a new level of government, the regions.

**The Institutional Life Cycle**

Table 8.2 (p. 167) shows a general typology for the institutional life cycle of creation, development, change, decline, and demise. It generalizes the empirical findings that were presented in Table 8.1. It must be kept in mind that not all institutions necessarily undergo all the phases indicated by this schema. Nor do they undergo them in this or any other particular chronological sequence. For example, institutions tend to become more extended over time and space rather than die. Others undergo multiple episodes of expansion and contraction. The general typology provides a general conceptual framework by which to understand institutional change and evolution. It also offers a set of testable hypotheses.

**Institutional Design, Civil Society, and the Self-Invention of Institutions**

Researchers claim that self-invented and self-developed institutions in which members create their own methods to solve their problems are more likely to be effective and just in the eyes of their constituents (Innes, Gruber, Neuman and Thompson 1994, Bellah, Madsen, Sullivan, Swidler, and Tipton 1991, Ostrom

**Table 8.2        Typology of institutional transformation**

| Type of change | Stimulus for change | Change to constituting image | Outcome of change |
|---|---|---|---|
| Demise | External threat, internal disregard | No image, Loss of image | Extinction |
| Decline/ Destructuring | Internal disregard, external threat | Loss of faith in existing image | Atrophy, decline |
| Evolution: Incremental change | | Maintain existing image | Stability within existing societal frame |
| Reform: Major change | | New image co-exists and/or competes with existing image | Stability-preserving change within new societal conditions, or instability (unintended result) |
| Creation | | New image | New institution |

1990, Giddens 1984). In the words of Robert Bellah and his collaborators these institutions are "warm". They pay more attention. Their internal and external environments are more connected. They inspire trust and commitment. Warm institutions are more whole (1991, 254–76).

"Cold" institutions do not possess these features, or possess them to a lesser degree. Cold institutions are more likely to be constituted from without, rather than being self-created. An example is national legislation that requires forming a local agency to resolve an issue. That issue may matter to the nation but not the locality. Another type of cold institution inherits long standing social traditions and fulfills them mechanically without feeling or commitment. These traditions are contradictory to extant conditions, leading to a crisis because institutional members do not hold the beliefs underlying the traditions. These institutions stem from inherited obligations rather than from self-created and self-imposed desire and will. Note that an old institution is not necessarily cold.

In Madrid the *Gran Sur* and *Madrid Region Metropolitana* were strategies that warmed the metropolitan planning and governing institutions that had for a generation been cold. COPLACO ideology, administrative structure, and processes were imposed from above by the central government. The gradual yet steady demise of COPLACO from its inception to abolition epitomized the chill that central government imparted. The planning required by the two 1984 *Comunidad de Madrid* laws was inherited without conviction. The non-fulfillment of the three planning instruments required by the 1984 laws reflected the lack of commitment to inappropriate institutional technology inherited from the past. In contrast, once the *Comunidad de Madrid* let go of these three planning instruments and marched forward with its two home grown strategies *Madrid Región Metropolitana* and the *Gran Sur*, it became a more effective agency.

How do we keep an institution from "catching cold"? Is institutional self-reliance the only remedy? Does an institution's warmth (or coldness) depend on the existence (or not) of a civic culture behind it as Robert Putnam (1993, 2000) suggested? Are there other factors at play? Can warmth be pre-installed or retrofitted, like central heating, using an institutional design approach? Or is it dependent on the warmth incrementally stoked by structuration?

These dualities—(1) self-reliance and imposition from above, (2) civic culture and absence of one, and (3) institutional design and structuration—interlace with each other to form an explanatory matrix. If these findings and those of others are corroborated by further empirical research, that is, if effectiveness and warmth can be correlated positively to the matrix of these three dualities, then we will step closer to an explanatory theory of institutions, their evolution, and their design.

In Madrid the planning institution has mattered during much of its modern history. When it was effective, people were committed to it because it was committed to improving their quality of life and made great strides in actually doing so. The institution mattered when it did not contradict social aims (as localized in Madrid) nor embrace the contradictions inherent to its central government. Another way of saying this is that the institution mattered when its constitutional image matched the internal images of individuals, the collective memory, and the external images projected in social media. When the institution mattered it maintained a high political profile and commanded significant resources. The institution has been able to flourish despite Madrid's historically weak civic culture (accounting for exceptional moments like the citizens' movement). This was possible due to the public sector's assumption of activities performed by the civil society and the private sector in other nations and cultures.

The duality that Madrid's planning institution never came to terms with is the balance between inventing its own methods and structures on one side and importing institutional technology from abroad and using it beyond its useful value on the other side. When the institution has been most effective, it has relied on its own innovations. Only occasionally has it successfully adapted imported techniques, and only when they were well suited (*concertación*, for example). Most often, imported methods were applied without carefully analyzing their appropriateness and long term impacts. Castro's expansion, mimetic of Cerdà's Barcelona expansion but without the latter's analysis, was criticized by Fernández de los Ríos, among others. The *Schema Director*, imported from France, was just one of COPLACO's aborted attempts. A question that has been missing from the debate on Spanish and Madrilenean planning has been: to what extent has the planning institution suffered arrested development due to the preference for imported theory and tools over self-developed techniques that respond to local conditions which decisively mold local planning? This is a question of institutional design and of local self reliance.

Has institutional design made a difference in Madrid? When it has been self-designed, yes. Yet the design of institutional "mechanics" (planning processes and administrative structures) was not enough. Thematic content, particularly moral content, was crucial. Was content designed up front? In at least two episodes it was. Both were noted for their distinct political ideologies. One case was the Bidagor plan for *Gran Madrid*, resonant of falangist ideals. The second was the socialist party's regional schemes of the 1980s, based on their ideals of attaining social equity along with economic competitiveness, environmental justice along with sustainable growth. Successfully designed infusion of thematic content (ideology) into the institution was realized only when goals were also widely held by society, particularly the governing class. Another type of infusion of ideology into the institution was not by design, but as the result of social mobilization. The goals of the urban social movement of the 1970s were widely held by all except those who tried to keep the Franco dictatorship alive.

Another way in which thematic content has been transferred across institutional episodes has been the ideas contained in city and metro plans (distinct from ideology, which was also contained in the plans and transmitted by them). See Table 6.3 for the continuity of planning ideas in Madrid plans. City plans accounted for the high degree of continuity in planning ideas, and these were perpetuated in administrative structures that also displayed a high degree of institutional continuity (see Tables 6.1 and 6.2). This stability was able to withstand the numerous changes in political regime types and political ideologies within and across regime types.

Wolach, for example, studied the impact of the French revolution on institutional structures in Paris and France. His findings parallel ours on numerous accounts. Wolach's analysis of new laws and new bureaus instituted in the aftermath of the revolution indicates that in some areas of French bureaucracy there was remarkable change (public education, conscription) while in others there was little change, and that which occurred did so slowly (public welfare). His study of legal documents in various fields of government activity disclosed a dialectic of institutional stability and change. Political change precedes administrative stability (Wolach 1994).

**The Image**

What is the image and where does it come from? Up to this point the word image has had two meanings. The first meaning was *design* or *external image*, the second meaning *mental* or *internal image*. The design (external) image is an outward projection of selected parts of a self or an object, a disembodied abstraction that represents using visual symbols. The external image could be a design rendering a neighborhood, a plan projecting a new city, a photograph of a building, a film telling a story, etcetera. In the *Gran Sur* the design images (Figures 4.3 to 4.7) portrayed a new vision for the southern metropolitan periphery. In the course of our investigation we also have referred to the *city plan image*. This is the plan map or city design drawing representing the planners' vision of the future. It is contained in an official document called a city plan. A plan may contain other visual images in it and may provoke mental images through language and imagery that it contains. The overall image that an entire plan may leave in a reader's mind may differ from the city plan image as drawn on the plan map or city design.

The mental (internal) image is the one the mind uses to organize its thinking. It is what the mind's eye sees. It is what a mathematician sees when working through a complex theorem. It is what an architect sees when visualizing a design. It is what everyone sees when they use their image-ination to dream about a loved one, their next vacation, or a childhood memory. It is mental sediment, a deposit that settles into the memory, which changes as we change. We recall these internal images into the slide tray of memory and project them in our imagination. In the *Gran Sur* the internal image was present in the minds of the politicians and policy makers as they conceived the project. A sketch of it is shown in Figure 4.6.

The relation between the internal and external images played a key role in the structuration of the metropolitan planning institution. In general, the design images (city and metropolitan plans) drawn up by the architect-planners were first assimilated by the technicians, later by policy makers and politicians, and finally by the development community and the public. In this way the planning institution

**Figure 8.1    Logo of the 1993 Draft General Plan for the City of Madrid**
*Source*: Oficina Municipal del Plan, Ayuntamiento de Madrid.

extended over time and space while maintaining fidelity to its technical-political core.

We have also specified another type of image called the *constitutional image*. The constitutional image captures the essence of an institution in mental images. It portrays the thematic and moral content of an institution. It symbolizes what the institution means. An effective constitutional image represents the origins, history, and mission of the institution. Not all constitutional images package all these features in one image. The constitutional image may be packaged into an external image for marketing and publicity purposes. Examples are the Big Blue logo of IBM and the Mickey Mouse image of Disney. In Madrid the closest the new regional government came to producing a constitutional image is Madrid Metropolitan Region. Madrid's municipal crest is a sort of constitutional image. The logo for the 1995 general plan for the city of Madrid (Figure 8.1) conveys images of centrality, *capitalidad*, and radial access to the city center. It is in the shape of a star with three concentric rings of increasing size. Each ring represents an era of physical growth of the historic city. Each era possesses its characteristic urban pattern distinguishable from other eras. Its imagery of centrality and radial access hearkens back to the *Gran Madrid* of Pedro Bidagor and Francisco Franco.

Images give visual shape to the ideas that an institution forms around. They spark the imagination and become the rallying point for action and agency that build the institution. Cognitive theories will be used later in this chapter to suggest that the mental image in the mind's eye needs to be changed in order to accept a new idea which becomes the kernel (and eventually the constitutional image) that a new institution coalesces around. A corollary is that the constitutional image needs to stay intact to maintain the continuity of the mental image of an existing institution. In this way images play key roles in the entire institutional life cycle.

In some instances during the growth and change of the urban planning institution in Madrid, the internal mental and the external design images co-evolved, as in the Great South. The new institution of regional planning co-evolved with them. In the Great South and Madrid Metropolitan Region strategies we see another face of the image. Words, in the form of metaphors, slogans, and rhetoric were part of the image package. The words Great South and Madrid Metropolitan Region were as potent as their strategies. In these cases words were worth a thousand pictures.

The dual nature of images—internal/external, mental/representative—points to their other qualities. Mental and representative images are malleable, transportable, and virtual. In our minds images are created, used, changed, and replaced. We are highly mobile beings and transport our images and exhibit a readiness to impart and import new ones wherever we go. We are adept at fabricating images in dreams, creativity, play, and other modes of image-ination.

External images are as transportable as mental ones, if not more so. They are highly and increasingly easy to manipulate in an increasingly digitized world. They are becoming as malleable as mental images. As reality becomes more virtual, it is more difficult to distinguish between internal and external images. We can speculate a future in which image creation, manipulation, and diffusion become increasingly institutionalized despite (because of) the decentralized network structure of institutions that rely on digital telecommunications. Images seem to exist for their own sake in a multi-media environment in which the digitized image is supplementing and supplanting the word, even as the word itself grows more digitized (blogs, Kindle, iPad). An institution uses images for its own purposes, to propagate its apparati and ideology. Ideology is replaced by image-ology in a scenario of virtual institutions. This sort of institution, of which the world wide web and the internet are but one form, would be omnipresent. It could marginalize traditional structures, processes, and content by transforming them into virtual, real time, on-line ones.

In his landmark studies on civilization and symbolization Carl Jung (1964, 1969a, 1969b) proffers a theory relating image, self, and society from a psychological-cultural perspective. According to him, symbols (external images) connect with our deep subconscious in powerful ways that shape the way we relate to the world. These symbols exert their power by their ability to form or reform internal mental images. The more the external and internal images correspond, the greater the power (meaning) of the symbol and the clearer the mental image.

Jung's studies led him to identify *archetypes*. For Jung an archetype has a restricted meaning, reserved for the most powerful and most basic mental images in the pantheon. His prototypical archetypes include mother, father, child, house, anima, animus, and several others. Archetypes have greater effect on the psyche than to shape how we think about houses, mothers, fathers, etcetera; whether they be our house, a house, or the concept of a house. It is their extension beyond the immediate manifestations that accord archetypes power. The word archetype has entered the common language and is applied to any object that embodies what is perceived to be the essence of the concept represented by the object. The notion of essence leads to the idea of transferability of the archetype across cultures. Jung postulated that his limited set of archetypes existed in all cultures. Jung called archetypes "primordial *images*" before he settled on the term archetype (Jung 1961).

Kenneth Boulding explores the meaning of the image in his 1956 book *The Image*. He strived to develop a theory of the image by asking what determines it. He makes a fundamental distinction between the internal mental image and the messages that reach it. "The meaning of the message is the change which it produces in the image" (Boulding 1956, 7). The way in which people change their knowledge of the world stems from how they reorganize their own mental images. Boulding stresses that the image is the property of a person and not an organization. These images, he goes on to say, are subjective and interpretive, the result of mental manipulation of messages. They are "value-based" (Boulding 1956).

How personal are these images, however? Are they only private affairs? Some of the qualities of the image give it a double identity: private and public. One of these qualities is its plasticity (capacity to be modified from the outside). Another is its value base (inter-subjectivity). These two qualities place the image into the public realm. It is not just an internal image, a private affair. Images are in large part derived from social experience, as Jung points out. The sharing of images creates public knowledge. External imagery and discourse facilitate sharing. Sharing can be implicit, via passive reception through collective media such as the internet, podcasts, television, radio, the cinema, the press, etc. It can also be explicit by public discourse. It matters not if the public discourse is formal—a public hearing perhaps, or informal—an after hours conversation. In these ways images are made public, and thus political. Politics can be thought of as a process that modifies collective images. Some may call these collective images, when fused with philosophically grounded values, ideologies (Boulding 1956).

In these ideas Boulding not only preceded Berger's and Luckmann's 1966 classic *The Social Construction of Reality: A Treatise in the Sociology of Knowledge*, and Marshall McLuhan's and Quentin Fiore's *The Medium is the Message*, but provided a deeper interpretation. Boulding highlights the role of images in the sociology of knowledge on page 78.

While Boulding does not set out to create a political theory, the political implications of his analysis are valuable. Persuasion has long been a political tool. For him, the "art of persuasion is the art of perceiving the weak spots in the images of others and prying them apart with well constructed symbolic messages" (1956, 134). In Madrid the lack of a positive identity of the southern fringe of the metropolis was the weak spot that planners filled with a clear and well-presented symbolic message of the *Gran Sur*. In this case, the change in peoples' images of the southern fringe was the key to adopting and implementing the new strategy. Changing the image was the essence of planning.

Kevin Lynch, in his classic text *The Image of the City*, shows us that people possess images of their city or neighborhood. These images vary from person to person in sophistication, meaning, and other measures. They are ready-made mental maps that orient and connect identity to place. It is this image of a city or neighborhood, deeply held and developed over time through personal experience, that must be changed for a plan to be effective. It is not a trivial matter. Yet these images can and do change, as the evidence from Madrid demonstrates. Note the analogy to Thomas Kuhn's theory of scientific revolutions and paradigm breakdown and replacement. The paradigm is the institution of science's stand-in for the image. Paradigms, in fact, have been captured in images: earth-centered and sun-centered universes, and gravity attracting a falling object. We could modify Kuhn's vocabulary without harming his thesis by saying that changing the image was essential to changing the paradigm.

## Image Sources

The image has many sources. In part, image is related to identity. Take a personal or self image. The more we know who we are and the better formed our identity, then the clearer the image we have of ourselves. We can project that identity/ image more clearly to others. People, according to Boulding, carry in their minds different types of images: spatial, temporal, relational, personal, and value images (1956, 47). Using Boulding's typology, another example of the sources of images combines Boulding's spatial and temporal image types. His spatial and temporal images are similar to Lynch's studies of the images that people have of places. Places have identities in the minds of their inhabitants and users. The identity of place is captured by a mental image (Violich 1996).

We advance a connection between the role of place imagery in modern Spanish planning and its role in history. Richard Kagan has provided some indications of this connection in his work on medieval and early modern images in Spanish and Spanish colonial (South American) cities. He found that medieval Spanish cultural identity was based on the literal image of their city and how that city was projected (represented) in society (Kagan 1989). Maurice Halbwachs suggests how this may come about in a chapter entitled "Space and the Collective Memory" (Halbwachs 1950). Inhabitants of a place recurringly circulate through its spaces. The spaces become part of the group's collective memory (see also Rykwert (1976) on the origins of settlements and images, identity, and memory.) "The group's image of its external milieu and its stable relationship with this environment becomes paramount in the idea it forms of itself [identity]. ... thus we understand why spatial images play so important a role in collective memory" (Halbwachs 1950, 130). In Madrid planners inserted designed spatial images into collective processes to alter the extant spatial images in the collective memory.

We hypothesize that the stronger the identity that people experience of a place, and therefore the stronger the internal image they have of it, the more likely they are to act on that place. In this case the image is ready-made and available for use. Planners do not have to create a new image. In other cases, where the identity is lacking or negative, planners have persuasive opportunities. If the new external images (city plans, physical designs) they create are clear and convincing, and are effectively employed in a viable planning process, then they have an opportunity to replace the negative, weak, or non-existent internal images.

Findings from the cognitive sciences, in particular from neurophysiology, support this view with data describing how the brain works. The various characteristics of a viewed object are recorded individually by the brain: motion, size, color, contrast, shape, and so on. The brain processes visual signals independently and then constructs the image we "see". It is worth quoting to grasp this discovery, which earned David Hubel and Torsten Weisel the Nobel Prize in Physiology and Medicine in 1981 (Hubel 1988).

> [V]isual information enters the cortex and is split up according to function (shape and so on), but there is no place in which the picture can be put back together again. This leaves us with only one option—the picture itself must result from a dynamic process carried out in a distributed fashion among many cortical areas. In other words the picture one "sees" does not exist as a single complete

representation somewhere in the brain. Rather, it is an emergent property of the system (Finkel 1992, 400).

In Madrid, as regional government constructed its strategies for the south (the *Gran Sur)* and the region *(Madrid Región Metropolitana)*, images were an emergent property of the system (metropolitan planning institution). Emergent properties are also explained by cognitive science. The human mind is made of multitudes of highly cooperative, non-homogeneous, distributed, and interconnected networks. Each network patterns (sees) the experiential world which we envision in images. When recurrent patterns break down, there is a transition between them during which there is no prevalent set of mental images of the world. There is a "rapid reciprocal cooperation and competition between distinct agents [images] activated by the current situation, vying with each other for differing modes of interpretation" (Varela 1992, 334). There is an evolutionary mental process whereby one cognitive framework becomes more prominent than another.

Once a new image replaces an old one, the neural network reforms itself into a new pattern "constituting a coherent cognitive framework and readiness for action" (Varela 1992, 334). Cognitive framework replacement is an evolutionary process enabling images to form, be re-formed, and be replaced. "Cognitive structures emerge from recurrent patterns of sensimotor activities" (Varela 1992, 335). In Madrid the evolution of the *Gran Sur* image articulated a new cognitive structure regarding the south that emerged in the successive steps of conceiving the image. These events find macro-social expression in Kuhn's paradigms and their breakdowns and micro-social expression in Boulding's strong images replacing weak ones.

## The Image and the Institutional Life Cycle

The power of images to shape events is not disputed (Boorstin 1962). Indeed the multi-billion dollar (in the United States alone) marketing and advertising industries are witnesses to this fact. In politics "image handlers" have risen to the highest levels of confidence and influence in presidential circles. In the planning of Madrid the image also shaped events and has exerted a decisive influence on the evolutionary life cycle of the planning institution.

If we link the life cycle of institutions hypothesis with cognitive theories of image formation and situate their synthesis within a frame of cognition as a means of structuring the institution, we arrive at a new theory of institutional evolution. In this concept, the constitutional image represents the essence of the institution's thematic content that is replicated over space and time via structures and processes. Changing the constitutional image in the minds of the institution's members and constituents effectively yields a change in the institution. Even outside the transformative episodes we have investigated, constitutional images evolve gradually and incrementally. Combining the two general categories of change in our theory, gradual and transformational, resembles an institutional version of the "punctuated equilibria" theory of evolution (Eldredge and Gould 1972).

We can think of an institution as an instrument of power to maintain order according to an idea. This idea organizes people and resources around itself and thus institutionalizes the idea. It also institutionalizes people and resources. As the idea collapses, the institution formed around it also collapses.

Images have power not only because of the roles that they play in the mind, not only because they saturate the airwaves and other media, not only because they are malleable and transportable, and not only because they are widely accepted currency in today's world. They exert power because they transcend boundaries due to their nature as currency, just as money transcends boundaries. Both are universal media. Images cross geographic, social, political, economic, and ideological boundaries. It does not matter if the borders are disciplinary, functional, (in planning functional means specific categories as housing, transportation, environment, infrastructure), sectoral (private, public, non-profit, joint), cultural, political party, or of any other category. Images dissolve boundaries.

The boundary dissolving property of images endows them with the capacity to carry out politics and governance by supplementing and strengthening traditional means of coordination. A coordination strategy based on the image enhances coordination processes and structures, whether formal or informal. Images are a cohering logic that can be used (and abused) to carry out the complex task of coordination among the myriad partners that plan a metropolis. They can be used for any multi-interest, multi-disciplinary intergovernmental policy program involving multiple and competing objectives. We can think of a "single image" negotiating technique alongside the "single text negotiating document" used in conflict resolution (Moore 2008).

### Application of Findings

We must be careful in extending the findings from Madrid to other contexts for several reasons. As national capital, politics is at the fore of social and public life, assuming a significance disproportionate in relation to other cities. Government in Madrid as in Spain is very interventionist by North American and most western standards. (Paris is another example of a highly interventionist approach to territorial planning.) Planning agencies occupy a privileged position in politics, policy, and public discourse. City and regional planning are at the top of the agenda for a number of non-governmental groups as well. Planning departments and their budgets are huge compared to their counterparts in the United States and Europe. City plans are meaningful and do not gather dust on shelves. They govern public works and private development. Cultural and social characteristics impart a distinct Spanish flavor to planning. Nonetheless there are general findings germane to government institutions and more specific ones suggestive to planning institutions.

The most transferable finding may be the implications of an image-based theory of institutional evolution. If the image is at the heart of institutional change, this suggests that in order to manage change, we must manage the image. The image becomes the object of change. This is well known by corporate and political marketing strategists. It is becoming increasingly known by those who market and sell images of cities and metro areas as part of their economic development programs (Goodman 1979, Kearns and Philo 1993). Using the image like the *Comunidad Autónoma de Madrid* did in the *Gran Sur* implies the ascendance of marketing in city planning (Neuman 1994).

What is not so easily transferable to the North American and other contexts is the style of planning specific to Madrid: highly interventionist, technical-political, and architect dominated. This style has two consequences. In a more decentralized and pluralist setting, where more interests and stakeholders are active participants in a more broadly defined planning institution, the plan (policy, strategy) making forums and arenas are more dispersed and more fragmented. In this setting the image has even greater potential due to its nature as the cohering logic of the institution. Ansell (1996) found that symbols functioned as a cohering logic in networks. The size, complexity, and unwieldiness of contemporary metropolitan planning institutions have proven stubbornly resistant to customary procedural and structural means for coordination.

The second consequence is that architects and other designers of places (landscape architects, urban designers, physical planners), whose working methods rely on the image, have a more important position to occupy in the institution than has normally been accorded to them. In addition to urban planners' positions as the designers of places, we can add their capabilities as designers of institutions.

This research suggests that a richer interpretation of metropolitan planning by a wider disciplinary scope of investigators is possible. This includes psychologists, cognitive scientists, media scientists, marketing scholars, among others. It is also relevant to urban planning at other scales (community, city, regional, provincial, state) and by other names (town, country, spatial, territorial, land use, environmental, landscape). Institutional theories of planning, policy and strategy making, and governance provide a firm framework to counterbalance the tendency of planning practice and theory to focus on process. This processual focus has been narrowed to discourse in much planning theory. The theory advanced here gives the tradition of considering historical, economic, political, and social influences on the planning enterprise is given an institutional home.

## "Incrementalism is Innovation's Worst Enemy"[1]

*Is it Planning's Worst Enemy?*

Muddling through has long been a hallmark of urban planning and public policy. Some have averred that we are "still muddling and not yet through" (Lindblom

---

1 Negroponte (1995, 188).

1979). Metropolitan planning in Madrid has highlighted the positive role institutional design and redesign plays in effective planning and governing. It also showed the negative effects that incremental adjustments has occasionally had in prolonging ill-suited institutional practices.

Incremental institutional evolution may suffice when societal conditions are stable and institutions are perceived to be effective and are in step with social, economic, environmental, and political realities. In Madrid these conditions were met during the first decades following Castro's expansion plan, the early years following Bidagor's plan, and the *Consejería's Gran Sur* and *Madrid Región Metropolitana* strategies. Those images corresponded with existing realities all the while they tried to change some of them. In times of change and turbulence, and in times of paradigm questioning, gradual and minor tinkering with the technical side of Madrid's planning institutions—their inner workings and their organizational structures—were to little or no avail in the face of new ideas and new ideals, or the loss of faith in existing ones. The constitutional images and/or city plan images in times of crisis were not consistent with the messages pervading society, leading to an institutional crisis. In several episodes we have shown how the image was fundamental in leading the planning institution out of a crisis, when that image was coupled to a legitimate social movement or institutional actor.

Planning based wholly on incrementalism sells itself short. It may have been appropriate in eras when planners typically operated in stable institutional settings, or in the reform of institutions within stable societal settings. This constituted the common, every day range of contexts in which urban planners and policy makers typically found themselves. In turbulent times such as these, when paradigms and realities change rapidly, planners and policy makers operate in radically different contexts. Given the starting point, that the institution is the locus of power (resources, knowledge, decisions, actions), then for planners to be effective institutional change agents, they must recognize the stage of the institutional life cycle, along with the constitutional image and its status.

This research places the planning episode within the institutional life cycle. It suggests an appropriate mode of planning for each stage in the life cycle. Comprehensive planning cannot be done continuously. We cannot make a grand plan to stir men's blood at any moment. The institution and broader society will not accept it. At the same time planners must not fail when the time is ripe for a new plan. This occurs when coincident social forces conspire for an entirely new approach, and perhaps for a new institution. Other activities of planning, typically associated with comprehensive planning, such as information gathering, scenario development, testing, and evaluation, can be done on a regular basis to support ongoing governing functions. Martin Meyerson called this the "intelligence function of planning" that provides a "middle-range bridge" between long term comprehensive planning and the daily routine (Meyerson 1956). These activities also anticipate and support the eventual preparation of a long term plan.

In addition to distinguishing the timing for plan making from other more routine aspects of planning, these findings imply another role for planning, institutional design. The institutional view is not a new one. In one form or another, planning is and always has been about the design of new political institutions that are meant to shape our land and city scapes. We have demonstrated this for the city and metropolitan region of Madrid.

In the United States, whether the actual city plans, zoning codes, and planning commissions begun in the progressive era; the Standard Planning Enabling Act, Standard Zoning Enabling Act, National Resources Planning Board, State Planning Boards, and the Tennessee Valley Authority of the New Deal; or the regional associations of government, river basin commissions, state planning programs, metropolitan planning organizations, and the multitude of other single or multiple purpose regional entities of the post-World War II era (just to mention some of the more prominent ones)—planning has been a significant agent of political institution formation outside the federal level in the last century. Leaders in planning have long recognized its essential link to democratic government, evidenced in Rexford Tugwell's *The Battle for Democracy* (1935) and Robert Walker's *The Planning Function in Urban Government* (1941). Institutional design was implicit in their formulations, and explicit in practice. Institutional design was and is a vital job of planning.

# Appendices

**Appendix 1: Madrid Interview Questionnaire**

The following list of questions was shared with some but not all of the interviewees listed in Appendix 2. In every interview, regardless whether the interviewee had seen them in advance or not, these questions were used as a baseline for data gathering. Each interview was open ended, so that all topics that may not have been suggested by these questions could have been, and were, explored. Thanks to Judy Innes, Judy Gruber, Bob Thompson, and Ricardo Goldman Angel for advice.

Planeamiento Territorial En Madrid

Intento comprender el planeamiento territorial del area metropolitana de Madrid desde el punto de vista de los protagonistas—a partir de los miembros de las instituciones públicas, agentes sociales y económicos, y los ciudadanos organizados—que estan metidos en el desarrollo del territorio de la Región.

Mis intereses principales son dos. Primero, la estructura de la institución, sus procesos de hacer política territorial, y las relaciones entre sus miembros. Segundo, mi enfoque es la manera de desarrollar política territorial: su redacción y concertación entre los miembros de dicha institución. Se entiende como proceso político.

1. ¿Cuál es la tarea más importante que ocupa la organización hoy en día?

2. ¿Cuáles son las otras organizaciones que también están intentado a resolver estos problemas?

3. ¿Hay otras organizaciones aparte de la Consejería de Política Territorial? Por ejemplo, comisiones especiales, comités, o organizaciones temporales que se ha habido compuesto para concertar la política territorial?

4. ¿Si existen, cómo se constituyen?

5. ¿Cuál es el papel de la coordinación en la redacción de política territorial?

5a. ¿Quiénes son los participantes de esta coordinación?

6. ¿Cuáles son los métodos de concertación y coordinación de planeamiento territorial?

7. ¿Cuál es la estructura interinstitucional de concertación y coordinación de la política territorial?

8. ¿Cuáles son los obstáculos que se encuentra la coordinación? ¿Que se precisa para lograr coordinación?

9. ¿Cuál es el papel de los políticos?

10. ¿Cuál es el papel de los ciudadanos, y las asociaciones de vecinos?

11. ¿Quien formula los objetivos de planeamiento?

12. ¿ Cuál es la relación entre los políticos y los profesionales?

13. ¿Por qué participan los agentes sociales y económicos, o sea, por qué no es solamente una operación de instituciones públicas?

14. Se habla de un corporativismo, un estilo propio en España, de hacer política. Si se puede hablar de corporativismo en politíca territorial, ¿cómo funciona?

15. En las reuniones interinstitucionales para concertar propuestas entre organizaciones, ¿cómo se hacen los acuerdos y se resuelven los desacuerdos?

15a. ¿Son los procesos de desarrollar planes y políticas diseñado en total desde el principio? ¿O son revisados *ad hoc* como respuesta a un crisis o cambio de circunstancias? ¿O son revisados cotidianamente por los propios instituciones? ¿En todo caso cuales son los criterios de revisión?

16. ¿Se produce cambios de percepción o imagen, del problema, y de los intereses a lo largo del proceso del desarrollo de las propuestas?

17. ¿Cuándo se crea o utiliza información nueva en el proceso? ¿De dónde viene esta información?

17a. ¿Cuál es el origen de *su* información sobre planeamiento territorial? (Por ejemplo, mesas redondas, jornadas de debate, artículos, libros, periódicos, las noticias, consultores, colegas, documentos del gobierno).

18. ¿Cómo se acuerdan las propuestas—mediante consenso o votación? ¿Cómo se hace exactamente?

19. ¿Cómo se hizo el acto de compatibilización entre la Comunidad de Madrid y los siete municipios del "Gran Sur"?

20. ¿Cuál es la interacción entre la Comunidad de Madrid y sus Estrategias Territoriales/borrador Plan Estratégico Territorial con el Ayuntamiento de Madrid y su Avance del Nuevo Plan General?

21. ¿Dónde reside el poder de hacer nuevas políticas de planeamiento territorial realmente?

22. ¿Cómo se ejerce el poder?, ¿manipulación?, ¿coacción?, ¿negociación?, ¿consenso?, ¿delegación?

23. ¿Qué porcentaje de su tiempo utiliza para el planeamiento territorial? ¿Otros asuntos regionales/metropolitanes? ¿Ha habido un cambio en este porcentaje desde 1980?, ¿1970?

24. ¿Cuáles son los foros (donde se debaten o discuten propuestas y políticas) regionales/metropolitanas mas importantes en cuanto a urbanismo y planeamiento territorial? ¿Cuales funcionan mejor?

25. ¿Cuáles son las arenas (donde se deciden políticas) regionales/metropolitanas más importantes? ¿Cuáles funcionan mejor?

26. ¿Dónde decide usted estos asuntos? Si tiene usted un cambio de opinión, ¿donde ocurre y cómo?

27. ¿Está la institución actual adecuada para la tarea de desarrollar, coordinar, y efectuar política territorial?

28. ¿Está usted satisfecho con el proceso?, ¿con las propuestas y/o las políticas? ¿Hace falta algo o alguien? ¿Hay demasiado de algo?

29. ¿Si hubiera tenido usted el encargo del diseño de la institución (en el sentido mas amplio de la palabra, no solamente el gobierno), como la habriá cambiado?

30. ¿Si hubiera tenido usted el encargo del diseño del proceso, cómo lo habría cambiado?

31. ¿Será el Plan Estratégico Territorial aprobado?

32. ¿Será el proyecto de la Ley del Suelo de la Comunidad de Madrid aprobado? Si lo será, ¿en qué manera va a influir o cambiar la estructura y el proceso de hacer planeamiento territorial?

**Appendix 2: Madrid 1993-1994 Interview and Conference List**

| | |
|---|---|
| 12/1–12/2/1993 | Two day conference on *"El Gran Sur Metropolitano Madrileño: ¿Una propuesta sostenible?"*, sponsored by ARPEGIO, S.A., *Comunidad Autónoma de Madrid* (CAM). |
| 12/9/1993 | Javier Hernández, CAM, Consejería de Política Territorial (CPT), Subdirección General de Arquitectura. |
| 12/13–12/14/1993 | Two day conference on *"Espacio Social y Periferia Urbana"*, sponsored by la Oficina de Coordinación y Actuaciones Preferentes (OCAP), CAM. |
| 12/20/1993 | Pedro García Alarcó, Jefe del Area, Ayuntamiento de Madrid, Oficina Municipal del Plan (OMP). |
| 12/20/1993 | Asociación Ecologista de Defensa de la Naturaleza (AEDENAT), a nationwide ecological organization, Madrid section weekly meeting of the Comisión de Urbanismo. |
| 12/21/1993 | María Roces, Responsable de Urbanismo y Vivienda, Federación Regional de Asociaciones de Vecinos (FRAV). |
| 12/22/1993 | Professor Jesús Leal, sociologist specializing in housing and regional planning, Universidad Complutense de Madrid. |
| 1/17/1994 | AEDENAT, weekly meeting of Comisión de Urbanismo. |
| 1/17/1994 | Mariano García Bachiller, jefe de sección de obras, Junta del distrito de Chamberí, Ayuntamiento de Madrid. |
| 1/25/1994 | Guadalupe Castro Lenza, administrative coordinator of AEDENAT. |
| 1/31/1994 | AEDENAT, weekly meeting of Comisión de Urbanismo. |
| 3/1/1994 | FRAV-sponsored jornada de debate *"Madrid a Debate"* re. Avance del Nuevo Plan General de Madrid. |
| 3/7/1994 | AEDENAT, attended quarterly Assembly. |
| 3/8/1994 | Alberto Leboreiro, subdirector general de la dirección general de planificación urbanística y concertación, CPT, CAM. |

| | |
|---|---|
| 3/8/1994 | Emilio Miralles, Viceconsejero de Transportes, CAM. |
| 3/9/1994 | Félix Arias, Director Técnico, MOPTMA (Ministerio de Obras Públicas, Transportes y Medio Ambiente). He worked previously with COPLACO, the Ayuntamiento de Madrid, and the Comunidad Autónoma de Madrid's Consejería de Política Territorial. |
| 3/11/1994 | Eduardo Mangada, Ex Consejero de CPT, CAM. |
| 3/14/1994 | Jesús Morón, Ex Viceconsejero de CPT, CAM. |
| 3/15/1994 | Ignacio Quintana, Director de Proyecto, ARPEGIO, S.A. |
| 3/15/1994 | Francisco López, Director del Servicio de Apoyo y Gestión al Planeamiento, Dirección General de Urbanismo, CPT, CAM. |
| 3/17/1994 | Pedro García Alarcó, Jefe del Area, OMP, Ayuntamiento de Madrid. |
| 3/23/1994 | Félix Arias, MOPTMA. |
| 3/25/1994 | Fernando de Terán, Catédratico de Urbanismo, Universidad Politécnica de Madrid. |
| 3/24/1994 | José María de la Riva, Secretario General del Grupo Socialista, Ayuntamiento de Madrid. |
| 3/24/1994 | Ignacio Solana, Viceconsejero de Presidencia, CAM. |
| 3/25/1994 | Pedro García Alarcó, OMP, Ayuntamiento de Madrid. |
| 3/25/1994 | Vicente Pérez, Director Tecnico, FRAV. |
| 3/25/1994 | Inés Sánchez, ARPEGIO, S. A. |
| 3/28/1994 | Jesús Neira, Concejal de Urbanismo, Municipio de Getafe. |
| 3/28/1994 | Ramón Fernández Duran, author, AEDENAT member, former staff member of COPLACO and CPT, CAM. |
| 3/28/1994 | Ignacio Solana, Viceconsejero de Presidencia. |

3/29/1994    José Ignacio Gómez, Consejero Técnico del Gabinete del Gerente, OMP, Ayuntamiento de Madrid.

3/29/1994    Jesús Leal, Profesor de Sociología de la Universidad Complutense.

3/29/1994    Augustin Herrero, Director de Carreteras, Consejería de Transportes, CAM.

3/30/1994    Javier Hernández, CAM, CPT.

7/6/1994    José María Ezquiaga, Director General de Planificación y Concertación Urbanística, CPT, CAM.

7/7/1994    Alberto Leboreiro, Sub-Director General de Planificación y Concertación Urbanística, CPT, CAM.

7/7/1994    Javier Echenagusía, Editor, *Alfoz*.

7/7/1994    Jesús Leal, Profesor de Sociología, Universidad Complutense de Madrid.

9/16/1994    Félix Arias, MOPTMA.

9/20/1994    Ignacio Solana, CAM.

9/20/1994    Javier Echenagusía, Editor, *Alfoz*.

**Appendix 3: Chronology of Planning in Madrid Since 1850**

| | |
|---|---|
| 1833 | Province of Madrid appears with the geographic configuration it has today. |
| 1854 | Demolition of city walls. |
| 1859 | *Plan del Ensanche* (Expansion) of the engineer Carlos de María Castro. |
| 1860 | Royal Decree adopts *Plan del Ensanche* de Madrid. |
| 1868 | Ayuntamiento publishes the Angel Fernández de los Ríos book *El Futuro Madrid*. |
| 1876 | *Ley General de 22 de diciembre de Ensanche de Poblaciones.* |
| 1877 | *Reglamento de 19 de febrero* implementing the 1876 law. |
| 1892 | *Ley de 26 de julio de Ensanche para las poblaciones de Madrid y Barcelona.* |
| 1895 | *Ley de 18 de marzo para el Saneamiento, Reforma y Ensanche Interior de las poblaciones de 30,000 o más almas.* |
| 1895 | *Comisión Especial para la Reforma del Suelo y Subsuelo de Madrid.* |
| 1905 | *Junta Consultiva* formed in the city government of Madrid. |
| 1907 | *Sección de la Dirección de Vias Públicas, Estudios de urbanismo* created. |
| 1909 | *Proyecto para la urbanización del extrarradio*, known as the Nuñez Granés Plan after its author the engineer Pedro Nuñez Granés. Expansion of existing *ensanche*. |
| 1916 | Nuñez Granés proyecto approved, never implemented. Implementation was pending a ley de urbanización which never was adopted. |
| 1924 | *Extensión General de Madrid* a new plan proposed by Nuñez Granés, which was never adopted nor implemented. |
| 1924 | *Estatuto Municipal de 8 de mayo* approved, to deal with the planning within city limits only, in response to article in *Arquitectura* (Madrid) |

of February 1924 by J.L. Sallaberry, P. Aranda, J. Lorite, J. Garcáa Cascales *"Plan General de Extensión de Madrid y su distribución en zonas. Applicación y modificaciones a establecer en el proyecto para urbanización extrarradio"*. This article called for a *Ley Especial*.

1928     *Sección de Urbanismo del Ayuntamiento de Madrid* created.

1929     The city published the *Plan General de Extensión* which was never adopted.

1929     International Competition for the *"reforma del interior y urbanización del extrarradio"* of Madrid. *Información Sobre la Ciudad*, Ayuntamiento de Madrid, information for competition.

1929     Zuazo-Jansen *esquema* (scheme) submitted to international competition, one of 12 entries. Jury declared competition void, no entrant fulfilled mandatory requirements, did not award any prizes. Only entry to receive mention by jury: Memoria del Proyecto Zuazo-Jansen, whose official title is *Anteproyecto del trazado viario y urbanización de Madrid*. Secundino Zuazo, Spanish (Madrid) and Herman Jansen, German planner. Moneo (1967) called the project a "moral winner" which "distinguishes itself, above all, for the clarity with which it planned" for the future growth of Madrid. It projected future development to the north: *Paseo de la Castellana, Nuevos Ministerios*, etc.

1931     *Plan General de Extensión*, Oficina Técnica Municipal, *Informe sobre el plan general de extensión de 1931*, José de Lorite Kramer, *arquitecto, Gerente de los servicios técnicos municipales*, published 1932 by the *Ayuntamiento de Madrid*.

1931     *Plan General de Extensión: Estudio para el Plan Regional*, published by *Oficina de Urbanización*.

1931     Beginning of second republic, for first time Madrid was formally declared as the capital of Spain.

1933     *Plan General de Extensión* approved by the *Ministerio de Gobernación* for just the portion within the city limits, because the Municipal Charter did not enable supra-municipal planning.

1937     Creation of the *Comité de Reforma, Reconstrucción y Saneamiento de Madrid* (CRRSM).

1938     *Servicio Nacional de Regiones Devastadas* created.

1939    Dirección General de Regiones Devastadas created.

1939    *Plan Regional de 1939, Comité de Reforma, Reconstrucción y Saneamiento de Madrid (CRRSM), Julian Besteiro, Presidente.* Influenced by regional planning movement of era, particularly Britain (Greater London Regional Planning Committee), and by legal-administrative framework of regional planning in Paris.

1939    *Esquema y Bases para Desarrollo del Plan Regional de Madrid*, CRRSM.

1939    *Plan General de Ordenación y Extensión de Madrid*, José Paz Maroto. Maroto was involved in the 1929 competition.

1939    *Orden de 27 de abril* named the *Junta de Reconstrucción de Madrid y su Provincia*, to prepare a plan for Madrid and environs.

1939    *Orden de 7 de octubre* constituting the *Junta de Reconstrucción de Madrid*, part of *Dirección General de Regiones Devastadas. Oficina Técnica de la Junta*, headed by Pedro Bidagor.

1939    *Dirección General de Arquitectura* created in the Ministerio de Gobernación. *Sección de Urbanismo* created in *Dirección General de Arquitectura*, Pedro Bidagor named head.

1941    *Plan General de Ordenación Urbana* (Bidagor Plan) printed. Bidagor inspired by 1929 Zuazo Proposal.

1942    *Memoria del Plan de 1941* made public at exposition in Royal Palace. *Junta de Reconstrucción* publishes *Plan General de Ordenación Urbana de Madrid y Sus Alrededores.*

1944    *Ley de Bases de 25 de noviembre para la Ordenación Urbana de Madrid y sus Alrededores.*

1946    *Ley Especial de 1 de marzo* approved *Plan General de Ordenación Urbana.* Created *Comisaría General para la Ordenación Urbana de Madrid y sus Alrededores.* Also created national *Comisión de Urbanismo.* First Commissioner Pedro Muruguza (one year), second Commissioner Francisco Moreno.

1947    *Reglamento de 17 de octubre*, implementing the 1946 law.

1948     *Municipio de Madrid* begins multi-year program to expand to its current size. It ends in 1954 after the annexation of 12 bordering towns, increasing in area from nearly 70 square kilometers to more than 600 square kilometers.

1949     *Jefatura Nacional de Urbanismo* created by Decreto de 22 de julio.

1951     *Decreto de 4 de enero: la Comisión de Urbanismo de Madrid se hace cargo del Plan General de la Ordenación Urbana de la Provincia de Madrid.*

1951     First draft of the national planning law, the *ley de regimen del suelo y ordenación urbana* (which was adopted in 1956).

1956     *Ley de 12 de mayo del Regimen del Suelo y Ordenación Urbana.*

1956     *Decreto de 25 de febrero creates Ministerio de la Vivienda* (Ministry of Housing), *Dirección General de Arquitectura y Urbanismo* part of ministry.

1956     *Consejo Nacional de Urbanismo*, and its permanent staff arm the *Comisión Nacional de Urbanismo* created.

1957     *Plan de Urgencia Social de Madrid.*

1957     *Decreto of 3 de octubre* creates "*Consejos Provinciales de Urbanismo, Arquitectura y Vivienda*" in each province, replacing "*Comisiones Provinciales de Urbanismo*".

1957     *Dirección General de Urbanismo* created, split off from the *Dirección General de Arquitectura y Urbanismo* in the *Ministerio de la Vivienda.*

1959     *Plan de Estabilización*, national economic development plan which concentrated industry in three regions: Madrid, Barcelona, Bilbao.

1961     Fifteen years after the official adoption (1946) of the Bidagor plan, a revision was begun to prepare a plan of the metropolitan area.

1961     *La Comisaría General para la Ordenación Urbana de Madrid y sus Alrededores* publishes *Plan General de Ordenación Urbana del Area Metropolitana de Madrid.*

1961     First *Plan Nacional de Vivienda*, National Housing Plan.

1961    *Plan de Absorción de Chabolas*, which created Unidad Vecinal de Absorción (UVA). The UVAs were called "*chabolismo oficial*" (official shanty town creation) and "campos de concentración" (concentration Camps). These two 1961 housing plans were contradictory.

1963    *Ley 121/1963 de 2 de diciembre* adopted *Plan General de Ordenación Urbana del Area Metropolitana de Madrid*. Rafael Moneo: 1963 plan a "weak imitation without conviction of 1941 Plan", beginning of a grey period in city planning.

1964    *Decreto 3088/1964 de 28 de septiembre*, adopted regulations implementing 1963 *Plan General del Area Metropolitana*. One area was designated: the *Area Metropolitana* comprised of 23 municipalities, and two organizations were created: the *Comisión de Planeamiento y Coordinación del Area Metropolitana de Madrid* (COPLACO), and the *Gerencia Municipal de Urbanismo* for the city of Madrid.

1971    Central government publishes *III Plan del Desarrollo*.

1972    COPLACO publishes *Avance del Esquema Director*, never adopted.

1972    *Decreto 2432/1972 de 18 de agosto, bases para concursos de ejecución de urbanizaciones en Madrid (Urbanismo Concertado).*

1975    *Ley de 2 de mayo Sobre Régimen del Suelo y Ordenación Urbana*, revising national planning law of 1956.

1975    COPLACO *Plan Especial de Protección del Medio Físico de la Provincia de Madrid*. A joint venture with INCONA, *Instituto Nacional de la Conservación de la Naturaleza*.

1975    COPLACO *Plan Especial del Grandes Equipamientos Comerciales de la Provincia de Madrid.*

1975    COPLACO *Plan Especial de Infraestructura de Transportes de la Provincia de Madrid.*

1976    COPLACO *Plan Especial de Infraestructuras Básicas de la Provincia de Madrid.*

1976    *Real Decreto 1346/1976 de 9 de abril Texto Refundido de la Ley sobre Régimen del Suelo y Ordenación Urbana*, revising 1975 national planning law.

1977     *Ministerio de Obras Públicas y Urbanismo* created, combining existing *Ministerio de Obras Públicas, Ministerio de la Vivienda,* and *Dirección General de Acción Territorial y Medio Ambiente.*

1977     National democratic institutions established.

1978     Constitution of Spain.

1978     *Real Decreto 2159/1978 de 23 de junio,* regulations implementing 1976 revision to the national ley del suelo.

1978     COPLACO publishes *Normas de Planeamiento para la Provincia de Madrid: Documento de Trabajo,* internal working document. Normas never adopted.

1978     COPLACO publishes *¿Qué Hacer con Madrid?*

1978     COPLACO publishes *Problemas y Perspectivas del Area Metropolitana de Madrid.* Looked for citizen input, got it.

1978     COPLACO starts publishing *Programas de Actuación Inmediatas* (PAIs).

1979     First local democratic elections.

1980     *Ayuntamiento de Madrid* publishes *Plan Especial de la Villa de Madrid.*

1980     COPLACO publishes *Informe sobre Ordenación del Territorio en el area metropolitana de Madrid.*

1980     *Ley-Decreto 11/1980 de 28 de septiembre, Revisión del Plan General de Ordenación Urbana del Area Metropolitana.* Metropolitan plan "will be realized through the elaboration and writing of [local] General Plans".

1981     COPLACO publishes *Directrices de Planeamiento Territorial Urbanístico para la Revisión del Plan General del Area Metropolitana de Madrid.*

1983     *Comunidad Autónoma de Madrid* adopts its constitution, *Ley Organica 3/1983 de 25 de febrero Estatuto de Autónomia de la Comunidad de Madrid.*

1983    *Comunidad Autónoma de Madrid* (CAM) created *Consejería de Ordenación Territorial, Medio Ambiente y Vivienda* (COTMAV) and *Comisión de Urbanismo y Medio Ambiente de Madrid*, the latter presided by the head of COTMAV.

1984    CAM adopts two laws governing planning. *Ley 10/1984 de 30 de mayo Ordenación Territorial de la Comunidad de Madrid*, and *Ley 4/1984 de 10 de febrero Medidas de Disciplina Urbanística*.

1985    COTMAV publishes *Directrices de Ordenación Territorial: Documento Previo*.

1986    Created *Oficina de Planeamiento Territorial* (OPT) within COTMAV.

1987    CAM combined COTMAV and the *Consejería de Obras Públicas y Transportes* into *Consejería de Política Territorial*, with more than half of CAM budget. Known as the "Superconsejería".

1988    *Comisión de Urbanismo y Medio Ambiente* split into two: *Comisión de Urbanismo* and *Agencia de Medio Ambiente*.

1988    *Consejería de Política Territorial* publishes *Directrices de Ordenación del Territorio: Bases*.

1991    CAM split *Consejería de Política Territorial* into a smaller *Consejería de Política Territorial* and *Consejería de Transportes*, and abolished the OPT when political changes caused Eduardo Mangada (Consejero of CPT) and Félix Arias (head of OPT) to resign.

1991    *Created Consejería de Cooperación* (from parts of *Consejería de Agricultura* and *Oficina de Cooperación*) which subsumed the *Agencia de Medio Ambiente*.

1992    *Real Decreto-Ley 11/992 de 26 de junio Texto Refundido [revised] sobre Régimen de Suelo y Ordenación Urbana*.

1994    CAM publishes and the *Consejo de Gobierno* approves *Proyecto de Ley de Medidas de Política Territorial, Suelo y Urbanismo de la Comunidad de Madrid*.

# References

Abellan, J.L. 1994. España invertebrada: Estado de la cuestion, in *El País*, February 1.

Abercrombie, P. 1911. Town planning in greater London: The necessity for cooperation, in *Town Planning Review*, 2, 261–80.

Ackoff, R. 1974. *Redesigning the Future: A System's Approach to Societal Problems*. New York: Wiley.

Adams, T. 1935. *Outline of Town and City Planning*. New York: Russell Sage.

Adizes, I. 1979. Organizational passages: diagnosing and treating life cycle problems in organization, in *Organizational Dynamics*, 9, 3–25.

Agnew, J. 1987. *Place and Politics: The Geographic Mediation of State and Society*. Boston: Allen and Unwin.

Aguilar, S. 1991. *Políticas de control y diseños institucionales en España y Alemania*. Madrid: Estudios Avanzadas en Ciencias Sociales, Working Paper 29.

Alabart, A., García, S. and Giner, S., eds 1994. *Clase, Poder y Ciudadanía*. Madrid: Siglo Veintiuno.

Albrechts, L. 1999. Planners as catalysts and initiators of change, in *European Planning Studies*, 7(5), 587–603.

Albrechts, L., Alden, J. and de Rosa Pires, A., eds 2001. *The Changing Institutional Landscape of Planning*. Aldershot: Ashgate.

Albrechts, L., Healey, P. and Kunzmann, K. 2003. Strategic spatial planning and regional governance in Europe, in *Journal of the American Planning Association*, 69(2), 113–29.

Alexander, C. 1964. *Notes on the Synthesis of Form*. Cambridge, MA: Harvard University Press.

Alexander, C. 1965a. A city is not a tree, Part I, in *Architectural Forum*, 122(1), 58–62.

Alexander, C. 1965b. A city is not a tree, Part II, in *Architectural Forum*, 122(2), 58–62.

Alexander, E. 1984. After rationality, what?, in *Journal of the American Planning Association*, 50(1), 62–9.

Alexander, E. 1993. Interorganizational coordination: Theory and practice, in *Journal of Planning Literature*, 7(4), 328–43.

Alinsky, S. 1969 [1947]. *Reveille for Radicals*, 2nd Edition. New York: Vintage Books.

Allison, G. 1971. *The Essence of Decision: Explaining the Cuban Missile Crisis*. Boston: Little Brown.

Allport, A. 1989. Visual attention, in M. Posner, ed. *Foundations of Cognitive Science*. Cambridge, MA: MIT Press.

Alpers, S. 1983. *The Art of Describing*. Chicago: University of Chicago Press.

Altshuler, A. 1965a. *The City Planning Process: A Political Analysis*. Ithaca, NY: Cornell University Press.

Altshuler, A. 1965b. The goals of comprehensive planning, in *Journal of the American Institute of Planners*, 186–97.

Alvar Ezquerra, A. 1989. *El Nacimiento de Una Capital Europea: Madrid entre 1561 y 1606*. Madrid: Turner Libros.

Anderson, B. 1983. *Imagined Communities: Reflections on the Origins and Spread of Nationalism*. London: Verso.

Ansell, C. 1997. Symbolic networks: The realignment of the French working class 1887–1894, in *American Journal of Sociology*, 103(2), 359–90.

Angelet, J. 1987. La Corporación Metropolitana de Barcelona en la encrucijada, in *Urbanismo*, 8(1), 32–8.

Anonymous, eds (nd). *Crisis Social de la Ciudad*. Madrid: Cidur Alfoz.

Anonymous, 1911. Datos Acerca la Ciudad Lineal, in *Madrid: Compania Madrileña de Urbanización*.

Área Metropolitana de Barcelona. 1991. *Memòria d'actuacions: 1987–1991*. Barcelona: Mancomunitat de Municipis del Área Metropolitana de Barcelona.

Área Metropolitana de Barcelona. 1995. *Memòria d'actuacions: 1991–1995*. Barcelona: Mancomunitat de Municipis del Área Metropolitana de Barcelona.

Área de Urbanismo y Ordenación Territorial. 1982. *Documentación Urbanística: Documentos para la Revisión del Plan General del Área Metropolitana de Madrid*. Six volumes. Madrid: Diputación de Madrid.

Arendt, H. 1958. *The Human Condition*. Chicago: University of Chicago Press.

Arendt, H. 1963. *On Revolution*. New York: Viking Press.

Arendt, H. 1972. On violence, in *Crisis of the Republic*. New York: Harcourt Brace Jovanovich.

Argyris, C. and Schön, D. 1978. *Organizational Learning: A Theory of Action Perspective*. Reading, MA: Addison-Wesley.

Argyris, C. 1982. *Reasoning, Learning, and Action: Individual and Organizational Double Loop Learning*. San Francisco: Jossey-Bass.

Argyris, C. 1990. *Overcoming Organizational Defenses*. Boston: Allyn and Unwin.

Argyris, C. 1993. *Knowledge for Action: A Guide to Overcoming Barriers to Organizational Change*. San Francisco: Jossey-Bass.

Arias, F. and Gago, V. 1987. Las estrategias territoriales de ámbito sub-regional, in *Urbanismo*, 8, 45–62.

Arias, F. 1988. Ciudad del sur, in *Alfoz*, 56, 23–6.

Aristotle. 1943. *Politics*. trans. Jowett, B. New York: Random House.

Arnheim, R. 1969. *Visual Thinking*. Berkeley: University of California Press.

ARPEGIO, S.A., no date. *Nuevo Sur Metropolitano: Un Proyecto para la Refundación del Sur*. Madrid: ARPEGIO.

ARPEGIO, S.A. no date. Arroyo Culebro: Programa de actuación urbanística, in brochure. Madrid: ARPEGIO.

ARPEGIO, S.A. no date (1993). *Madrid Gran Sur Metropolitano: Territorio, Desarrollo Regional y Medio Ambiente*. Madrid: Comunidad de Madrid. Two versions: one in Spanish, one in Spanish and English.

ARPEGIO, S.A. 1993. *Madrid Gran Sur Metropolitano: Territorio, Desarrollo Regional y Medio Ambiente*. Madrid: Comunidad de Madrid.

ARPEGIO, S.A. 1994. *1993 Annual Report*. Madrid: Comunidad de Madrid.

Axelrod, R. 1984. *The Evolution of Cooperation*. New York: Basic Books.

Ayuntamiento de Barcelona, no date. *Barcelona Año 2000: Estudio de Ordenación Urbana*. Barcelona: Ayuntamiento de Barcelona.

Ayuntamiento de Madrid. 1910. *Proyecto para la urbanización del extrarradio de dicha villa*. Madrid: Imprenta Municipal.

Ayuntamiento de Madrid. 1925. *Ordenanzas Municipales de la Villa de Madrid*. Madrid: Imprenta de Madrid.

Ayuntamiento de Madrid. 1929a. *Bases: Concurso Urbanístico de Anteproyectos para la Urbanización del Extrarradio y Estudio de la Reforma Interior y de la Extensión de la Ciudad*. Madrid: Imprenta Municipal.

Ayuntamiento de Madrid. 1929b. *Información de la Ciudad*. Madrid: Artes Gráficas Municipales.

Bache, I. and Flinders, M. eds 2004. *Multi-level Governance*. Oxford: Oxford University Press.

Bachelard, G. 1969 [1957]. *The Poetics of Space*. Boston: Beacon Press.

Bachrach, P. and Baraty, M. 1962. Two faces of power, in *American Political Science Review*, 56, 451–60.

Bacon, E. 1967. *Design of Cities*. New York: Viking Press.

Bak, P., Chen, K. and Creutz, M. 1989. Self-organized criticality and the "game of life", in *Nature*, 342, 780–2.

Bakhtin, M.M. 1981. *The Dialogic Imagination*, edited by Holquist, M. trans. Emerson, C. and Holquist, M. Austin: University of Texas Press.

Balducci, A. 2000. Le nuove politiche della *governance* urbana [The new policies of urban governance], in *Territorio*, 13, 7–15.

Ball, T. 1992 [1988]. New faces of power, in T. Wartenberg, ed. *Rethinking Power*. Albany, NY: SUNY Press.

Banerjee, T. 1971. Urban experience and the development of the city image, Ph.D. dissertation, Department of Urban Studies and Planning, MIT.

Banerjee, R. and Southworth, M., eds 1990. *City Sense and City Design: Writings and Projects of Kevin Lynch*. Cambridge, MA: MIT Press.

Banfield, E. 1961a. *Urban Government: A Reader in Politics and Administration*. New York: The Free Press.

Banfield, E. 1961b. *Political Influence: A New Theory of Urban Politics*. New York: The Free Press.

Barber, B. 1984. *Strong Democracy: Participatory Politics for a New Age*. Berkeley: University of California Press.

Barnard, C. 1938. *The Functions of the Executive*. Cambridge, MA: Harvard University Press.

Barnett, J. 2003. *Redesigning Cities: Principles, Practices, Implementation*. Chicago: Planner's Press.

Bateson, G. 1972. *Steps to an Ecology of Mind*. New York: Ballantine Books.

Bateson, G. 1979. *Mind and Nature: A Necessary Unity*. New York: Dutton.

Baudrillard, J. 1981 [1972]. *For a Critique of the Political Economy of the Sign*, translated with an introduction by Charles Levin. St. Louis: Telos Press.

Beckhard, R. and Harris, R. 1977. *Managing Complex Change*. Reading, MA: Addison-Wesley.

Bellah, R., Madsen, R., Sullivan, W., Swidler, A. and Tipton, S. 1985. *Habits of the Heart*. Berkeley: University of California Press.

Bellah, R., Madsen, R., Sullivan, W., Swidler, A. and Tipton, S. 1991. *The Good Society*. New York: Alfred Knopf.

Bendix, R. 1964. *Nation Building and Citizenship*. New York: Wiley.

Bendor, J. and Hammond, T. 1992. Rethinking Allison's models, in *American Political Science Review*, 86(2), 301–22.

Benevolo, L. 1967. *The Origins of Modern Town Planning*. Cambridge, MA: MIT Press.

Benson, K. 1975. The interorganizational network as political economy, in *Administrative Science Quarterly*, 20, 229–49.

Benveniste, G. 1983. *Bureaucracy*, 2nd Edition. San Francisco: Boyd and Fraser.

Benveniste, G. 1987. *Professionalizing the Organization: Reducing Bureaucracy to Enhance Professionalization*. San Francisco: Jossey-Bass.

Benveniste, G. 1989. *Mastering the Politics of Planning: Crafting Credible Plans and Policies that Make a Difference*. San Francisco: Jossey-Bass.

Berger, P. and Luckmann, T. 1966. *The Social Construction of Reality: A Treatise in the Sociology of Knowledge*. New York: Doubleday.

Berger, S., ed. 1981. *Organizing Interests in Western Europe: Pluralism. Corporatism and the Transformation of Politics*. Cambridge: Cambridge University Press.

Bermeo, N. 1994. Sacrifice, sequence, and strength in successful dual transitions: lessons from Spain, in *Journal of Politics*, 56(3), 601–27.

Bernstein, R. 1991. *The Ethical-Political Horizons of Modernity/Postmodernity*. Cambridge, MA: MIT Press.

Bidagor, P. 1964. Situación general del urbanismo en España, in *Arquitectura*, 62.

Bidagor, P. 1969. La Coyuntura actual del urbanismo en España, in *Revista de Estudios de la Vida Local*, 162.

Blanco, H. 1989. *Pragmatism: A Conceptual Framework for Planning*, Ph.D. Dissertation. Berkeley: University of California.

Blasé, M. 1973. *Institution Building: A Sourcebook*. Washington DC: U.S. AID.

Blau, P. 1964. *Exchange and Power in Social Life*. New York: Wiley.

Blyth, M. 2002. *Great Transformations: Economic Ideas and Institutional Change in the Twentieth Century.* Cambridge: Cambridge University Press.

Bohigas, O. 1985. *Reconstrucciò de Barcelona.* Barcelona: Ediciones 62.

Bohigas, O. 1989a. *Desde los Años Inciertos.* Barcelona: Editorial Anagrama.

Bohigas, O. 1989b. *Combat D'Incertaeses: Dietari de Records.* Vol. I. Barcelona: Ediciones 62.

Bohigas, O. 1992. *Dit o Fet: Dietari de Records.* Vol. II. Barcelona: Ediciones 62.

Bolan, R. 1980. The Practitioner as theorist: the phenomenology of the professional episode, in *Journal of the American Planning Association*, 46(3), 261–74.

Bolan, R. 1991. Urban planning in shared power settings, in J. Bryson and R. Einsweiler, eds *Shared Power: What is it? How Does it Work? How Can We Make it Better?.* Lanham, MD: University Press of America.

Bolan, R. 1992. Planning and institutional design, in *Planning Theory*, 516, 7–34.

Bolan, R. 1994. Planning and the Dialectics of Institutional Design, paper presented at the annual conference of the Association of Collegiate Schools of Planning, Pheonix, Arizona.

Bollens, S. 1993. Restructuring land use governance, in *Journal of Planning Literature*, 7(3), 211–26.

Boorstin, D. 1980 [1962]. *The Image: or, What Happened to the American Dream.* New York: Atheneum.

Borges, J.L. 1971 [1941]. El jardín de senderos que se bifurcan, in *Ficciones.* Madrid: Alianza.

Borja, J. 1977. Urban movements in Spain, in M. Harloe, ed. *Captive Cities.* Chicester: Wiley.

Borja, J., Castells, M., Dorado, R. and Quintana, I., eds 1990. *Las Grandes Ciudades en la Decada de los Noventa.* Madrid: Editorial Sistema.

Bosselman, F. and Callies, D. 1971. *The Quiet Revolution in Land Use Control.* Washington DC: Government Printing Office.

Bosselman, F., Feurer, D. and Siemon, C. 1976. *The Permit Explosion: Coordination of the Revolution.* Washington DC: The Urban Land Institute.

Boulding, K. 1956. *The Image: Knowledge in Life and Society.* Ann Arbor: University of Michigan Press.

Boulding, K. 1970. *Primer on Social Dynamics.* New York: Free Press.

Bourdieu, P. 1977 [1972]. *Outline of a Theory of Practice, New York.* Cambridge: Cambridge University Press.

Bourdieu, P. 1986. The forms of capital, in J. Richardson, ed. *Handbook of Theory and Research for the Sociology of Education.* New York: Greenwood Press.

Bourdieu, P. 1990. *The Logic of Practice.* Stanford: Stanford University Press.

Bourdieu, P. 1991 [1982]. *Language and Symbolic Power*, edited with an introduction by John Thompson, trans. by Gino Raymond and Matthew Adamson. Cambridge: Harvard University Press.

Boyer, C. 1983. *Dreaming the Rational City: The Myth of American City Planning.* Cambridge, MA: MIT Press.

Boyer, C. 1994. *The City of Collective Memory: Its Historical Imagery and Architectural Entertainments.* Cambridge, MA: MIT Press.

Bozeman, B. 1987. *All Organizations Are Public: Bridging Public and Private Organization Theories.* San Francisco: Jossey Bass.

Brennan, G. 1943. *The Spanish Labyrinth.* London: Macmillan.

Brenner, N. 1999. Globalisation as reterritorialisation: The re-scaling of urban governance in the European Union, in *Urban Studies*, 36(3), 431–51.

Brightman, R. 1995. Forget culture: Replacement, transcendence, relexification, in *Cultural Anthropology*, 10(4), 509–46.

Brooks, D. 1994. *The Unity of the Mind.* New York: Saint Martin's Press.

Brower, D., Godschalk, D. and Porter, D. 1989. *Understanding Growth Management: Critical Issues and a Research Agenda.* Washington DC: Urban Land Institute.

Bryson, J. and Einsweiler, R., eds 1991. *Shared Power: What is it? How Does it Work? How Can We Make it Better?* Lanham, MD: University Press of America.

Bryson, J. and Crosby, B. 1992. *Leadership for the Common Good: Tackling Public Problems in a Shared Power World.* San Francisco: Jossey Bass.

Buchanan, J. and Tullock, G. 1965. *The Calculus of Consent: Logical Foundations of Constitutional Democracy.* Ann Arbor: University of Michigan Press.

Burns, L. and Friedmann, J., eds 1985. *The Art of Planning: Selected Essays of Harvey S. Perloff.* New York: Plenum Press.

Calthorpe, P. 1993. *The Next American Metropolis: Ecology, Community, and the American Dream.* New York: Princeton Architectural Press.

Calvino, I. 1974 [1972]. *Invisible Cities.* New York: Harcourt Brace and Co.

Cameron, K.S. and Whetten, D.A. 1981. Perceptions of organizational effectiveness over organizational life cycles, in *Administrative Science Quarterly*, 26, 525–44.

Campbell, H. 2003. Planning: An idea of value, in *Town Planning Review*, 73(3), 271–88.

Campos Venuti, G. 1978. *Urbanistica e Austerita.* Milan: Feltrinelli.

Campos Venuti, G. 1991. *L'urbanistica Riformista: Antologia di Scritti, Lezioni. e Piani*, Oliva, F., ed. Milan: Etaslibri.

Carson, R. 1962. *Silent Spring.* Boston: Houghton Mifflin.

Casquiero, J. 1993. Ocho municipios del sur revisan su urbanismo para regenerar el paisaje, in *El País*, 10 May.

Casquiero, J. 1994. El pulmón del sur, in *El País*, April 4.

Castells, M. 1969. Vers une théorie sociologique de la planification urbaine, in *Sociologie du Travail*, 11, 413–43.

Castells, M. 1971a (1968). Hay una sociología urbana?, in M. Castells, *Problemas de Investigación en Sociología Urbana.* Madrid: Siglo XXI de España Editores, 17–44.

Castells, M. 1971b. Hacia una teoría sociológica de la planificación urbana, in M. Castells, *Problemas de Investigación en Sociología Urbana*. Madrid: Siglo XXI de España Editores, 195–233.

Castells, M. 1977a. *Ciudad, Democracia, Socialismo: La Experiencia de las Asociaciones de vecinos de Madrid*. Madrid: Siglo XXI.

Castells, M. 1977b (1972). *The Urban Question*. Cambridge, MA: MIT Press.

Castells, M. 1981. *Crisis Urbana y Cambio Social*. Madrid: Siglo XXI Editores.

Castells, M. 1983. *The City and the Grassroots*. Berkeley: University of California Press.

Castells, M. 1984. Planeamiento urbano y gestión municipal: Madrid, 1979–1982, in *Ciudad y Territorio*, 59, 13–40.

Castells, M. 1989. *The Informational City: Information Technology. Economic Restructuring and the Urban–Regional Process*. Cambridge, MA: Basil Blackwell.

Castells, M. 2000. *Towards a Network Society*, 2nd Edition. Malden, MA: Blackwell.

Castells, M. 2004. *The Power of Identity*, 2nd Edition. Malden, MA: Blackwell.

Castells, M. and Hall, P. 1994. *TechnoPoles of the World: The Making of Twenty-first Century Industrial Complexes*. London: Routledge.

Castles, F. 1989. *The Comparative History of Public Policy*. New York: Oxford University Press.

Castro, C.M. 1860a. *Anteproyecto del Ensanche de Madrid*. Madrid: Ayuntamiento de Madrid.

Castro, C.M. 1860b. *Memoria descriptiva del anteproyecto de ensanche de Madrid*, Madrid, Imprenta de D. José de la Peña, Reprinted in a new edition by the *Colegio Oficial de Arquitectos de Madrid*, 1978, with an introduction by Antonio Bonet Correa.

Cawson, A., ed. 1985. *Organized Interests and the State: Studies in Meso-Corporatism*. Beverly Hills: Sage.

Cerdà, I. 1978 [1867]. *Teoría General de la Urbanización y Aplicación de sus Principios y Doctrinas a la Reforma y Ensanche de Barcelona*. Madrid: Imprenta Española.

Chadwick, G. 1971. *A Systems View of Planning: Towards a Theory of the Urban and Regional Planning Process*. Oxford: Pergamon.

Chamorro, E. 1986. *Enrique Tierno: El Alcalde*. Madrid: Cambio 16.

Chandler, A. 1977. *The Visible Hand: The Managerial Revolution in American Business*. Cambridge, MA: Harvard University Press.

Chandler, A. 1990. *Scale and Scope: The Dynamics of Industrial Capitalism*. Cambridge, MA: Harvard University Press.

Cheema, G. and Rondinelli, D., eds 2007. *Decentralizing Governance: Emerging Concepts and Practices*. Cambridge, MA: JFK School, Harvard University and Washington, DC: Brookings Institution Press.

Chisholm, D. 1989. *Coordination Without Hierarchy: Informal Structures in Multi-Organizational Systems*. Berkeley: University of California Press.

Choay, F. 1965. *L'urbanisme: Utopies et Réalités, Une Anthologie*. Paris: Seuil.
Choay, F. 1996 [1980]. *The Rule and the Model: On the Theory of Architecture and Urbanism*. Cambridge, MA: MIT Press.
Chomsky, N. 1968. *Language and Mind*. New York: Harcourt, Brace and World.
Chomsky, N. 1986. *Knowledge and Language: Its Nature, Origins and Use*. New York: Praeger.
Chomsky, N. 1995. Language and nature, in *Mind*, 104, 413, 1–61.
Christensen, K. 1999. *Cities and Complexity: Making Intergovernmental Decisions*. Newbury Park, CA: Sage.
Clausewitz, C.V. 1968. *On War*, trans. Col. J.J. Graham. London: Routledge and Kegan Paul.
Clavel, P. 1986. *The Progressive City: Planning and Participation, 1969–1984*. New Brunswick, NJ: Rutgers University Press.
Cohen, S. 1969. *Modern Capitalist Planning: The French Model*. Cambridge, MA: Harvard University Press.
Coleman, J. 1990a. *Foundations of Social Theory*. Cambridge, MA: Harvard University Press.
Coleman, J. 1990b. Commentary: social institutions and social theory, in *American Journal of Sociology*, 55(3), 333–40.
COAM. 1976. Texto de la alegación presentada por el COAM ante COPLACO in relación con el *Plan Especial de Infraestructuras de Transporte de la Provincia de Madrid*. Madrid: Colegio Oficial de Arquitectos de Madrid (COAM).
Comisaría General de Ordenación Urbana de Madrid y sus Alrededores (CGOUMA). 1944. *Plan General de Ordenación Urbana de Madrid*. Madrid: Ministerio de la Gobernación.
Comisaría General para la Ordenación Urbana de Madrid y sus Alrededores. 1953. *Gran Madrid, Boletín*, 23(3). Madrid: Ministerio de la Gobernación.
Comisaría General para la Ordenación Urbana de Madrid y sus Alrededores. 1955. *Reportario Legislativo de la Comisaría de Urbanismo 1948–1955*. Madrid: Ministerio de la Gobernación.
Comisaría General para la Ordenación Urbana de Madrid y sus Alrededores. 1961. *Plan General de Ordenación Urbana del Área Metropolitana de Madrid*. Madrid: Ministerio de Vivienda.
Comisaría de Urbanismo. 1947. Reglamento de 17 de octubre de 1947 para el desarrollo orgánico de la Ley de Ordenación Urbana de Madrid y sus Alrededores. Madrid: Ministerio de la Gobernación.
Comisaría de Urbanismo. 1948. *Disposiciones Legislativas Dictadas para la Ordenación Urbana de Madrid y sus Alrededores*. Madrid: Ministerio de la Gobernación.
Comité de la Reforma, Reconstrucción y Saneamiento de Madrid. 1939. *Esquema y Bases para el Desarrollo del Plan Regional de Madrid*. Madrid: Ministerio de Obras Públicas.

Comunidad Autónoma de Madrid. 1983. Ley Orgánica 3/1983 de 25 de febrero, de Estatuto de Autonomía de la Comunidad de Madrid. Madrid: Comunidad Autónoma de Madrid.

Comunidad Autónoma de Madrid. 1984a. Ley 10/1984 de 30 de mayo, sobre Ordenación Territorial de la Comunidad de Madrid. Madrid: Comunidad Autónoma de Madrid.

Comunidad Autónoma de Madrid. 1984b. Ley 4/1984 de 10 de febrero, sobre Medidas de Disciplina Urbanística. Madrid: Comunidad Autónoma de Madrid.

Consejería de Ordenación del Territorio, Medio Ambiente y Vivienda. 1985. *Directrices de Ordenación Territorial: Documento Previo*. Madrid: Comunidad de Madrid.

Consejería de Política Territorial. 1985. *Directrices del Ordenación Territorial: Documento Previo*.

Consejería de Política Territorial. 1988a. *Una Estrategia para la Zona Sur Metropolitana*.

Consejería de Política Territorial. 1988b. *Directrices de Ordenación del Territorio: Bases*.

Consejería de Política Territorial. 1989a. *Madrid Región Metropolitana: Estrategia Territorial: Zona Oeste Metropolitana*.

Consejería de Política Territorial. 1989b. *Madrid Región Metropolitana: Estrategia Territorial: Corredor de Henares*.

Consejería de Política Territorial. 1989c. *Medidas Sobre Política de Suelo*.

Consejería de Política Territorial. 1989d. *Estrategias de Transportes en la Región Metropolitana*.

Consejería de Política Territorial. 1990a. *Madrid Región Metropolitana: Actuaciones y Estrategias: Catálogo de Actuaciones*.

Consejería de Política Territorial. 1990b. *Madrid Región Metropolitana: Actuaciones y Estrategias: Objetivos y Propuestas*.

Consejería de Política Territorial. 1990c. *Los Planes de Ordenación Urbana de Madrid*.

Consejería de Política Territorial. 1991a. Madrid Región Metropolitana (MRM): *Compendio de Actuaciones Estructurantes*, Madrid: Comunidad de Madrid.

Consejería de Política Territorial. 1991b. *MRM: Estrategia Territorial y Actuaciones*.

Consejería de Política Territorial. 1994a. Proyecto de la Ley de Medidas de Política Territorial, Suelo y Urbanismo. Madrid: Comunidad de Madrid.

Consejería de Política Territorial. 1994b. La necesidad de nuevos instrumentos de política territorial. Bases: objetivos estratégicos, in *Working Document*. Madrid: Comunidad de Madrid.

Cooke, P. 2007. Regional innovation systems, assymetric knowledge, and the legacies of learning, in R. Rutten and F. Boekema, eds *The Learning Region: Foundations, State of the Art, Future*. Cheltenham: Edward Elgar, 184–205.

COPLACO. 1972. *Madrid 2000: Avance del Esquema Director de la Subregión Central*. Madrid: Ministerio de la Vivienda.

COPLACO. 1975a. *Plan Especial de Infraestructura de Transportes de la Provincia de Madrid*. Madrid: Ministerio de la Vivienda.

COPLACO. 1975b. *Plan Especial de Protección del Medio Físico de la Provincia de Madrid*. Madrid: Ministerio de Obras Públicas y Urbanismo.

COPLACO. 1975c. *Plan Especial de Grandes Equipamientos Comerciales de la Provincia de Madrid*. Madrid: Ministerio de Obras Públicas y Urbanismo.

COPLACO. 1976. *Plan Especial de Infraestructuras Básicas de la Provincia de Madrid*. Madrid: Ministerio de Obras Públicas y Urbanismo.

COPLACO. 1977. *Informe sobre Participación Pública en el Planeamiento Metropolitano*. Madrid: Ministerio de Obras Públicas y Urbanismo.

COPLACO. 1978. *¿Qué Hacer con Madrid?* Madrid: Ministerio de Obras Públicas y Urbanismo.

COPLACO. 1979a. *Análisis de Problemas y Oportunidades: Planeamiento Vigente y Suelo Urbanizado*. Madrid: Ministerio de Obras Públicas y Urbanismo.

COPLACO. 1979b. *Informe al Pleno de la Comisión sobre la situación del Programa de Planeamiento de la Provincia de Madrid*. 2 volumes. Madrid: Ministerio de Obras Públicas y Urbanismo.

COPLACO. 1980. *Informe Sobre Ordenación del Territorio en la Área Metropolitana de Madrid*. Madrid: Ministerio de Obras Públicas y Urbanismo.

COPLACO. 1981. *Directrices de Planeamiento Territorial Urbanístico para la Revisión del Plan General del Área Metropolitana de Madrid*. Madrid: Ministerio de Obras Públicas y Urbanismo.

Cosier, R. 1991. Organizational life cycles: structural implications for OSD, in *Public Affairs Quarterly*, 225–38.

Couto, R. 1993. Narrative, free space, and political leadership in social movements, in *Journal of Politics*, 55(1), 57–79.

Crary, J. and Kwinter, S., eds 1992. *Incorporations*. Cambridge: MIT Press, Zone 6 (serial).

Crawford, S. and Ostrom, E. 1995. A grammar of institutions, in *American Political Science Review*, 89(3), 582–600.

Crouch, D., Garr, D. and Mundigo, A. 1982. *Spanish City Planning in North America*. Cambridge, MA: MIT Press.

Crozier, M. 1964. *The Bureaucratic Phenomenon*. Chicago: University of Chicago Press.

Crozier, M. 1965. Pour une analyse sociologique de la planification française, in *Revue française de Sociologie*, VI, 147–63.

Crozier, M. 1975. *The Crisis of Democracy: Report on the Governability of Democracies*. New York: New York University Press.

Crozier, M. 1984. *The Trouble With America*, trans. Peter Heinegg. Berkeley: University of California Press.

*Cuadernos para el Dialogo*. 1970. Special issue on Madrid, Madrid (serial).

Cullingworth, B. 1993. *The Political Culture of Planning; American Land Use Planning in Comparative Perspective*. New York: Routledge.

Cyert, R. and March, J. 1963. *A Behavioral Theory of the Firm*. Englewood Cliffs: Prentice Hall.

Dahl, R. 1957. The concept of power, in *Behavioral Science*, 2, 201–15.

Dahl, R. 1961. *Who Governs? Democracy and Power in an American City*. New Haven: Yale University Press.

Dahl, R. and Tufte, E. 1973. *Size and Democracy*. Palo Alto: Stanford University Press.

Dahl, R. 1989. *Democracy and its Critics*. New Haven: Yale University Press.

Danielson, M. and Doig, J. 1982. *The Politics of Urban and Regional Development*. Berkeley: University of California Press.

Davidoff, P. and Reiner, T. 1962. A choice theory of planning, in *Journal of the American Institute of Planners*, 28(2), 102–9.

Davidoff, P. 1965. Advocacy and pluralism in planning, in *Journal of the American Institute of Planners*, 31(4), 103–15.

Davoudi, S. and Strange, I., eds 2009. *Conceptions of Space and Place in Strategic Spatial Planning*. New York and London: Routledge.

Dawkins, R. 1976. *The Selfish Gene*. New York: Oxford University Press.

D'Cuckoo. 1994. One of four fates, in *Umoja* [music album], San Francisco: RGB Records.

Decreto/Ley de 1 de marzo de 1946. Ley de Ordenación Urbana de Madrid y sus Alrededores.

Decreto de 17 de octubre de 1947. Por el que se aprueba el Reglamento para el desarrollo orgánico de la Ley de Ordenación Urbana de Madrid y sus Alrededores.

Decreto de 25 de febrero de 1956. Por el que se crea el Ministerio de la Vivienda.

Decreto de 26 de abril de 1957. Por el que se aprueba el Reglamento Orgánico Provisional del Ministerio de la Vivienda.

Decreto 1674/1963, de 11 de julio. Por el que se aprueba el Texto Articulado de la Ley que establece un Régimen Especial para el Municipio de Madrid.

Decreto 3655/1963, de 26 de diciembre. Por el que se aprueba el Plan General de Ordenación Urbana del Área Metropolitana de Madrid.

Decreto 3088/1964, de 28 de septiembre. Sobre el Reglamento de la Ley sobre el Área Metropolitana.

Decreto 2432/1972, de 18 de agosto de 1972. Sobre Bases para concursos de ejecución de urbanizaciones en Madrid.

Decreto 561/1974, de 1 de marzo. Sobre la Comisión de Planeamiento y Coordinación del Área Metropolitana de Madrid: Organización.

Decreto 68/1983, de 30 de junio. Por el que se crea la Comisión de Urbanismo y Medio Ambiente de Madrid y se aprueba su Reglamento de Organización y Funcionamiento.

DeGrove, J. 1984. *Land: Growth and Politics*. Chicago: APA Press.

DeGrove, J. 1992. *Emerging State and Regional Roles in Growth Management.* Cambridge, MA: Lincoln Institute for Land Policy.

DeGrove, J. 2005. *Planning, Policy and Politics: Smart Growth and the States.* Cambridge, MA: Lincoln Institute for Land Policy.

del Corral, J. 1990. *Madrid 1561: La Capitalidad.* Madrid: Ediciones La Librería.

de Jong, M., Konstantinos, L. and Mamadouh, V., eds 2002. *The Theory and Practice of Institutional Transplantation: Experiences with the Transfer of Policy Institutions.* Dordrecht: Kluwer.

de Lorite Kramer, J. 1932. *Informe Sobre el plan General de Extensión de 1931.* Madrid: Artes Gráficas Municipales.

de Neufville, J.I. and Barton, S. 1987. Myths and the definition of policy problems: an exploration of home ownership and public-private partnerships, in *Policy Sciences*, 20, 181–206.

Departamento de Política Territorial i Obras Públicas. 1992. *Pla Territorial Metropolità de Barcelona.* Barcelona: Generalitat de Cataluña.

de Roo, G. and Porter, G., eds 2007. *Fuzzy Planning: The Role of Actors in a Fuzzy Governance Environment.* Aldershot: Ashgate.

Derthick, M. 1974. *Between State and Nation: Regional Organizations of the United States.* Washington, DC: Brookings.

de Souza Briggs, X. 2008. *Democracy as Problem Solving: Civic Capacity in Communities Across the Globe.* Cambridge, MA: MIT Press.

de Terán, F. 1968. *La Ciudad Lineal: Antecedente de un Urbanismo Actual.* Madrid: Editorial Ciencia Nueva.

de Terán, F. 1982. *Planeamiento Urbano en la España Contemporánea (1900/1982).* Madrid: Alianza Editorial.

de Terán, F. 1999. *Historia del Urbanismo en España III: siglos XIX y XX.* Madrid: Cátedra.

de Terán, F. and Sanchez de Madariaga, I. 1999. *Madrid: Ciudad-Región. Entre la Ciudad y el Terrritorio, en la segunda mitad del siglo XX.* Madrid: Comunidad de Madrid.

de Tocqueville, A. 1899 [1835]. *Democracy in America.* Volume 1, trans. Henry Reeve. New York: Colonial Press.

de Tocqueville, A. 1966 [1840]. *Democracy in America.* Volume 2, trans. Henry Reeve. New Rochelle: Arlington House.

de Torres i Cappell, M. 1992. Barcelona: Planning problems and practices in the Jaussely era, in *Planning Perspectives*, 7, 211–33.

Deutsch, K. 1953. *Nationalism and Social Communication: An Inquiry into the Foundations of Nationality.* Cambridge, MA: MIT Press.

Diaz, L. 1992. *Madrid: Tabernas, Botillerías y Cafés 1476–1991.* Madrid: Espasa Calpe.

Diaz, M., Fransciso, J. 1976. La estructura institucional del urbanismo de Madrid: origen y evolución de la COPLACO del área metropolitana de Madrid, in *Ciudad y Territorio*, 2(3), 195–202.

Dideon, J. 1993. The golden land, in *The New York Review of Books*, XL, 17, 85–95.

DiMaggio, P. 1983. Organizations as institutions, in S. Bacharach, ed. *Research in Organizational Behavior*. Greenwich, CT: JAI Press.

DiMaggio, P. 1987. Institutional theories of organizations, in *Annual Review of Sociology*, 13, 443–64.

DiMaggio, P. and Powell, W. 1983. The iron cage revisited: institutional isomorphism and collective rationality in organizational fields, in *American Sociological Review*, 48, 147–60.

Dodge, W. and Montgomery, K. 1996. *Shaping a Region's Future: A Guide to Strategic Decision Making for Regions*. Washington, DC: National League of Cities.

Dolšak, N. and Ostrom, E. 2003. *The Commons in the New Millennium: Challenges and Adaptation*. Cambridge, MA: MIT Press.

Donald, S. and Gammack, J. 2007. *Tourism and the Branded City: Film and Identity in the Pacific Rim*. Aldershot: Ashgate.

Douglas, M. 1970. *Natural Symbols: Explorations in Cosmology*. New York: Pantheon.

Douglas, M. 1986. *How Institutions Think*. Syracuse: Syracuse University Press.

Downs, A. 1957. *An Economic Theory of Democracy*. New York: Harper and Brothers.

Downs, A. 1967. *Inside Bureaucracy*. Boston: Little, Brown.

Dryzek, J. 1987. *Rational Ecology: Environment and Political Economy*. London: Basil Blackwell.

Dryzek, J. 1990. *Discursive Democracy: Politics, Policy and Political Science*. New York: Cambridge University Press.

Duany, A. and Plater-Zyberk, E. 1991. *Towns and Town-making Principles*, edited by A. Krieger. New York: Rizzoli.

Dylan, B. 1974. Idiot Wind, in *Blood on the Tracks* [music album]. New York: Columbia Records.

Easton, D. 1990. *The Analysis of Political Structure*. New York: Routledge.

Echenagusia, J. 1991. *Madrid: Punto Seguida*. Madrid: Cidur/Alfoz.

Eco, U. 1976. *A Theory of Signs*. Bloomington: University of Indiana Press.

Eco, U. 1984. *Semiotics and the Philosophy of Language*. Bloomington: University of Indiana Press.

Edelman, G. 1990. *The Remembered Present: A Biological Theory of Consciousness*. New York: Basic Books.

Edelman, G. 1993. *Bright Air, Brilliant Fire: On the Matter of the Mind*. New York: Basic Books.

Edelman, M. 1964. *The Symbolic Uses of Politics*. Urbana: University of Illinois Press.

Edelman, M. 1971. *Politics as Symbolic Action: Mass Arousal and Quiescence*. New York: Academic Press.

Editors. 1930. Concurso urbanístico internacional de Madrid, in *Arquitectura*, XII: 140, cover page (December).

Editors. 1989. Entrevista a Eduardo Mangada, in *Urbanismo*, 7, 25–37.

Editors. 1991. Debate: Always and again, housing, in *Alfoz*, 76, 76.

Eigen, M. 1992. *Steps Toward Life: A Perspective on Evolution*. Trans. Paul Woolley. Oxford: Oxford University Press.

Eisenstadt, S.N. 1968. *Max Weber: On Charisma and Institution Building*. Chicago: University of Chicago Press.

Eldredge, N. and Gould, S. 1972. Punctuated equilibria: An alternative to phyletic gradualism, in T.J.M. Schopf, ed. *Models in Paleobiology*. San Francisco: Freeman, Cooper.

Eliadis, P., Hill, M. and Howlett, M., eds 2005. *Designing Government: From Instruments to Governance*. Montreal: McGill University Press.

Ellis, A. 1956. *The Penny Universities: A History of the Coffee Houses*. London: Secker and Warburg.

Elorza, A. 1990. *La Modernización Política in España: Ensayos de Historia de Pensamiento Político*. Madrid: Ediciones Endymion.

Elster, J. 1983. *Sour Grapes: Studies in the Subversion of Rationality*. Cambridge: Cambridge University Press.

Elster, J. 1989a. *The Cement of Society: A Study of Social Order*. New York: Cambridge University Press.

Elster, J. 1989b. *Solomonic Judgments: Studies in the Limitations of Rationality*. New York: Cambridge University Press.

Emirbayer, M. and Goodwin, J. 1994. Network analysis, culture, and the problem of agency, in *American Journal of Sociology*, 99(6), 1411–54.

Erikson, E. 1963. *Childhood and Society*. New York: Norton.

Estevan, A. (1991) 1988. Crisis social de la ciudad, in J. Echenagusía, ed. *Madrid: Punto Seguido*. Madrid: Cidur Alfoz.

Etzioni, A. 1961. *A Comparative Analysis of Complex Organizations: On Power. Involvement and Their Correlates*. New York: The Free Press.

Evans, P., Ruescbmeyer, D. and Skocpol, T. 1985. *Bringing the State Back In*. New York: Cambridge University Press.

Eyerman, R. and Jamison, A. 1991. *Social Movements: A Cognitive Approach*. University Park, PA: Penn State University Press.

Eymeri-Douzans, J.-M. and Pierre, J., eds 2010. *Administrative Reforms and Democratic Governance*. New York and London: Routledge.

Ezquiaga, J.M. 1989. De la recuperación de la ciudad a la articulación del espacio metropolitano, in *Alfoz*, 62–3, 75–101.

Ezquiaga, J.M. 1993. Madrid: nuevos instrumentos de política territorial, in *Ciudad y Territorio y Estudios Territoriales*, 95–6, 107–21.

Fabre, J. 1989. *Barcelona: La Construccio d'una Ciutat*. Barcelona: Plaza and Janes.

Fainstein, S. 1983. *Restructuring the City: The Political Economy of Redevelopment*. New York: Longman.

Faludi, A. 1987. *A Decision-centred View of Environmental Planning*. Oxford: Pergamon Press.

Faludi, A. 1996. Framing with images, in *Environment and Planning B: Planning and Design*, 23, 93–108.

Faludi, A. and Korthals Altes, W. 1994. Evaluating communicative planning: a revised design for performance research, in *European Planning Studies*, 2(4), 403–18.

Faludi, A. and van der Valk, A.J. 1994. *Rule and Order: Dutch Planning Doctrine in the Twentieth Century*. Dordrecht: Kluwer Academic Publishers.

Feagin, J., ed. 1979 [1973]. *The Urban Scene: Myth and Reality*, second edition. New York: Random House.

Federación Socialista Madrileña. 1987. Madrid Región Metropolitana, in *Alfoz*, 41, 52–66.

Fernandez, J., ed. 1991. *Beyond Metaphor: The Theory of Tropes in Anthropology*. Stanford: Stanford University Press.

Fernández de los Ríos, A. 1989 [1868]. *El Futuro Madrid: Paseos Mentales por la Capital de España, tal cual es y tal cual debe dejarla transformada la revolución*, with an introduction by Antonio Bonet Correa. Madrid: Libros de la Frontera.

Fernández Duran, R. 1993. *La Explosión del Desorden: La Metrópoli como Espacio de la Crisis Global*. Madrid: Editorial Fundamentos.

Fernández García, A., ed. 1993. *Historia de Madrid*. Madrid: Editorial Complutense.

Fernández, R. and Ramón, T. 1974. *El Urbanismo Concertado y la Reforma de la Ley del Suelo*. Madrid: Instituto de Estudios Administrativos, Cuadernos de Administración Pública.

Filley, A., House, R. and Kerr, S. 1976. *Managerial Process and Organizational Behavior*. New York: Scott Foresman.

Finkel, L. 1992. The construction of perception, in J. Crary and S. Kwinter, eds *Incorporations*. Cambridge, MA: MIT Press.

Fischer, F. and Forester, J., eds 1993. *The Argumentative Turn in Policy Analysis and Planning*. Durham: Duke University Press.

Fisher, R. and Ury, W. 1981. *Getting to Yes*. Boston: Houghton Mifflin.

Fishkin, J. 1991. *Democracy and Deliberation: New Directions for Democratic Reform*. New Haven: Yale University Press.

Flyvbjerg, B. 1998. *Rationality and Power*. Chicago: University of Chicago Press.

Forester, J. 1980. Critical theory and planning practice, in *Journal of the American Planning Association*, 46, 275–86.

Forester, J. 1989. *Planning in the Face of Power*. Berkeley: University of California Press.

Forester, J. and Krumholz, N. 1990. *Making Equity Planning Work*. Philadelphia: Temple University Press.

Forester, J. 1993. Learning from practice stories: The priority of practical judgment, in F. Fischer and J. Forester, eds *The Argumentative Turn in Policy Analysis and Planning*. Durham: Duke University Press.

Forester, J. 1999. *The Deliberative Practitioner: Encouraging Participatory Planning*. Cambridge, MA: MIT Press.

Foucault, M. 1970 [1966]. *The Order of Things: An Archeology of the Human Sciences*. New York: Random House.

Foucault, M. 1972 [1969]. *The Archeology of Knowledge*. New York: Pantheon.

Foucault, M. 1978. Politics and the study of discourse, in *Ideology and Consciousness*, 3.

Foucault, M. 1979. Governmentality, in *Ideology and Consciousness*, 6, 5–21.

Foucault, M. 1980. *Power/Knowledge*. Edited by C. Gordon. New York: Pantheon.

Frampton, K. 1983. Towards a critical regionalism: six points for an architecture of resistance, in H. Foster, ed. *The Anti-Aesthetic: Essays on Postmodern Culture*. Port Townsend: Bay Press.

Frederickson, H.G. 1991. Towards a theory of the public for public administration, in *Administration and Society*, 22(4), 395–417.

Freire, P. 1970. *The Pedagogy of the Oppressed*. New York: Continuum.

Fuentes Quintana, E. 1990. De los pactos de la Moncloa a la constitución (julio 1977–diciembre 1978), in J.L. Delgado, ed. *Economía española de la transición y la democracia*. Madrid: Centro de Investigaciones Sociológicas.

Friedland, R. and Alford, R. 1991. Bringing society back in, in W. Powell and P. DiMaggio, eds 1991. *The New Institutionalism in Organizational Analysis*. Chicago: University of Chicago Press.

Friedmann, J. 1973. *Retracking America: A Theory of Transactive Planning*. Norwell: Anchor Press.

Friedmann, J. 1987. *Planning in the Public Domain: From Knowledge to Action*. Princeton: Princeton University Press.

Friedmann, J. 1998. Planning theory revisited, in *European Planning Studies*, 6(3), 245–54.

Friedmann, J. 2005. Globalization and the emerging culture of planning, in *Progress in Planning*, 64, 183–234.

Gabinete de Análisis Sociológica. 1993. *Estudio de Base: Nuevo Sur Metropolitano*, vol. 1. Madrid: ARPEGIO, S.A.

Gage, R. and Mandell, M. 1990. *Strategies for Managing Intergovernmental Networks*. New York: Praeger.

Gago, J. and Leira, E. 1979. Política de suelo: requisito para una nueva política de vivienda, in *Información Comercial Española*, 548, 73–89.

Gago, V. and Castanyer Vila, J. 1976. La administración urbanística en la provincia de Madrid, in *Ciudad y Territorio*, 2(3), 202–7.

Gamson, W. 1992. *Talking Politics*. New York: Cambridge University Press.

García Pablos, R. 1985. Directrices de ordenación territorial: documento previo, in *Alfoz*, 18/19, 91–106.

Garfinkel, H. 1967. *Studies in Ethnomethodology*. Englewood Cliffs: Prentice Hall.

Garreau, J. 1991. *Edge Cities: Life on the Frontier*. New York: Doubleday.

Gawthrop, L. 1993. Images of the Common Good, in *Public Administration Review*, 53(6), 508–15.

Geddes, P. 1915. *Cities in Evolution*. London: Williams and Norgate.

Geertz, C. 1973. *The Interpretation of Cultures*. New York: Basic Books.

Geertz, C. 1983. *Local Knowledge*. New York: Basic Books.

Gellner, E. 1994. *Conditions of Liberty: Civil Society and its Rivals*. London: Penguin.

Gere, C. 2002. *Digital Culture*. London: Reaktion Books.

Gerring, J. and Thacker, S. 2008. *A Centripetal Theory of Democratic Governance*. Cambridge: Cambridge University Press.

Giddens, A. 1979. *Central Problems in Social Theory: Action, Structure, and Contradiction in Social Analysis*. Berkeley: University of California Press.

Giddens, A. 1984. *The Constitution of Society: An Outline of a Theory of Structuration*. Berkeley: University of California Press.

Gibson, J. 1950. *The Perception of the Visual World*. Boston: Houghton Mifflin.

Gibson, J. 1979. *The Ecological Approach to Visual Perception*. Boston: Houghton Mifflin.

Giner, S. and Sevilla, E. 1984. Spain from corporatism to corporatism, in A. Williams, ed. *Southern Europe Transformed: Political and Economic Change in Greece, Italy, Portugal and Spain*. London: Harper and Row.

Giner, S. 1994. Ciudad y política en la Europa meridional: algunas reflexiones históricas y sociológicas, in A. Alabart, S. García and S. Giner, eds *Clase, Poder y Ciudadanía*. Madrid: Siglo Veintiuno.

Glynn, S., ed. 2009. *Where the Other Half Lives: Lower Income Housing in a Neoliberal World*. New York, NY: Palgrave Macmillan.

Goffman, E. 1974. *Frame Analysis: An Essay on the Organization of Experience*. Cambridge, MA: Harvard University Press.

Goodin, R.E., ed. 1996. *The Theory of Institutional Design*. Cambridge: Cambridge University Press.

Goodman, R. 1979. *The Last Entrepreneurs*. New York: Basic Books.

Gottdiener, M. and Lagopoulos, A., eds 1986. *The City and the Sign: An Introduction to Urban Semiotics*. New York: Columbia University Press.

Gottmann, J. 1961. *Megalopolis: The Urbanization of the Northeastern Seaboard of the United States*. New York: Twentieth Century Fund.

Gould, S.J. 1989. *Wonderful Life: The Burgess Shale and the Nature of History*. New York: W.W. Norton.

Grafstein, R. 1992. *Institutional Realism: Social and Political Constraints on Rational Actors*. New Haven: Yale University Press.

Gruber, J., Innes, J., Neuman, M. and Thompson, R. 1993. Coordinating growth management through consensus building: incentives and the generation of social, intellectual and political capital, presented at the annual conference of the American Political Science Association.

Gualini, E. 2001. *The Intelligence of Institutions*. Aldershot: Ashgate.

Gualini, E. 2004. *Multi-Level Governance and Institutional Change: The Europeanization of Regional Policy in Italy*. Aldershot: Ashgate.

Gunther, R. 1980. *Public Policy in a No-Party State: Spanish Planning and Budgeting in the Twilight of the Franquist Era*. Berkeley: University of California Press.

Gunther, R., ed. 1993. *Politics, Society, and Democracy: The Case of Spain*. Boulder: Westview Press.

Habermas, J. 1970. *Towards a Rational Society*. Boston: Beacon Press.

Habermas, J. 1971. *Knowledge and Human Interests*. Boston: Beacon Press.

Habermas, J. 1974. *Theory and Practice*. Boston: Beacon Press.

Habermas, J. 1975. *Legitimation Crisis*. Boston: Beacon Press.

Habermas, J. 1979. *Communication and the Evolution of Society*, trans. Thomas McCarthy. Boston: Beacon Press.

Habermas, J. 1983. *Philosophical-Political Profiles*. Cambridge, MA: MIT Press.

Habermas, J. 1984. *Theory of Communicative Action: Reason and the Rationalization of Society*, volume one. Boston: Beacon Press.

Habermas, J. 1987. *The Theory of Communicative Action: Lifeworld and System: A Critique of Functionalist Reason*, volume two. Boston: Beacon Press.

Habermas, J. 1989. *The Structural Transformation of the Public Sphere: An Inquiry and into a Category of Bourgeois Society*. Cambridge, MA: MIT Press.

Hack, G., Birch, E. and Silver, M. 2009. *Local Planning: Contemporary Principles and Practices*. Washington, DC: International City/County Management Association.

Hajer, M. and Wagenaar, H., eds 2003. *Deliberative Policy Analysis: Understanding Governance in a Network Society*. Cambridge: Cambridge University Press.

Halbwachs, M. 1980 [1950]. *The Collective Memory*, with an introduction by Mary Douglas. New York: Harper and Row.

Haldane, J.B.S. 1928. On being the right size, in J.B.S. Haldane, *Possible Worlds*. New York: Harper.

Hall, P.A. 1986. *Governing the Economy: The Politics of State Intervention in Britain and France*. New York: Oxford University Press.

Hall, P.G. 1966. *The World Cities*. New York: McGraw-Hill.

Hall, P.G. 1982. *Urban and Regional Planning*, 3rd Edition. London: George Allen and Unwin.

Hall, P.G. 1988. *Cities of Tomorrow: An Intellectual History of Urban Planning in the Twentieth Century*. Oxford and New York: Basil Blackwell.

Hall, P.G. and Pfeiffer, U. 2001. *Urban Future 21: A Global Agenda for Twenty-first Century Cities*. London: E & FN Spon.

Hamilton, A., Madison, L. and Jay, J. 1961 [1787–1788]. *The Federalist Papers*. New York: New American Library.

Hannay, A. 1971. *Mental Images: A Defence*. London: George Allen and Unwin.

Hardin, R. 1982. *Collective Action*. Baltimore: Johns Hopkins University Press.

Hardin, G. 1968. Tragedy of the commons, in *Science*, 162, 1243–8.

Harper, T. and Stein, S. 1992. The centrality of normative ethical theory to contemporary planning theory, in *Journal of Planning Education and Research*, 11, 105–16.

Harper, T. and Stein, S. 2006. *Dialogical Planning in a Fragmented Society*. New Brunswick: CUPR Press.

Harvey, D. 1989. *The Condition of Postmodernity*. Oxford: Blackwell.

Hartz, L., et al. 1964. *The Founding of New Societies*. New York: Harcourt Brace & World.

Hatt, P. and Reiss, A., Jr., eds 1957 [1951]. *Cities and Society: The Revised Reader in Urban Sociology*. New York: The Free Press of Glencoe.

Haughton, G., Allmendinger, P., Counsell, D. and Vigar, G. 2010. *The New Spatial Planning: Territorial Management with Soft Spaces and Fuzzy Boundaries*. London, New York: Routledge.

Havel, V. 1985. The power of the powerless, in V. Havel, *The Power of the Powerless: Citizens against the State in Central–Eastern Europe*. Armonk: M.E. Sharpe.

Havel, V. 1992. *Summer Meditations*. New York: Alfred Knopf.

Haworth, L. 1963. *The Good City*. Bloomington: Indiana University Press.

Hayward, J. and Watson, M., eds 1975. *Planning, Politics and Public Policy: The British, French and Italian Experience*. Cambridge: Cambridge University Press.

Healey, P. 1988. The British planning system and managing the urban environment, in *Town Planning Review*, 59(4), 397–417.

Healey, P. et al. 1988. *Land Use Planning and the Mediation of Urban Change*. Cambridge: Cambridge University Press.

Healey, P. 1990. Places, people and policies: plan making in the 1990s, in *Local Government Policy Making*, 17(2), 29–39.

Healey, P. 1992a. A planner's day: knowledge and action in communicative practice, in *Journal of the American Planning Association*, 58(1), 9–20.

Healey, P. 1992b. Planning through debate: the communicative turn in planning theory, in *Town Planning Review*, 63(2), 143–62.

Healey, P. 1993. The communicative work of development plans, in *Environment and Planning B: Planning and Design*, 20, 83–104.

Healey, P. 1997. *Collaborative Planning: Shaping Places in Fragmented Societies*. London: Macmillan.

Healey, P. 2006. *Collaborative Planning: Shaping Places in Fragmented Societies*, 2nd Edition. New York: Palgrave Macmillan.

Healey, P. 2007. *Urban Complexity and Spatial Strategies: Towards a Relational Planning for our Times*. London: Routledge.

Healey, P., Khakee, A., Motte, A. and Needham, B. 1997. *Making Strategic Spatial Plans: Innovation in Europe*. London: University College London Press.

Hechter, M., Opp, K.D. and Wippler, R., eds 1990. *Social Institutions, Their Emergence, Maintenance, and Effects.* New York: Aldine de Gruyter.

Hedetoft, U. 1998. *Political Symbols, Symbolic Politics: European Identities in Transformation.* Aldershot: Ashgate.

Heidegger, M. 1971 [1954]. Building, dwelling, thinking, in *Poetry, Language, Thought.* New York: Harper and Row.

Heidegger, M. 1977 [1953]. The question concerning technology, in D. Krell, ed. and trans., *Martin Heidegger: Basic Writings.* New York: Harper and Row.

Heil, J. 1983. *Perception and Cognition.* Berkeley: University of California Press.

Heinett, H. and Kübler, D. 2009. *Metropolitan Governance in the 21st Century: Capacity, Democracy and the Dynamics of Place.* New York and London: Routledge.

Heinett, H., Sweeting, D. and Getimis, P., eds 2009. *Legitimacy and Urban Governance: A Cross-National Comparative Study.* New York and London: Routledge.

Hernández Fernández de Bobadilla, M. 1994. Personal communication, August 25.

Hillier, J. 2007. *Stretching Beyond the Horizon: A Multiplanar Theory of Spatial Planning and Governance.* Aldershot: Ashgate.

Hine, R.V. 1992. *Josiah Royce: From Grass Valley to Harvard.* Norman: University of Oklahoma Press.

Hirschman, A.O. 1970. *Exit, Voice, and Loyalty: Responses to Decline in Firms, Organizations, and States.* Cambridge: Harvard University Press.

Hobbes, T. 1964 [1651]. *Leviathan: Or the Matter, Forme, and Power of a Commonwealth Ecclesiasticall and Civil,* abridged and edited by Francis Randall. New York: Washington Square Press.

Hobsbawm, E. and Ranger, T., eds 1983. *The Invention of Tradition.* Cambridge: Cambridge University Press.

Hoch, C. 1994. *What Planners Do: Power, Politics, and Persuasion.* Chicago: Planners Press, American Planning Association.

Hoffman, A., et al. 1990. Structure, context, and centrality in interorganizational networks, in *Journal of Business Research*, 20(4), 333–47.

Hollis, A. and Sweetman, A. 2001. The life-cycle of a microfinance institution: the Irish loan funds, in *Journal of Economic Behavior and Organization*, 46(3), 291–311.

Holyoak, K. and Thagard, P. 1995. *Mental Leaps: Analogy in Creative Thought.* Cambridge, MA: MIT Press.

Howard, E. 1898. *To-Morrow: A Peaceful Path to Real Reform,* re-issued as *Garden Cities of To-Morrow,* 1902. London: Schwan Sonnenschein.

Howe, E. 1992. Normative ethics in planning, in *Journal of Planning Literature*, 5(2), 123–50.

Hubel, D. 1988. *Eye, Brain, and Vision.* New York: Scientific American Library.

Huntington, S. 1968. *Political Order in Changing Societies*. New Haven: Yale University Press.

Hult, K. and Walcott, C. 1989. Organizational design as public policy, in *Policy Studies Journal*, 17(3), 469–94.

Immergut, E. 1992. *Health Politics: Interests and Institutions in Western Europe*. New York: Cambridge University Press.

Innes, de Neufville, J. 1983. Planning theory and practice: bridging the gap, in *Journal of Planning Education and Research*, 3(1), 35–45.

Innes de Neufville, J. 1987. Knowledge and action: making the link, in *Journal of Planning Education and Research*, 6(2), 86–92.

Innes de Neufville, J. 1990. *Knowledge and Public Policy: The Search for Meaningful Indicators*, second expanded edition. New Brunswick: Transaction Publishers.

Innes, J. 1992. Group process and the social construction of growth management: Florida, Vermont, and New Jersey, in *Journal of the American Planning Association*, 58(4), 440–53.

Innes, J. 1995. Planning theory's emerging paradigm: communicative action and interactive practice, in *Journal of Planning Education and Research*, 14(3), 183–9.

Innes, J. and Booher, D. 2010. *Planning with Complexity: An Introduction to Collaborative Rationality for Public Policy*. London: Routledge.

Instituto de Estudios de Administración Local (IEAL). 1945. *El Futuro Madrid*. Madrid: IEAL.

Jacobs, A. 1978. *Making City Planning Work*. Chicago: American Society of Planning Officials.

Jacobs, J. 1984. *Cities and the Wealth of Nations: Principles of Economic Life*. New York: Random House.

Jameson, F. 1981. *The Political Unconscious*. Ithaca: Cornell University Press.

Janaway, C. 1995. *Images of Excellence*. New York: Oxford University Press.

Janowitz, M. 1969. *Institution Building in Urban Education*. New York: Russell Sage.

Jaynes, J. 1976. *The Origins of Consciousness in the Breakdown of the Bicameral Mind*. Boston: Houghton Mifflin.

Jones, B. 1994. *Reconceiving Decision Making in Democratic Politics: Attention, Choice and Public Policy*. Chicago: University of Chicago Press.

J.R.S. 1976. Se reparten Madrid, in *Doblon*, July 10–16, 17–27.

Jung, C.G. 1961. *Memories, Dreams, Reflections*, recorded and edited by Aniela Jaffe, trans. Richard and Clara Winston. New York: Random House.

Jung, C.G. 1969a (1934). *The Archetypes and the Collective Unconscious*. Princeton: Princeton University Press.

Jung, C.G. 1969b (1960), *The Structure and Dynamics of the Psyche*. Princeton: Princeton University Press.

Jung, C.G. 1964. *Man and His Symbols*. Garden City: Doubleday.

Jung, C.G. 1982. *Aspects of the Feminine*. Princeton: Princeton University Press.

Jung, C.G. 1982. On the concept of the archetype, in *Aspects of the Feminine*. Princeton: Princeton University Press.

Junta de Reconstrucción de Madrid. 1942. *Ordenación General de Madrid*. Madrid: Ministerio de Gobernación.

Kagan, R., ed. 1989. *Spanish Cities of the Golden Age: The Views of Anton van den Wyngaerde*. Berkeley: University of California Press.

Kantor, P. 2000. Can regionalism save poor cities? Politics, institutions, and interests in Glasgow, in *Urban Affairs Review*, 35(6), 794–820.

Kaplan, T. 1992. *Red City Blue Period: Social Movements in Picasso's Barcelona*. Berkeley: University of California Press.

Katz, P. 1994. *The New Urbanism: Toward an Architecture of Community*. New York: McGraw-Hill.

Kauffman, S. 1993. *The Origins of Order*. Oxford: Oxford University Press.

Kaufman, H. 1976. *Are Government Organizations Immortal?* Washington, DC: Brookings.

Kaufman, H. 1985. *Time, Chance, and Organizations*. Chatham, NJ: Chatham House.

Kean, T. 1989. *The Politics of Inclusion*. New York: Basic Books.

Kearns, G. and Philo, C., eds 1993. *Selling Places: The City as Cultural Capital, Past and Present*. Oxford: Pergamon.

Kelbaugh, D., ed. 1990. *The Pedestrian Pocket Book: A New Suburban Design Strategy*. Princeton: Princeton Architectural Press.

Kelman, S. 1992. Adversary and cooperationist institutions for conflict resolution in public policymaking, in *Journal of Policy Analysis and Management*, 11(2), 178–206.

Kemmis, D. 1990. *Community and the Politics of Place*. Norman: University of Oklahoma Press.

Kennedy, P. 1987. *The Rise and Fall of the Great Powers: Economic Change and Military Conflict from 1500–2000*. New York: Random House.

Kent, T.J. 1964. *The Urban General Plan*. San Francisco: Chandler.

Keohane, R. 1989. *International Institutions and State Power: Essays on International Relations Theory*. Boulder: Westview.

Keyes, J., et al. 1991. Land use planning and the control of development in Spain, Reading, England: Centre for European Property Research, University of Reading.

Kimberly, J.R. and Miles, R.H. 1980. *The Organizatjonal Life Cycle: Issues in the Creation, Transformation and Decline of Organizations*. San Francisco: Jossey-Bass.

King, A. 1990. *Global Cities: Post-Imperialism and the Internationalization of London*. London: Routledge.

Knight, J. 1992. *Institutions and Social Conflict*. New York: Cambridge University Press.

Knoke, D. 1990. *Political Networks: The Structural Perspective*. New York: Cambridge University Press.

Koeble, T. 1995. The new institutionalism in political science and sociology, in *Comparative Politics*, 27(2), 231–43.

Korthals Altes, W. 1992. How do planning doctrines function in a changing environment?, in *Planning Theory*, 7–8, 100–15.

Kosslyn, S. 1980. *Image and Mind*. Cambridge: Harvard University Press.

Kostof, S. 1991. *The City Shaped: Urban Patterns and their Meanings Through History*. Boston: Little Brown and Company.

Krier, L. 1992. *Architecture and Urban Design 1967–1992*, edited by R. Economakis. New York: St. Martins.

Kubik, J. 1994. *The Power of Symbols Against the Symbols of Power: The Rise of Solidarity and the Fall of State Socialism in Poland*. University Park: Penn State University Press.

Kuhn, T. 1962. *The Structure of Scientific Revolutions*. Chicago: University of Chicago Press.

Laba, R. 1990. *The Roots of Solidarity: A Political Sociology of Poland's Working Class Democratization*. Princeton: Princeton University Press.

Landau, M. 1971. Linkage, coding, and intermediacy: A strategy for institution building, in *Journal of Comparative Administration*, 4(2), 401.

Lane, R. 1990. Concrete theory: an emerging political method, in *American Political Science Review*, 84(3), 927–40.

LaPorte, T., ed. 1975. *Organized Social Complexity: Challenge to Politics and Policy*. Princeton: Princeton University Press.

LaPorte, T. 1994. Shifting vantage and conceptual puzzles in understanding public organizational networks, paper presented to the Conference on Public Network Analysis and Innovation, Madison, Wisconsin, October 1994.

Lasswell, H. and Leites, N. 1949. *The Language of Politics: Studies in Quantitative Semantics*. New York: George Stewart.

Lasswell, H., Lerner, D. and De Sola Pool, I. 1952. *The Comparative Study of Symbols: An Introduction*. Stanford: Stanford University Press.

Lavoie, D. and Culbert, S.A. 1978. Stages in organizations and development, in *Human Relations*, 31, 417–38.

Leal Maldonado, J. 1987. El "boom" inmobilario madrileño: Precios altos para rentas bajas, in *Alfoz*, 46.

Leblebici, H., Salancik, G., Copay, A. and King, T. 1991. Institutional change and the transformation of interorganizational fields: An organizational history of the U.S. radio broadcasting industry, in *Administrative Science Quarterly*, 36, 333–63.

Ledrut, R. 1968a. *L'Espace Social de la Ville: Problèmes de Sociologie Appliquée à l'Aménagement Urbain*. Paris: Anthropos.

Ledrut, R. 1968b. *Sociologie Urbaine*. Paris: Presses Universitaires de France.

Ledrut, R. 1973. *Les Images de la Ville*. Paris: Anthropos.

Lefebvre, H. 1991 [1974]. *The Production of Space*. Oxford: Blackwell.

Leira, E., Gago, J. and Solana, I. 1976. Madrid: Cuarenta años de crecimiento urbano, in *Ciudad y Territorio*, 2(3), 43–66; reprinted in Ayuntamiento de

Madrid. 1981. *Madrid: Cuarenta Años de Desarrollo Urbano 1941–1981*, Madrid, 136.

Leira, E. 1989. El plan general de Madrid: una apuesta por la transformación, in *Urbanismo*, 7, 456.

Lévi-Strauss, C. 1975 [1955]. *Tristes Tropiques*, trans. John and Doreen Weightman. New York: Atheneum.

Levine, R.A. 1972. *Public Planning: Failure and Redirection*. New York: Basic Books.

Lewin, R. 1992. *Complexity: Life at the Edge of Chaos*. New York: Macmillan.

Ley General del Ensanche de Poblaciones de 22 de diciembre de 1876.

Ley de 26 de julio de 1892. Ley del Ensanche para las poblaciones de Madrid y Barcelona.

Ley de 18 de marzo de 1895. Ley de Saneamiento, Reforma y Mejora Interior de las Poblaciones de 30,000 o más almas.

Ley de 23 de noviembre de 1944. Ley de Ordenación Urbana de Madrid y sus Alrededores.

Ley de 12 de mayo de 1956. Régimen del Suelo y Ordenación Urbana.

Ley de 13 de noviembre de 1957. Sobre Plan de Urgencia Social de Madrid.

Ley 121/1963, de 2 de diciembre. Sobre el Área Metropolitana de Madrid.

Ley 9/1995 de 28 de marzo de Medidas de Política Territorial, Suelo y Urbanismo. Madrid: Comunidad de Madrid.

Ley 9/2001 de 17 de julio del Suelo. Madrid: Comunidad de Madrid.

Ley Decreto 1541/1972, de 15 de junio de 1972. Del Plan del Desarrollo Económico y Social.

Ley Decreto, 1984. *Ley Sobre Medidas de Disciplina Urbanista*. Madrid: Comunidad de Madrid.

Ley Decreto 3102, 1986. *Evaluación de Impacto Ambiental*. Government of Spain.

Lindblom, C.E. 1979. Still muddling, not yet through, in *Public Administration Review*, 39(6), 517–26.

Linz, J. 1981. A century of politics and interests in Spain, in S. Berger, ed. *Organizing Interests in Western Europe*. Cambridge: Cambridge University Press.

Lipset, S.M. 1963. *The First New Nation: The United States in Historical and Comparative Perspective*. New York: Basic Books.

Llinás, R. 1987. Mindness as a functional state of the brain, in C. Blakemore and S. Greenfield, eds *Mindwaves: Thoughts on Intelligence, Identity and Consciousness*. Oxford: Basil Blackwell.

Lopez Sallaberry, J., Aranda, P., de Lorite Kramer, J. and García Cascales, J. 1923. *Informe sobre la urbanización del Extrarradio*. Madrid: Artes Gráficas Municipales.

Lovejoy, A. 1936. *The Great Chain of Being: The Study of the History of an Idea*. Cambridge, MA: Harvard University Press.

Low, N. 1991. *Planning, Politics and the State: The Political Foundations of Planning Thought*. London: Unwin and Hyman.

Lukes, S. 1974. *Power, A Radical View*. London: Macmillan.

Lukes, S. 1977. *Essays in Social Theory*. New York: Columbia University Press.

Lukes, S. 1978. Power and authority, in T. Bottomore and R. Nisbit, eds *A History of Sociological Analysis*. New York: Basic Books.

Lukes, S. 1987. Perspectives on authority, in J.R. Pennock and J. Chapman, eds *Authority Revisited*. New York: New York University Press.

Lyden, F.J. 1975. Using Parson's functional analysis in the study of public organizations, in *Administrative Science Quarterly*, 20(1), 59–70.

Lynch, K. 1960. *The Image of the City*. Cambridge, MA: MIT Press.

Lynch, K. and Appleyard, D. 1972. *What Time is This Place?* Cambridge, MA: MIT Press.

Lynch, K. 1976. *Managing the Sense of a Region*. Cambridge, MA: MIT Press.

Lynch, K. 1981. *A Theory of Good City Form*. Cambridge, MA: MIT Press.

Lynch, K. 1990. Reconsidering the image of the city, in T. Banerjee and M. Southworth, eds *City Sense and City Design: Writings and Projects of Kevin Lynch*. Cambridge, MA: MIT Press.

MacIntyre, A. 1984. *After Virtue: A Study in Moral Theory*. South Bend: University of Notre Dame Press.

MacIntyre, A. 1988. *Whose Justice? Which Rationality?* South Bend: University of Notre Dame Press.

Madanipour, A., Hull, A. and Healey, P., eds 2001. *The Governance of Place: Space and Planning Processes*. Aldershot: Ashgate.

Mandelbaum, S. 1985. The institutional focus of planning theory, in *Journal of Planning Education and Research*, 5(1), 3–9.

Mandelbaum, S. 1990. Reading plans, in *Journal of the American Planning Association*, 56(3), 350–6.

Mandelbaum, S. 1991. Telling stories, in *Journal of Planning Education and Research*, 10(3), 209–14.

Mandelbaum, S., Mazza, L. and Burchell, R., eds 1996. *Explorations in Planning Theory*. New Brunswick: Center for Urban Policy Research.

Mandelbaum, S. 2000. *Open Moral Communities*. Cambridge, MA: MIT Press.

Mangada, E. 1981. Del convenio urbanístico a la negociación colectiva en la gestión de la ciudad, in Ayuntamiento de Madrid, ed. *El Urbanismo Heredado: El Convenio Urbanístico Como Instrumento de Gestión*. Madrid: Ayuntamiento de Madrid.

Mangada, E. 1994. Personal correspondence to the author.

Mannheim, K. 1936 [1929]. *Ideology and Utopia*, trans. L. Wirth and E. Shils, preface by L. Wirth. New York: Harcourt Brace.

Mannheim, K. 1950. *Freedom, Power, and Democratic Planning*. Oxford: Oxford University Press.

Mansbridge, J. 1980. *Beyond Adversary Democracy*. Chicago: University of Chicago Press.

Maravall, J.M. 1981. *La Política de la Transición*. Madrid: Taurus.

March, J., ed. 1965. *The Handbook of Organizations*. Chicago: Rand McNally.

March, J. and Olsen, J. 1984. The new institutionalism: organizational factors in political life, in *American Political Science Review*, 78(3), 734–49.

March, J. and Olsen, J. 1989. *Rediscovering Institutions: The Organizational Basis of Politics*. New York: The Free Press.

March, J. and Simon, H. 1993 [1958]. *Organizations*, second edition. Cambridge, MA: Blackwell.

Margolis, H. 1987. *Patterns, Thinking and Cognition*. Chicago: University of Chicago Press.

Markusen, A. 1985. *Profit Cycles, Oligopoly and Regional Development*. Cambridge, MA: MIT Press.

Markusen, A. 1987. *Regions: The Economics and Politics of Territory*. Totowa, NJ: Rowman and Littlefield.

Marr, D. 1982. *Vision*. San Francisco: W.H. Freeman.

Marris, P. 1987. *Meaning and Action: Community Planning and Conceptions of Change*. London: Routledge and Kegan Paul.

Martinez-Alier, J. and Roca, J. 1987. Spain after Franco: from corporatist ideology to corporatist reality, in *International Journal of Political Economy*, 177(4), 56–87.

Maure Rubio, M. 1991. *La Ciudad Lineal de Arturo Soria*. Madrid: Colegio Oficial de Arquitectos de Madrid.

McDowell, J. 1994. *Mind and World*. Cambridge, MA: Harvard University Press.

McKelvey, B. 1982. *Organizational Systematics: Taxonomy, Evolution, Classification*. Berkeley: University of California Press.

McLaughlin, J.B. 1969. *Urban and Regional Planning: A Systems Approach*. London: Faber and Faber.

McLuhan, M. and Fiore, Q. 1967. *The Medium is the Message*. New York: Random House.

McMahon, C. 1994. *Authority and Democracy: A General Theory of Government and Management*. Princeton: Princeton University Press.

Meadows, D. and Club of Rome. 1972. *The Limits to Growth*. New York: Universe Books.

Melnick, R. 1991. Introduction to the symposium on the new politics of public policy, in *Journal of Policy Analysis and Management*, 10(3), 363–8.

Metaxas, T. 2009. Place marketing, strategic planning and competitiveness: The case of Malta, in *European Planning Studies*, 17(9), 1357–78.

Metcalf, H. and Urwick, L., eds 1941. *Dynamic Administration: Collected Papers of Mary Parker Follett*. London: Sir Isaac Pitman and Sons.

Meyerson, M. and Banfield, E. 1955. *Politics, Planning and the Public Interest*. New York: The Free Press.

Meyerson, M. 1956. Building a middle range bridge for planning, in *Journal of the American Institute of Planners*, 22(2), 58–64.

Meyerson, M. 1961. Utopian traditions and the planning of cities, in *Deadalus*, 90(1), 180–93.

Michael, D. 1973. *Learning to Plan and Planning to Learn*. San Francisco: Jossey Bass.

Miller, D. 1989. *Lewis Mumford: A Life*. New York: Weidenfeld and Nicholson.

Mills, C.W. 1956. *The Power Elite*. Oxford and New York: Oxford University Press.

Ministerio de Vivienda. 1959. Setenta mil viviendas: plan de urgencia social de Madrid, documentary film, 7'36", black and white, sound. Madrid: Ministerio de la Vivienda.

Mintzberg, H. 1979. *The Structuring of Organizations*. Englewood Cliffs: Prentice-Hall.

Mollenkopf, J. 1983. *The Contested City*. Princeton: Princeton University Press.

Monclús, J. 1992. Planning and history in Spain, in *Planning Perspectives*, 7, 101–5.

Monclús, J. and Guàrdia, M., eds 2006. *Culture, Urbanism and Planning*. Aldershot: Ashgate.

Moneo, R. 1967. Madrid: los últimos veinticinco años (1940–1965), in *Información Comercial Española*, no. 4,021, in Oficina Municipal del Plan. 1981. *Madrid: Cuarenta Años de Desarrollo Urbano 1940–1980*. Madrid: Ayuntamiento de Madrid, 79–94.

Moneo, R. 1970. El desarrollo urbano de Madrid en los años sesenta, in *Cuadernos para el Dialogo*, special issue on Madrid, in Oficina Municipal del Plan. 1981. *Madrid: Cuarenta Años de Desarrollo Urbano 1940–1980*. Madrid: Ayuntamiento de Madrid, 101–12.

Moore, C. 1986. *The Negotiation Process: Practical Strategies for Resolving Conflict*. San Francisco: Jossey-Bass.

Moore, C. 2008. *The Mediation Process: Practical Strategies for Resolving Conflict*, 3rd edition, revised. San Francisco: Jossey-Bass.

Morgan, C.L. 1923. *Emergent Evolution*. London: Williams and Northgate.

Morgan, G. 1986. *Images of Organization*. Beverly Hills: Sage.

Morgan, G. 1993. *Imaginization: The Art of Creative Management*. Newbury Park: Sage.

Morris, A.E.J. 1972. *History of Urban Form: Pre-History to the Renaissance*. London: George Goodwin.

Murray, W., MacGregor, K. and Bernstein, A., eds 1994. *The Making of Strategy: Rulers, States and Wars*. New York: Cambridge University Press.

Nadler, D.A. and Tushman, M.L. 1989. Organizational frame bending: principles for managing reorientation, in *Academy of Management Executive*, 3, 194–202.

Nadler, D.A. and Tushman, M.L. 1990. Beyond the charismatic leader: leadership and organizational change, in *California Management Review*, 32(2), 77–97.

Naredo, J.M. 1988. Sobre la naturaleza de la actual recuperación económica madrileña: in *Economía y Sociedad*, 1.

Naredo, J.M. 1990. Los limites de crecimiento, in *Alfoz*, 74–5, 40–8.

Nasar, J. 1997. *The Evaluative Image of the City*. Thousand Oaks: Sage.

Neacsu, M.C. 2009. The city image and the local public administration: a working tool in urban planning, in *Transylvanian Review of Administrative Sciences*, 27(E), 172–88.

Negroponte, N. 1995. The balance of trade of ideas, in *Wired*, 3(4), 188.

Neisser, U. 1976. *Cognition and Reality*. San Francisco: W.H. Freeman.

Neuman, M. 1991. Utopia, dystopia, diaspora, in *Journal of the American Planning Association*, 57(3), 344–7.

Neuman, M. 1993. Land use mediation in Florida and New Jersey, in *Land Use Forum*, 2(3), 200–5.

Neuman, M. 1994. El eslabón débil, in *Alfoz*, 107, 129–36.

Neuman, M. 1995a. La imagen y la ciudad, in *Ciudad y Territorio y Estudios Territoriales*, III, 104, 377–94.

Neuman, M. 1995b. Museum with a message, in *Journal of the American Planning Association*, 61(4), 518–20.

Neuman, M. 1996a. The imaginative institution: planning and politics in Madrid, in *Planning Theory*, 15, 120–31.

Neuman, M. 1996b. Images as institution builders: metropolitan planning in Madrid, in *European Planning Studies*, 4(3), 293–312; also in P. Healey, et al., eds 1997. *Making Strategic Plans: Innovation in Spatial Planning in Europe*. London: University College London Press.

Neuman, M. 1997. The imaginative institution: planning and institutions in Madrid, in *Berkeley Planning Journal*, 12, 159–60.

Neuman, M. 1998a. Planning, governing and the image of the city, in *Journal of Planning Education and Research*, 18, 61–71.

Neuman, M. 1998b. Does planning need the plan?, in *Journal of the American Planning Association*, 64(2), 208–20.

Neuman, M. 2000. Regional design: recovering a landscape architecture and urban planning tradition, in *Landscape and Urban Planning*, 47, 115–28.

Neuman, M. and Gavinha, J. 2005. The planning dialectic of continuity and change: the evolution of metropolitan planning in Madrid, in *European Planning Studies*, 13(7), 985–1012.

Neuman, M. 2007. Multi-scalar large institutional networks in regional planning, in *Planning Theory and Practice*, 8(3), 319–44.

Neuman, M. 2009. Spatial planning leadership by infrastructure: an American view, in *International Planning Studies*, 14(2), 201–17.

Neuman, M. and Hull, A. 2009. The futures of the city region, in *Regional Studies*, 43(6), 777–87.

Neuman, M. and Hull, A., eds 2010. *The Futures of the City Region*. New York and London: Routledge.

Neustadt, R. 1990. *Presidential Power and the Modern Presidents: The Politics of Leadership from Roosevelt to Reagan*. New York: Maxwell Macmillan.

New Jersey State Planning Commission. 1992. *Communities of Place: The New Jersey State Development and Redevelopment Plan*. Trenton: State Planning Commission.

Newman, P. and Herrschel, T. 2002. *Governance of Europe's City Regions: Planning, Policy and Politics*. London and New York: Routledge.

Nisbet, R. 1953. *The Quest for Community: A Study in the Ethics of Order and Freedom*. New York: Oxford University Press.

Noria, N. and Eccles, R., eds 1992. *Networks and Organizations: Structure, Form and Action*. Boston: Harvard Business School Press.

North, D. 1990. *Institutions. Institutional Change and Economic Performance*. New York: Cambridge University Press.

Nuevo Estatuto Municipal de 8 de marzo de 1924 del Municipio de Madrid.

Nuñez Granés, P. 1924. *La extensión general de Madrid*. Madrid: Imprenta Municipal.

Oficina Municipal del Plan. 1981. *Madrid: Cuarenta Años de Desarrollo Urbano 1940–1980*. Madrid: Ayuntamiento de Madrid.

Oficina Municipal del Plan. 1985. *Plan General de Ordenación Urbana de Madrid*, various volumes, particularly *Memoria General*, *Memoria de Participación*, and *Memoria de Compatibilización*. Madrid: Ayuntamiento de Madrid.

Oficina Municipal del Plan. 1988. *Normas Urbanísticas*. Madrid: Ayuntamiento de Madrid.

Oficina Municipal del Plan. 1990. *Avance Sobre la Revisión del Plan General de Madrid*. Madrid: Ayuntamiento de Madrid.

Oficina Municipal del Plan. 1991. *Revisión de Plan General de Ordenación Urbana de Madrid: Fase de Avance*. Madrid: Ayuntamiento de Madrid.

Oficina Municipal del Plan. 1992. *Directrices de Actuación*. Madrid: Ayuntamiento de Madrid.

Oficina Municipal del Plan. 1993. *Revisión del Plan General de Ordenación Urbana de Madrid: Avance 1993*. Madrid: Ayuntamiento de Madrid.

Oficina Municipal del Plan. 1993. *El Proceso de Participación en el Nuevo Plan General Madrid: Avance 1993*. Madrid: Ayuntamiento de Madrid.

Oficina Municipal del Plan. 1994. *Avance del Nuevo Plan General: Proceso de Participación Ciudadana: Documentación Relativa a las Sugerencias Presentadas en la Exposición al Público*. Madrid: Ayuntamiento de Madrid.

Olson, M. 1965. *The Logic of Collective Action: Public Goods and the Theory of Groups*. Cambridge: Harvard University Press.

Ortega y Gasset, J. 1922. *España Invertebrada: Bosquejo de Algunos Pensamientos Históricos*. Madrid: Calpe.

Osborne, D. and Gaebler, T. 1992. *Reinventing Government: How the Entrepreneurial Spirit is Transforming the Public Sector*. Reading, MA: Addison Wesley.

Osborne, S., ed. 2009. *The New Politics of Governance? Emerging Perspectives on the Theory and Practice of Public Governance*. New York and London: Routledge.

Ostrom, E. 1990. *Governing the Commons: The Evolution of Institutions for Collective Action*. Cambridge: Cambridge University Press.

Ostrom, E. 1991. Rational choice theory and institutional analysis: toward complementarity, in *American Political Science Review*, 85(1), 237–43.

Ostrom, E. 1995. New horizons in institutional analysis, in *American Political Science Review*, 89(1), 174–8.

Ostrom, E., Dietz, T., Dolšak, N., Stern, P., Stonich, S. and Weber, E.U., eds 2002. *The Drama of the Commons*. Washington, DC: National Academy Press.

Ostrom, V., Feeny, D. and Picht, H., eds 1988. *Rethinking Institutional Analysis and Development: Issues. Alternatives and Choices*. San Francisco: ICS Press.

Padilla, S., ed. 1975. *Tugwell's Thoughts on Planning*. Puerto Rico: University of Puerto Rico Press.

Pagden, A. 1995. *Lords of All the World: Ideologies of Empire in Spain, Britain and France c.1500–c.1800*. New Haven: Yale University Press.

Panofsky, E. 1955. *Meaning in the Visual Arts*. Garden City: Doubleday.

Parmentier, R. 1994. *Signs in Society: Studies in Semiotic Anthropology*. Bloomington: University of Indiana Press.

Parra Baño, T. 1988. Madrid centro y periferia del empleo, in Anonymous, eds *Crisis Social de la Ciudad*. Madrid: Cidur Alfoz.

Parsons, T. 1937. *The Structure of Social Action*. New York: McGraw Hill.

Parsons, T. 1960. *Structure and Process in Modern Societies*. Glencoe, IL: Free Press.

Parsons, T. 1990 [1934]. Prolegomena to a theory of social institutions, in *American Sociological Review*, 55(3), 319–33.

Paz Maroto, J. 1939. *Plan General de Ordenación y Extensión de Madrid*. Madrid: Artes Gráficas Municipales.

Peirce, C. 1931–1958. *Collected Papers*. Cambridge, MA: Harvard University Press.

Pérez-Diaz, V. 1994. interview in *El País*, 27 February.

Pérez-Diaz, V. 1990. *Governability and the Scale of Governance: Mesogovermnents in Spain*. Working Paper 5, Madrid: Centro de Estudios Avanzados en Ciencias Sociales.

Pérez-Diaz, V. 1993. *The Return of Civil Society: The Emergence of Democratic Spain*. Cambridge: Harvard University Press.

Perrow, C. 1972. *Complex Organizations: A Critical Essay*. Glenview, IL: Scott, Foresman.

Perrucci, R. and Potter, H. 1989. *Networks of Power: Organizational Actors at the National, Corporate, and Community Levels*. New York: A. de Gruyter.

Pessoa, F. 1984 [1982]. *Libro de Desasosiego*. Barcelona: Seix Barral.

Peterson, P. 1981. *City Limits*. Chicago: University of Chicago Press.

Pettit, P. 1993. *The Common Mind: An Essay on Psychology, Society, and Politics*. New York: Oxford University Press.

Pfeffer, J. and Salanick, G. 1978. *The External Control of Organizations*. New York: Harper and Row.

Pierre, J., ed. 2000. *Debating Governance*. Oxford, New York: Oxford University Press.

Pi i Margall, F. 1982 [1854]. *La Reacción y la Revolución*. Barcelona: Anthropos.

Pitkin, H. 1967. *The Concept of Representation*. Berkeley: University of California Press.

Popper, F. 1988. Understanding American land use regulation since 1970: a revisionist interpretation, in *Journal of the American Planning Association*, 54(3), 291–301.

Porter, M. 1980. *Competitive Strategy: Techniques for Analyzing Industries and Competitors*. New York: Free Press.

Porter, M. 1985. *The Competitive Advantage: Creating and Sustaining Superior Performance*. New York: Free Press.

Powell, W. 1990. Neither market nor hierarchy: network forms of organizations, in *Research in Organizational Behavior*, 12, 295–36.

Powell, W. and DiMaggio, P., eds 1991. *The New Institutionalism in Organizational Analysis*. Chicago: University of Chicago Press.

Prelec, D. and Herrnstein, R.J. 1991. Preferences or principles: alternative guidelines for choice, in R. Zeckhauser, ed. *Strategy and Choice*. Cambridge, MA: MIT Press.

Preston, P. 1986. *The Triumph of Democracy in Spain*. New York: Methuen.

Promadrid. 1993. *Madrid Futuro: Plan Estratégico de Madrid*. Madrid: Promadrid.

Putnam, R. 1993. *Making Democracy Work: Civic Traditions in Modern Italy*. Princeton: Princeton University Press.

Putnam, R. 2000. *Bowling Alone: The Collapse and Revival of American Community*. New York: Simon and Schuster.

Quinn, R.H. and Cameron, K. 1983. Organizational life cycles and shifting criteria of effectiveness: some preliminary evidence, in *Management Science*, 29, 33–51.

Rabinow, P., ed. 1984. *The Foucault Reader*. New York: Pantheon.

Rabinow, P. 1989. *French Modern: Norms and Forms of the Social Environment*. Cambridge, MA: MIT Press.

Rachlin, H. 1994. *Behavior and Mind*. New York: Oxford University Press.

Rasmussen, S.E. 1951. *Towns and Building Described in Drawings and Words*. Cambridge, MA: Harvard University Press.

Real Decreto de 8 de Abril de 1857. Nombramiento de la Comisión para el estudio del Proyecto de ensanche de Madrid.

Real Decreto 1346/1976, de 9 de abril. Texto refundido de la Ley sobre Régimen del Suelo y Ordenación Urbana.

Real Decreto-Ley 11/1980, de 26 de septiembre. Sobre la revisión del Plan General de Ordenación Urbana del Área Metropolitana de Madrid.

Real Decreto Legislativo 1/1992, de 26 de junio. Por el que se aprueba el Texto Refundido de la Ley sobre el Régimen del Suelo y Ordenación Urbana.

Redondo de la Serna, A. 1988. La evolución de la marginación social en Madrid, in Anonymous, eds *Crisis Social de la Ciudad*. Madrid: Cidur Alfoz.

Regional Plan Association. 1996. *A Region at Risk*. New York: Regional Plan Association.

Reglamento de Obras y Servicios Municipales de 14 de julio de 1924. Del Municipio de Madrid.

Rehfeld, A. 2005. *The Concept of Constituency: Political Representation, Democratic Legitimacy, and Institutional Design*. Cambridge: Cambridge University Press.

Reich, R. 1990. *The Power of Public Ideas*. Cambridge: Harvard University Press.

Rein, M. 1987. *Stagnation and Renewal in Social Policy: The Rise and Fall of Policy Regimes.* Armonk: M.E. Sharpe.

Reiner, T. 1963. *The Place of the Ideal Community in Urban Planning*. Philadelphia: University of Pennsylvania Press.

Ridruejo Brieva, J.A. 1978. *Madrid y su Gestión Urbana Metropolitana*, 4 volumes. Madrid: COPLACO.

Riera, P. 1991. The practice of land use planning in Spain, in *Planning Practice and Research*, 6(2), 11–8.

Rittel, H. and Webber, M. 1973. Dilemmas in a general theory of planning, in *Policy Sciences*, 4, 155–69.

Roberts, N. 1991. Towards a synergistic model of power, in J. Bryson and R. Einsweiler, eds *Shared Power: What is it? How Does it Work? How Can We Make it Better?* Lanham: University Press of America.

Roca, J. 1987. Neo-corporatism in post-Franco Spain, in I. Scholten, ed. *Political Stability and Neo-Corporatism*. London: Sage.

Rodowick, D.N. 1991. Reading the figural, in *Camera Obscura*, 24.

Rogers, L. 1995. Take your place in the ECUs, in *RIBA Journal*, 102(2), 6–9.

Rorty, R. 1989. *Contingency, Irony, and Solidarity*. Cambridge: Cambridge University Press.

Ross, C., ed. 2009. *Megaregions: Planning for Global Competitiveness*. Washington, DC: Island Press.

Rossi, A. 1982 [1966]. *The Architecture of the City*. Cambridge, MA: MIT Press.

Royce, J. 1886. *California, From the Conquest in 1846 to the Second Vigilance Committee in San Francisco: A Study in American Character*. Boston: Houghton Mifflin.

Rueda Laffond, J.C. 1993. El desarrollo de la ciudad y la política urbanística, in A. Fernández García, *Historia de Madrid*. Madrid: Editorial Complutense, 579–601.

Rutten, R. and Boekema, F., eds 2007. *The Learning Region: Foundations, State of the Art, Future*. Cheltenham: Edward Elgar.

Ruíz Gimenez, J. 1916. Mejoras e intereses de Madrid, in *El Liberal*, Madrid, June 17, 1916.

Rykwert, J. 1988. *The Idea of a Town: The Anthropology of Urban Form in Rome: Italy and the Ancient World*, 2nd Edition. Cambridge, MA: MIT Press.

Salisbury, H. 1992. *Interests and Institutions: Substance and Structure in American Politics*. Pittsburgh: University of Pittsburgh Press.

Sale, K. 1980. *Human Scale*. New York: Coward, McCann, & Geoghegan.

Salet, W., Thornley, A. and Kreukels, A., eds 2003. *Metropolitan Governance and Spatial Planning: Comparative Case Studies of European Regions*. London: Spon.

Salvador y Carreras, A. 1923. Problemas madrileños: la urbanización del extrarradio, in *Boletin de la Sociedad Central de Arquitectos*, Madrid, 147, 3.

Sandercock, L. 2004. Towards a planning imagination for the 21st Century, in *Journal of the American Planning Association*, 70(2), 133–41.

Sanyal, B. 2005. *Comparative Planning Cultures*. London: Routledge.

Sassen, S. 1991. *The Global City: New York, London, Tokyo*. Princeton: Princeton University Press.

Sassen, S. 2007. *Deciphering the Global: Its Scales, Spaces, and Subjects*. New York and London: Routledge.

Savitch, H.V. 1988. *Post Industrial Cities: Politics and Planning in New York, London and Paris*. Princeton: Princeton University Press.

Saxenian, A. 1994. *Regional Advantage: Culture and Competition in Silicon Valley and Route 128*. Cambridge: Harvard University Press.

Scharpf, F. 1993. *Games in Hierarchies and Networks*. London: Westview.

Schattschneider, E.E. 1935. *Politics, Pressure and the Tariff*. Englewood Cliffs: Prentice Hall.

Schattschneider, E.E. 1960. *The Semisovereign People: A Realist's View of Democracy in America*. New York: Holt, Reinhart, and Winston.

Schmitter, P. and Lehmbruch, G. 1979. *Trends Toward Corporatist Intermediation*. Beverly Hills: Sage.

Schmitter, P. 1981. Interest intermediation and governability in Western Europe and North America, in S. Berger, ed. *Organizing Interests in Western Europe: Pluralism, Corporatism and the Transformation of Politics*. Cambridge: Cambridge University Press.

Schneider, A. and Ingram, H. 1993. Social construction of target populations: implications for politics and policy, in *American Political Science Review*, 87(2), 334–47.

Schneider, V. 1992. The structure of policy networks, in *European Journal of Political Research*, 21(1–2), 109–30.

Schön, D. and Rein, M. 1994. *Frame Reflection: Towards the Resolution of Intractable Policy Controversies*. New York: Basic Books.

Schwartz, R. 1994. *Vision: Variations on Some Berkeleian Themes*. Oxford: Basil Blackwell.

Schweers Cook, K. and Levi, M., eds 1990. *The Limits of Rationality*. Chicago: University of Chicago Press.

Scott, W.R. 1988. The adolescence of institutional theory, in *Administrative Science Quarterly*, 32, 493–511.

Searing, D. 1991. Roles, rules, and rationality in the new institutionalism, in *American Political Science Review*, 85(4), 1239–60.

Searle, J. 1969. *Speech Acts*. Cambridge: Cambridge University Press.

Searle, J. 1992. *The Rediscovery of the Mind*. Cambridge, MA: MIT Press.

Searle, J. 1995a. *The Construction of Social Reality*. New York: The Free Press.
Searle, J. 1995b. The mystery of consciousness, in *The New York Review of Books*, XLII, 17 and 18, 60–66 and 54–61.
Segberg, K., ed. 2007. *The Making of Global City Regions: Johannesburg, Mumbai, São Paolo, Shanghai*. Baltimore: Johns Hopkins University Press.
Selznick, P. 1949. *TVA and the Grassroots*. Berkeley: University of California Press.
Selznick, P. 1957. *Leadership in Administration: A Sociological Interpretation*. Berkeley: University of California Press.
Selznick, P. 1992. *The Moral Commonwealth: Social Theory and the Power of Community*. Berkeley: University of California Press.
Sennett, R. 1990. *The Conscience of the Eye: The Design and Social Life of Cities*. New York: Knopf.
Serratosa, A. 1979. *Objetivos y Metodologías de un Plan Metropolitano*. Barcelona: Oikos–Tau Ediciones.
Sewell, Jr., W. 1992. A theory of structure: duality, agency, and transformation, in *American Journal of Sociology*, 98(1), 1–29.
Shepsle, K. 1989. Studying institutions: some lessons from the rational choice approach, in *Journal of Theoretical Politics*, 1, 131–47.
Shubert, A. 1990. *A Social History of Modern Spain*. London: Unwin Hyman.
Simancas, V. and Elizalde, J. 1969. Madrid, siglo XX, in *El Mito del Gran Madrid, Madrid*. Editorial Guadiana; in Ayuntamiento de Madrid, 1981, *Madrid: Cuarenta Años de Desarrollo Urbano 1941–1981*.
Simón, F. 1994. Un pulmón para el sur, in *El País*, April 4, 4–5.
Simon, H. 1952. A behavioral model of rational choice, in *Quarterly Journal of Economics*, 69, 98–118.
Simon, H. 1957. *Models of Man*. New York: Wiley.
Simon, H. 1976. *Administrative Behavior*, 3rd Edition. New York: The Free Press.
Singh, J., ed. 1990. *Organizational Evolution: New Directions*. Newbury Park: Sage.
Sitte, C. 1945 [1889]. *The Art of Building Cities: City Building According to its Artistic Principles*. New York: Reinhold.
Skocpol, T. 1979. *States and Social Revolutions*. Cambridge: Cambridge University Press.
Skocpol, T. 1985. Bringing the state back in, in P. Evans, D. Ruescbmeyer and T. Skocpol, *Bringing the State Back In*. New York: Cambridge University Press.
Smith, B.A. 1971. The Image of the City Ten Years Later, MA Thesis. Department of Urban Studies and Planning, MIT.
Solomon, D. 1992. *Rebuilding*. New York: Princeton Architectural Press.
Sorensen, E. and Torfing, J., eds 2004. *Theories of Democratic Network Governance*. Basingstoke and New York: Palgrave Macmillan.
Spirn, A. 1984. *The Granite Garden: Urban Nature and Human Design*. New York: Basic Books.

Starr, P. 1982. *The Social Transformation of American Medicine*. New York: Basic Books.

Stein, S. 1993. Wittgenstein, Davidson, and the myth of incommensurability, in J. Couture and K. Nelson, eds *Meta-Philosophie Reconstructing Philosophy: New Essays on Metaphilosophy*. Calgary: University of Calgary Press.

Steinbeck, J. 1962. *Travels with Charley: In Search of America*. New York: Viking Press.

Steinmo, S., Thelen, K. and Longstreth, F., eds 1992. *Structuring Politics: Historical Institutionalism in Comparative Politics*. Cambridge: Cambridge University Press.

Stinchcombe, A. 1965. Social structure and organizations, in J. March, ed. *The Handbook of Organizations*. Chicago: Rand McNally, 142–93.

Stone, C. 1989. *Regime Politics: Governing Atlanta, 1946–1988*. Lawrence: University of Kansas Press.

Stone, C. 1993. Urban regimes and the capacity to govern, in *Journal of Urban Affairs*, 15(1), 1–28.

Subias, X. 1989. El plan territorial general de Cataluña, in *Urbanismo*, 9, 63–72.

Subirats, E. 1993. *Después de la Lluvia: Sobre la Ambigua Modernidad Española*. Madrid: Ediciones Temas de Hoy.

Susskind, L. 1981. Citizen participation and consensus building in land use planning: a case study, in J. Innes de Neufville, ed. 1981. *The Land Use Policy Debate in the United States*. New York and London: Plenum.

Susskind, L. and Cruikshank, J. 1987. *Breaking the Impasse: Consensual Approaches to Resolving Public Disputes*. New York: Basic Books.

Swensen, P. 2004. Varieties of capitalist interests: power, institutions, and the regulatory welfare state in the United States and Sweden, in *Studies in American Political Development*, 18, 1–29.

Swidler, A. 1986. Culture in action: symbols and strategies, in *American Sociological Review*, 51, 273–86.

Tafuri, M. 1980. *Theories and Histories of Architecture*. New York: Harper and Row.

Tainter, J. 1988. *The Collapse of Complex Societies*. Cambridge: Cambridge University Press.

Tarrow, S. 1994. *Power in Movement: Social Movements, Collective Action, and Politics*. New York: Cambridge University Press.

Taylor, M. 1989. Structure, culture and action in the explanation of social change, in *Politics and Society*, 17, 115–62.

Teisman, G., van Buuren, A. and Gerrits, L., eds 2009. *Managing Complex Governance Systems*. New York and London: Routledge.

Thagard, P. 1992. *Conceptual Revolutions*. Princeton: Princeton University Press.

Thagard, P. 2005. *Mind: Introduction to Cognitive Science*. Cambridge, MA: MIT Press.

Thibault, P. 1991. *Social Semiotics as Practice: Text, Social Meaning Making, and Nabakov's Ada*. Minneapolis: University of Minnesota Press.

Thierstein, A. and Förster, A., eds 2008. *The Image and the Region: Making Megacity Regions Visible!* Baden: Lars Muller Publishers.

Thompson, J. 1967. *Organizations in Action.* New York: McGraw Hill.

Thompson, M., Ellis, A. and Wildavsky, A. 1990. *Cultural Theory.* Boulder: Westview Press.

Throgmorton, J. 1996. *Planning as Persuasive Storytelling: The Rhetorical Construction of Chicago's Electric Future.* Chicago: University of Chicago Press.

Tierno Galván, E. 1981. *Cabos Sueltos.* Barcelona: Bruguera.

Tierney, W., ed. 2006. *Governance and the Public Good.* Albany: State University of New York Press.

Tudela, M. 1984. *Aquellas Tertulias de Madrid.* Madrid: Avapies.

Tugwell, R. 1935. *The Battle for Democracy.* New York: Columbia University Press.

Tugwell, R. 1940. Implementing the general interest, in *Public Administration Review*, 1, 32–49.

Tursman, R. 1995. Cognition as a dynamic system, in *Transactions of the Charles S. Peirce Society*, XXXI, 2, 358–72.

Ullman, S. 1979. *The Interpretation of Visual Motion.* Cambridge, MA: MIT Press.

United Nations Centre for Human Settlements (UNCHS). 2006. *State of the World's Cities 2006/7.* London: Earthscan.

Vale, L. and Warner, S.B., eds 2001. *Imaging the City: Continuing Struggles and New Directions.* New Brunswick: CUPR Press.

Varela, F. 1992. The reenchantment of the concrete, in J. Crary and S. Kwinter, eds *Incorporations.* Cambridge, MA: MIT Press.

Various authors. 1916. *Papers in Honor of Josiah Royce on his Sixtieth Birthday.* Boston: Longman, Green and Company.

Various authors. 1970. *Cuadernos para el dialogo.* Madrid: special issue on Madrid.

Various authors. 1976. *Ciudad y Territorio*, nos. 2–3. Madrid: special double issue on Madrid.

Various authors. 1989. *Urbanismo*, 8, COAM, special issue on territorial planning.

Various authors. 1991. *Urbanismo*, 13, COAM, special issue on the preliminary plan revisions for the general plan of Madrid.

Vasconcelos, L. and Reis, A. 1994. The Plan Making Process: The Case Study of Lisbon, unpublished manuscript. New University of Lisbon.

Vaughan, D. 1995. *The Challenger Launch Decision: Risky Technology, Culture, and Deviance.* Chicago: University of Chicago Press.

Vázquez Montalbán, M. 1992. *Barcelonas*, translated by Andy Robinson, London: Verso.

Venturi, R., Scott Brown, D. and Izenour, S. 1972. *Learning From Las Vegas.* Cambridge, MA: MIT Press.

Venturi, R. 1977 [1967]. *Complexity and Contradiction in Modern Architecture*. New York: Museum of Modern Art.

Vickers, G. 1973. *Making Institutions Work*. New York: John Wiley and Sons.

Vygotsky, L. 1962 [1934]. *Thought and Language*. Cambridge, MA: MIT Press.

Violich, F. 1998. *The Bridge to Dalmatia: A Search for the Meaning of Place*. Baltimore: Johns Hopkins University Press.

Walker, R. 1950. *The Planning Function in Urban Government* 2nd Edition. Chicago: University of Chicago Press.

Walzer, M. 1983. *Spheres of Justice: A Defense of Pluralism and Equality*. New York: Basic Books.

Wartenberg, T., ed. 1992. *Rethinking Power*. Albany: State University of New York Press.

Waste, R. 1989. *The Ecology of City Policymaking*. New York: Oxford University Press.

Webber, M. 1964. The urban place and the non-place urban realm, in M. Webber, ed. *Explorations in Urban Structure*. Philadelphia: University of Pennsylvania Press.

Weber, M. 1946. Bureaucracy, in H.H. Gerth and C.W. Mills, eds *From Max Weber: Essays in Sociology*. Oxford: Oxford University Press.

Weber, M. 1958 [1921]. *The City*, trans. Don Martindale and Gertrud Neuwirth. Glencoe, IL: The Free Press.

Weller, M. and Wolff, S., eds 2005. *Autonomy, Self-Governance and Conflict Resolution: Innovative Approaches to Institutional Design in Divided Societies*. New York and London: Routledge.

Weiss, J. 1987. Pathways to cooperation among public agencies, in *Journal of Policy Analysis and Management*, 7(1), 94–117.

Wheeler, W. 1928. *Emergent Evolution and the Development of Societies*. New York: W.W. Norton.

Wiewel, W. and Gerrit-Knaap, J., eds 2005. *Partnerships for Smart Growth: University-Community Collaboration for Better Public Places*. Armonk: M.E. Sharpe; Cambridge, MA: Lincoln Institute of Land Policy.

Wildavsky, A. 1973. If planning is everything, maybe it's nothing, in *Policy Sciences*, 4, 127–53.

Wildavsky, A. 1987. Choosing preferences by constructing institutions: a cultural theory of preference formation, in *American Political Science Review*, 81, 3–21.

Wildavsky, A. 1989. If institutions matter, why don't we hear about them from moral philosophers?, in *American Political Science Review*, 83(4), 1343–50.

Williamson, O. 1975. *Markets and Hierarchies*. New York: Free Press.

Williamson, O., ed. 1990. *Organizational Theory: From Chester Barnard to the Present and Beyond*. Oxford: Oxford University Press.

Wilson, D. 1993. Organizational perspectives and urban spatial structure: a review and appraisal, in *Journal of Planning Literature*, 7(3), 228–37.

Wilson, J.Q. 1968. *City Politics and Public Policy*. New York: Wiley.

Wittgenstein, L. 1958. *Philosophical Investigations*. Oxford: Basil Blackwell.

Wolach, I. 1994. *Transformations of the French Civic Order, 1789–1820s*. New York: W.W. Norton.

Woods, T.D., et al. 1972. *Institution Building: A Model for Applied Social Change*. Cambridge, MA: Schenkman.

Xu, J. and Yeh, A. 2010. *Governance and Planning of Mega-City Regions: An International Comparative Perspective*. New York and London: Routledge.

Yishai, Y. 1993. Public ideas and public policy: abortion politics in four democracies, in *Comparative Politics*, 25(2), 207–28.

Zarza, D. 1991. *Arroyo Culebro: Estudio de Estructura y Ordenación Territorial del Sur Metropolitano Para Madrid Región*. Madrid: ARPEGIO, S.A.

Zeckhauser, R., ed. 1991. *Strategy and Choice*. Cambridge, MA: MIT Press.

Zeisel, J. 1976. Negotiating a shared community image, in *Ekistics*, 42(251), 224–7.

Zito, A., ed. 2010. *Learning and Governance in the EU Policy Making Process*. New York and London: Routledge.

Zuazo, S. de. and Jansen, H. 1929–1930. Anteproyecto del trazado viario y urbanización de Madrid.

Zucker, L. 1991. The role of institutionalism in cultural persistence, in W. Powell and P. DiMaggio, eds *The New Institutionalism in Organizational Analysis*. Chicago: University of Chicago Press, 83–107.

# Index